WHEN AN ORIGINAL IS NOT ORIGINAL

WHEN AN ORIGINAL IS NOT ORIGINAL

The Originality Requirement in Belgian Law

Niels VANDEZANDE

intersentia
Cambridge – Antwerp – Chicago

KU LEUVEN CiTiP
CENTRE FOR IT & IP LAW

Intersentia Ltd
Sheraton House | Castle Park
Cambridge | CB3 0AX | United Kingdom
Tel.: +44 1223 370 170 | Fax: +44 1223 370 169
Email: mail@intersentia.co.uk
www.intersentia.com | www.intersentia.co.uk

Distribution for the UK and Ireland:
NBN International
Airport Business Centre, 10 Thornbury Road
Plymouth, PL6 7 PP
United Kingdom
Tel.: +44 1752 202 301 | Fax: +44 1752 202 331
Email: orders@nbninternational.com

Distribution for Europe and all other countries:
Intersentia Publishing nv
Groenstraat 31
2640 Mortsel
Belgium
Tel.: +32 3 680 15 50 | Fax: +32 3 658 71 21
Email: mail@intersentia.be

Distribution for the USA and Canada:
Independent Publishers Group
Order Department
814 North Franklin Street
Chicago, IL60610
USA
Tel.: +1 800 888 4741 (toll free) | Fax: +1312 337 5985
Email: orders@ipgbook.com

ISBN 978-1-78068-760-5
ISBN 978-1-78068-761-2 (pdf)
D/2019/7849/8
NUR 827

British Library Cataloguing in Publication Data. A catalogue record for this book is available from the British Library.

This research was conducted within the framework of a research project supported by the Flanders Research Foundation (FWO grant no. G055015N).

CONTENTS

CHAPTER I
INTRODUCTION

1. STATE OF THE ART

1. There are several branches of Belgian law that impose specific originality requirements. These different incarnations of the originality requirement, however, have very little in common. To the best of our knowledge, no research has been conducted into establishing a common root or common elements between these different notions of originality. Moreover, the last two decades have seen the introduction of several initiatives aimed at introducing electronic information processes into law. Examples include the electronic signature in material and procedural law and the possibility to substitute paper invoices with electronic ones. In most cases, these electronic information processes are technological translations of traditional paper concepts. This means that there is a clear reliance on the presumption that electronic representations of information can be considered as equal to their paper counterparts when certain requirements are met. However, such presumptions can be found to conflict with the notion of originality. For instance, the originality requirement may become difficult to apply as electronic information should be considered as a manifestation or as the result of the interaction between the stored digital object and the technology used at the time of consultation. An example here is the digitalization and preservation of original documents under administrative law. Important elements of this matter currently remain unaddressed and could result in legal uncertainty regarding the fulfillment of the originality requirement in different branches of law. Therefore, there is a clear need for more comprehensive research on how to correctly interpret the originality requirement in terms of those ongoing digitalization processes.

2. OBJECTIVES

2. The research conducted here serves two main objectives. First, it is our aim to analyze a select number of the originality requirement's different incarnations in specific branches of Belgian law in order to identify their potential common elements. Second, these findings will be applied to the ongoing introduction of

digitalization processes into law, in order to establish how the different concepts of originality should be interpreted in light of those processes. The main goal of this research, then, is to seek whether we can establish a more uniform definition of the originality notion in law.

3. The first part of the research will serve to introduce the notion of originality and some of its different incarnations in current Belgian law as it exists at present. The main question here is whether or not these often-divergent notions of originality can be traced back to a common root and whether or not this might lead to the establishment of a common understanding of the originality requirement to be applied throughout different branches of law. In order to maintain the manageability of this study, it is important to determine a clear delineation of the scope from the outset. As a result, only three select branches of law will be included in the present study. First, the originality requirement as found in the Belgian Civil Code will be analyzed, given that this constitutes one of the main cases in which originality plays an important role in law. Second, the focus will be put on administrative law. Here, the concept of originality will be analyzed from the point of view of its role in fulfilling the requirements imposed on public administrative documents and their publication requirements. Aspects of archival law will be particularly important in this respect. Third, fiscal law will also be analyzed as there are clear references to the need to preserve original information within it, such as the original information contained in invoices. The inclusion of fiscal law in this study is especially important for the second goal of this study, given that fiscal law demonstrates an advanced integration of digitalization possibilities. In this analysis, the roots of the different incarnations of the originality requirement studied will be traced in an attempt to establish the commonalities between these different branches of law, the aim of which is to establish the core elements for a more comprehensive definition of the originality requirement in law.

4. The findings of the first part will be applied to digitalization processes introduced in law in the second part of this study. For instance, electronic signatures have been introduced in the Belgian Civil Code to allow for evidence to be provided by electronic means. Under administrative law, public administrative documents are being digitalized and published electronically. Fiscal law has demonstrated advanced efforts in this field, establishing clear rules on the substitution of paper documents by electronic versions, particularly with regard to invoices. However, the main question that remains to be answered here is how the respective originality requirements, present in those three branches of law, should be understood in light of their ongoing digitalization processes. It is, for instance, clear that paper document processes rely on the transfer of information, whereby one party loses possession of that information and another

party gains possession. This is not the case in the realm of electronic information, as electronic information is essentially duplicated when transferred. This means that the classic interpretations of originality may be difficult to uphold in the process of digitalization. Under administrative law, for instance, it may become difficult to assess whether or not electronic versions of information can satisfy the preservation and publication requirements of the paper documents they are intended to substitute.

5. Ultimately, it is our aim to construe a more uniform definition of the notion of originality by bringing the findings of the two main parts of this research together. Can the notion of originality in law be defined in a way that facilitates its application to different branches of law, while also allowing for its application to the ongoing processes of digitalization in law?

6. This research addresses specific issues confronting law introduced by the process of digitalization. While different branches of law have divergent definitions for their respective originality requirements, it is clear that the process of digitalization affects all of these branches of law in the same manner. Therefore, the direct impact of a more uniform definition would be its potential for broader application, thus serving to enhance legal certainty in other branches of law in which digitalization raises concerns about the fulfillment of the originality requirement. While digitalization has been going on for a while, concerns regarding originality still remain unanswered. Legal doctrine provides no clear answer to this matter and practice has demonstrated the adoption of scattered *ad hoc* solutions to this problem. A fundamental approach is, therefore, needed to provide a more satisfying solution.

3. METHODOLOGY

7. The general methodology to be used in the research proposed here will include legal theoretical analyses and historical research, as well as the critical assessment of the findings of such research. A normative approach will be maintained in attempting to establish a more uniform definition for the originality requirement in law. Legal theoretical research will be conducted to analyze how digitalization processes are currently implemented in the three different branches of law selected for this research. Methods of legal historical research will be used to guide the research when trying to establish the origins of the different notions of originality analyzed here. A critical assessment will be provided on how the introduction of digitalization processes affects the notion of originality in those three branches of law. For feasibility purposes, it was decided upon to focus solely on Belgian law. Cross-border comparative research in this

field would significantly enlarge the scope of this project beyond its means, given that this topic touches upon elements mainly regulated by national law, while the different branches of law selected here demonstrate substantial national differences.

8. An initial and broad study of legal literature on the concept of originality will be conducted, given that the main focal point of this research is to analyze a specific topic of legal theory on a conceptual level. From this study, the current scholarly definition of this concept will be derived. The broad nature of this initial research into originality will also serve in further defining the scope of the rest of the research, which is necessary for feasibility purposes. Similarly, an initial theoretical study of the notion of digitalization will be conducted to gain a better understanding of what this notion entails. What constitutes digitalization will briefly and broadly be analyzed as well as what its driving forces are and how this evolution has been implemented into law in recent decades. This will serve to provide an initial idea of the main issues that stem from this matter, or from the way it has been introduced into law. In so doing, this analysis will help in establishing the main grounds for the conflict between digitalization and originality. The results of this exercise can be found in chapter II.

9. Next, we will analyze the incarnations of the notions of originality and digitalization in three specific domains of Belgian law: civil law (chapter III), administrative law (chapter IV) and fiscal law (chapter V).

10. Belgian civil law was chosen as it contains some of the most important provisions concerning the need for original documents, as currently found in Belgian law. The rules on evidence form the clearest domain in which the notion of originality in law conflicts with digitalization processes. As part of this study's historical research, the roots for this requirement and its evolution over the years will be traced. This will serve to identify the core elements associated with originality under the Belgian Civil Code. With regards to the introduction of digitalization in the Belgian Civil Code, the focus will be put on the introduction of electronic signatures and digital records. More importantly, how the originality notion maintained here is affected by the introduction of such digitalization techniques will be critically assessed.

11. Administrative law was chosen for its practical display of a need for an approach that can reconcile its originality requirement with digitalization processes. Here, the emphasis will be put on the requirement of originality when preserving and publishing public administrative documents. Given the focus on the preservation of such original information, it will be analyzed whether – and if so, how – archival law influences this originality requirement. Similarly, it will be analyzed how digitalization processes regulate the substitution of public administrative documents by their electronic counterparts and the relation of preservation and publication requirements herewith. The main question to be answered here is how the notion of originality, as embedded into administrative law, can be maintained in light of this digitalization processes.

12. As noted previously, fiscal law – especially with regard to the invoice – includes digitalization processes to a significant extent. This domain could, therefore, provide insight into how to reconcile originality and digitalization. Particularly, the focus will be put on the example of the invoice, where significant legislative initiative was taken to allow for the substitution of paper document procedures by fully digital processes. Fiscal law could provide useful knowledge on how to reconcile the originality requirement with digitalization processes, given the more advanced state of implementation of digitalization processes.

13. Additionally, chapter VI will briefly look at blockchain-related processes. In assessing the potential value of this much-debated technology for this project, it can be concluded that blockchain has at least the potential to add another dimension to the project's work plan. To recapitulate, the project – as outlined above – aims to first look at the notion of originality as traditionally found in Belgian civil law, administrative law and fiscal law. Second, the project aims to look at the introduction of the processes of digitalization to these branches of law. These two stages can be taken to represent the past and the present, since law before digitalization can, at present, by now be considered as a matter of the past, while digitalization processes – to some extent still ongoing – are clearly a matter of the present. However, this omits the dimension of future processes, which go beyond the digitalization figures known in law today. While the electronic signature – and particularly the technique of the digital signature commonly used in advanced and qualified electronic signatures – is an important figure in law today with relation to the originality notion, it may be questioned how potential future techniques – such as blockchain – relate to the originality notion. Much of this is of course tentative: blockchain is a new technology that can still evolve in many ways, and the extent to which this technology will prove to have a tangible impact on society still remains to be seen. Nevertheless, given its potential, it was decided to include a brief assessment thereof within this project.

14. Concluding the research is a critical assessment of the previously reported findings, reported in chapter VII. In tracing the historical roots of the originality requirements analyzed here, whether or not a common origin can be found will be assessed. casein the event that this proves true, whether the differentiations that have developed along the way can still be upheld and whether the common origin could lead to the formulation of a uniform definition of originality must be assessed critically. The main risk to this aspect of the research is that no common origin can be established. This risk does not affect the outcome of our research, as a possible future convergence of the different notions of originality can still be pursued. Therefore, these findings will be used in an attempt to construe a uniform definition for the originality requirement. This part of the research also includes a comparative scope, as it aims to integrate the findings of the previous analyses of the different branches of law selected here. The primary goal of this comparison is to identify the common elements that could serve the later attempt toward the formulation of a uniform definition of originality. Last, we will attempt to formulate a more uniform definition of originality. This exercise will go completely beyond the current state of the art and, in doing so, will start with the critical assessment and integration of the research results. Moreover, in attempting to construct a uniform definition of the notion of originality, a normative approach will need to be adopted. In terms of normative criteria, a uniform definition of the notion of originality should first and foremost lead to legal certainty regarding the compliance of digitalization processes with the originality requirement of different branches of law. A uniform definition of originality should also be inclusive, meaning that it can be applied to different branches of law and does not solely serve a single branch. Last, such definition needs to be weighed against proportionality, meaning that it should not lead to the establishment of requirements that are too burdensome for the citizen. If anything, a more uniform definition of originality should facilitate the ongoing implementation of digitalization processes into different branches of law and should not be counterproductive to such evolution.

CHAPTER II
ORIGINALITY AND DIGITALIZATION

1. ORIGINALITY

15. Originality generally defines something as having the quality or state of being fresh and novel, something or someone that displays independent creative thought or action.[1] Original, in turn, can be considered as the first form or source of something, that from which other work is derived or copied.[2] The notion of originality rose to particular importance during the period of Romanticism in the 18th century.[3] It was in that period that this concept became linked to the notion of authorship, which in turn would form the basis of modern copyright law.[4]

16. Modern copyright law – from its origins in the 1710 Statute of Anne[5], throughout further developments in US constitutional law[6] and at the

1 "originality, n." (2015) *OED Online*, Oxford University Press; "originality" (2015) *Merriam-Webster.com*, Merriam-Webster; "originality" (2015) *Collins English Dictionary*, HarperCollins Publishers; "originality" (2015) *Cambridge Advanced Learners Dictionary & Thesaurus*, Cambridge University Press.

2 "original, adj. and n." (2015) *OED Online*, Oxford University Press; "original" (2015) *Merriam-Webster.com*, Merriam-Webster; "original" (2015) *Collins English Dictionary*, HarperCollins Publishers; "original" (2015) *Cambridge Advanced Learners Dictionary & Thesaurus*, Cambridge University Press.

3 Rose, M. (1988) "The Author as Proprietor: Donaldson v. Becket and the Genealogy of Modern Authorship", *Representations*, 56.

4 Rosenthal Kwall, R. (2007) "Originality in context", *Houston Law Review*, 871–872; Jaszi, P. (1994) "On the Author Effect: Contemporary Copyright and Collective Creativity", in: Woodmansee, M., Jaszi, P., *The construction of authorship: textual appropriation in law and literature*, Durham: Duke University Press, 29–32; Jaszi, P. (1991) "Toward a Theory of Copyright: The Metamorphoses of "Authorship", *Duke Law Journal*, 455–502. Note that these authors are fairly critical of the Romanticist idea of authorship. Rosenthal Kwall, for instance, puts forward a more Postmodernist view that all authors inevitably borrow from their cultural fabric in producing their work, yet also criticizes this view in not taking into account the author's unique efforts and contributions. An in-depth discussion of the precarious relationship between authorship and originality is, however, beyond the scope of our research. It is also in the sense of originality's connotation in copyright law that Black's Law Dictionary defines this notion as *"the quality or state of being the product of independent creation and having a minimum degree of creativity"*. "originality" (2009) *Black's Law Dictionary* (9th ed.), Thomson Reuters.

5 An Act for the Encouragement of Learning, by Vesting the Copies of Printed Books in the Authors or Purchasers of such Copies, during the Times therein mentioned of 5 April 1710, *c.19*.

6 Via the so-called Copyright Clause: Article I, Section 8, Clause 8 of the United States Constitution.

international level[7] – has sought to strike a balance between the "*rights of authors and publishers on one hand and the rights of users and consumers on the other*".[8] In order to benefit from the protection offered by copyright law, one of the defining criteria is that a work must be deemed original.[9] In US copyright law, the long-held belief was that the originality requirement meant that original work must be "*the fruits of intellectual labor*".[10] The focus was then put on the author's contribution, which must be the "*personal reaction of an individual upon nature*".[11] Important to note here is that this standard does not require a particular degree of novelty or ingenuity.[12] The latter became particularly apparent when considering the originality of compilations, where US courts found that compilations can be copyrighted if there has been sufficient effort to establish originality.[13] This "*sweat of the brow*" doctrine was later rejected in the landmark *Feist* case, in which the US Supreme Court established the need for a minimum degree of creativity.[14] In Continental European copyright law, an originality test was developed providing that a work must express the author's personality.[15] For compilations or databases – where such personality is hard to find – the standard was put at the author's creative choices.[16] This approach, developed by the French courts, has been followed in several EU Member States.[17]

---

7 For instance, the Convention for the Protection of Literary and Artistic Works, signed at Berne on 9 September 1886.

8 Abrams, H.B. (1992) "Originality and creativity in copyright law", *Law and Contemporary Problems*, vol. 55, 3.

9 *Ibid.*, 4; Judge, E.F., Gervais, D. (2009) "Of silos and constellations: comparing notions of originality in copyright law", *Cardozo Arts and Entertainment*, vol. 27, 376; Hariani, K., Hariani, A. (2011) "Analyzing "Originality" in Copyright Law: Transcending Jurisdictional Disparity", *IDEA The Intellectual Property Law Review*, vol. 51, 1–2.

10 United States *v.* Steffens, United States *v.* Witteman, and United States *v.* Johnson, 100 US 82 (1879), at 94; Abrams, H.B. (1992) "Originality and creativity in copyright law", *Law and Contemporary Problems*, vol. 55, 6.

11 Bleistein *v.* Donaldson Lithographing Co., 188 US 239 (1903), at 250.

12 Rosenthal Kwall, R. (2007) "Originality in context", *Houston Law Review*, 876; Hariani, K., Hariani, A. (2011) "Analyzing "Originality" in Copyright Law: Transcending Jurisdictional Disparity", *IDEA The Intellectual Property Law Review*, vol. 51, 8; Abrams, H.B. (1992) "Originality and creativity in copyright law", *Law and Contemporary Problems*, vol. 55, 7.

13 Abrams, H.B. (1992) "Originality and creativity in copyright law", *Law and Contemporary Problems*, vol. 55, 8.

14 Feist Publications *v.* Rural Telephone Service, 499 US 340 (1991), at 345; Rosenthal Kwall, R. (2007) "Originality in context", *Houston Law Review*, 876–877.

15 Hariani, K., Hariani, A. (2011) "Analyzing "Originality" in Copyright Law: Transcending Jurisdictional Disparity", *IDEA The Intellectual Property Law Review*, vol. 51, 12; Judge, E.F., Gervais, D. (2009) "Of silos and constellations: comparing notions of originality in copyright law", *Cardozo Arts and Entertainment*, vol. 27, 378.

16 Judge, E.F., Gervais, D. (2009) "Of silos and constellations: comparing notions of originality in copyright law", *Cardozo Arts and Entertainment*, vol. 27, 379. Thus, it rejects a strictly mechanical approach as under the "*sweat of the brow*" doctrine.

17 Though not all demonstrate an equally advanced level of protection. Judge, E.F., Gervais, D. (2009) "Of silos and constellations: comparing notions of originality in copyright law", *Cardozo Arts and Entertainment*, vol. 27, 381.

It has also found its way into EU law.[18] Apart from copyright law, originality has also always been one of the core requirements of patent law.[19] The originality requirement in patent law, however, could be regarded as stricter than that of copyright law.[20]

17. While the notion of originality is mainly linked to the development of intellectual property law, there are also several other branches of law in which an originality requirement can be found. European Napoleonic civil law, for instance, reserves a specific place for original instruments in its rules on evidence. As will be explored further on in chapter III, copies are generally accorded a lower probative value than originals.[21] This iteration of the originality requirement also found its way into other branches of law. Administrative law, and within this field especially archival law, has clear requirements on the keeping of original records.[22] Similar provisions can be found in fiscal law, where original invoices must be kept for a certain period of time.[23] Although the

---

18 See, for instance case law at the EU: European Court of Justice, Eva-Maria Painer *v.* Standard VerlagsGmbH and Others, C-145/10, at 88–89; European Court of Justice, Infopaq International A/S *v.* Danske Dagblades Forening, C-5/08, at 45. See also legislative acts: Article 2(2) Council Directive 87/54/EEC of 16 December 1986 on the legal protection of topographies of semiconductor products, *OJ* L 24 of 27 January 1987, 36–40; Article 3(1) Directive 96/9/EC of the European Parliament and of the Council of 11 March 1996 on the legal protection of databases, *OJ* L 77 of 27 March 1996, 20–28; Article 1(3) Council Directive 91/250/EEC of 14 May 1991 on the legal protection of computer programs, *OJ* L 122 of 17 May 1991, 42–46. With the latter directive, the EU rejected the stricter approach maintained by German courts that required a higher level of creativity: Bundesgerichtshof, Urt. *v.* 09.05.1985, *Az.* I ZR 52/83; Dumortier, J., Graux, H., Debusseré, F. (2013) *ICT-Recht*, Leuven: Acco, 221. However, this case law and EU law does not necessarily truly create a single originality standard in EU intellectual property rights law. Framing its position in international law could lead to the establishment of the author's creative choices as a standard, to be applied according to the technicality of the work: Judge, E.F., Gervais, D. (2009) "Of silos and constellations: comparing notions of originality in copyright law", *Cardozo Arts and Entertainment*, vol. 27, 387–388.

19 Liivak, O. (2005) "The Forgotten Originality Requirement: A Constitutional Hurdle for Gene Patents", *Journal of the Patent and Trademark Office Society*, vol. 87, 265.

20 In patent law, for instance, the natural products doctrine prohibits the patenting of what is found in nature, as it is not invented by the person applying for the patent. In copyright law, however, it is accepted that an author bases their work on observations of nature. Liivak, O. (2005) "The Forgotten Originality Requirement: A Constitutional Hurdle for Gene Patents", *Journal of the Patent and Trademark Office Society*, vol. 87, 268–269.

21 For instance, following article 1334 Belgian Civil Code.

22 In Belgium, public governments are obliged to submit their archival records to the State Archives. Article 1 of the Belgian Archival Act of 24 June 1955, *Belgian State Gazette* 12 August 1955. While the notion of 'archival records' is not defined in law, it is generally accepted to include original documents. The exception to this rule is when the law specifically allows for the substitution of original documents. Den Teuling, A.J.M. (2003) *Archiefterminologie voor Nederland en Vlaanderen*, 's-Gravenhage: Stichting Archiefpublicaties, nr. 8; Boudrez, F., Dekeyser, H. (2004) *Handboek Digitaal archiefbeheer in de praktijk*, Antwerpen: Stadsarchief, 22.

23 Article 60 of the Belgian VAT Code must be interpreted as referring to original invoices: Federal Public Service Finance (2007) "I. Verplichting tot bewaring", *FisconetPlus*, nr. 557/2–558.

focus of our research is limited to continental European law, similar originality requirements can also be found in the rules on evidence in common law. In the US, for instance, the best-evidence rule requires that the original writing must be produced to prove the contents of that writing.[24] The original of a writing or recording can then be defined as "*the writing or recording itself or any counterpart intended to have the same effect by the person who executed or issued it*".[25]

18. The question is then whether all of these originality requirements, found throughout different branches of law, stem from the same origin or whether they are fundamentally different. From a high-level view, it could be posited that the originality requirements in civil law, administrative law and fiscal law at least serve the same overall purpose. That would be to discourage the use of copies or other non-original documents, especially in a probative context, as copies are historically considered to not provide a fully trustworthy record of the original document. From the same high-level view, it could also be posited that intellectual property law has a similar purpose in providing protection to the originator – be it the author under copyright law or the inventor under patent law – of original content. However, there are fundamental differences in the ways in which these originality requirements are operationalized. As will be discussed further on in our research, the originality requirement in European civil law relies on the fulfillment of formal requirements. These do not include any 'intellectual labor', 'personal reaction' or even any creativity whatsoever. By contrast, copyright law relies on precisely those elements, while not caring too much about the formalities – any form in which the original idea has been expressed will do.[26] While it might therefore be concluded that the originality requirements in European civil law and in copyright law do have a core purpose in common at their most basic level – namely the protection of originals against copies – there is a substantial difference in how these branches of law operationalize that requirement.

2. DIGITALIZATION

19. As will be shown in chapter III, the rules on evidence in the Napoleonic Civil Code are very much focused on paper document processes. The obvious reason for this is that in 1804 handwritten paper documents were practically the only means available for drafting private instruments. Copies of these

---

24 "best-evidence rule" (2009) *Black's Law Dictionary* (9th ed.), Thomson Reuters. See also Fed. R. Evid. 1002.

25 Fed. R. Evid. 1001(d). Here, the production of documents that are not original is the exception to the rule: Fed. R. Evid. 1004.

26 Note that there can also be formalities in copyright law. Until the US joined the Berne Convention in 1989, it did require a copyright notice – such as the ©-symbol – to be used in order to gain copyright protection.

documents were handwritten as well, thus leaving room for forgery or mistakes. This is the main reason why a higher probative value was accorded to originals. Moreover, handwritten documents had to be exchanged physically between parties. In the meantime, however, several waves of technological innovation have significantly changed the way in which information is drafted, copied and exchanged between parties.

20. First, there have been several developments in how documents between parties are drafted. An early example is the typewriter, diminishing the need for handwritten documents. Currently, private instruments between parties are almost exclusively drafted using word processing software on computers. These computers have also brought about a paradigm shift in the relation between information and its carrier. While the information is inextricably linked to the carrier with paper documents, this is no longer the case when using computers. Here, the information is stored in a computer file – which in itself is a collection of data and resource files coupled with metadata[27] – and is manifested as a result of the interaction of the hardware and software used for the consultation with that file. The file can be moved freely, and is therefore not bound to a particular information carrier.

21. Second, there have been developments in how information is copied. Long gone is the time during which the production of a duplicate of a document required manual labor. By the 19th century the production of duplicates was facilitated by carbon paper. In the 20th century, the invention of the photocopier – or Xerox – allowed for the quick production of reliable copies. The use of computers – combined with printers – also greatly facilitated the production of larger numbers of originals or duplicates thereof.

22. Third, technology has changed the way in which information is exchanged between parties. From the fax to the Internet, technology has significantly reduced the need for parties to meet in order to arrange a physical transfer of information. Currently, as information is increasingly created electronically, together with the advent of electronic procedures to guarantee the authenticity and integrity of that information, the electronic transfer of information between parties has become standard practice.

23. Fourth, the societal shift toward the creation of electronic information has also resulted in the creation of new information types. Agreements between parties are no longer solely concluded in what can be considered as documents in the strict sense – either in paper or electronic form. These new information types include e-mails, text messages, social media posts and blogs. New information

---

27 Siracusa, J. (2003) "About the Finder…", *Ars Technica*, 2 April 2003.

types are also not constricted to be purely text-based information; they can also include pictures – on platforms such as Instagram and Snapchat – and video – including so-called vlogs.

24. These technological changes in how information is drafted, copied and transferred, as well as the development of new information types, pose a clear challenge to the 19th-century rules on evidence found in Napoleonic civil law. Handwritten documents have become a rarity; handwritten signatures cannot be applied to electronic information and electronic information exchange deviates from the classic notion of one party losing possession over that information. The process of society's embrace of electronic information can be referred to as the digitalization process, and it poses obvious challenges to lawmakers who found law to be increasingly at odds with this process. New legislation therefore seemed in order.[28]

25. One example of such new legislation relates to the electronic signature. As noted previously, handwritten documents are becoming a rarity, thus also posing a challenge to the notion of signatures. After all, how should a handwritten signature be affixed to information consisting of computer bits? The electronic signature, therefore, provides a way to satisfy the requirements and goals of a handwritten signature in an electronic manner. One of the earliest examples of such electronic signature in law can be found in the US State of Utah, in 1995.[29] Here, cryptographic means – more specifically a hashing function and a public key interface (PKI), also known as a digital signature – were used to establish an equivalence between a handwritten and electronic signature. This model was subsequently adopted in Germany[30] and Italy[31], and became the inspiration for an EU-wide legal framework on electronic signatures.[32] The EU followed a more technology-neutral approach, but it still reserved a specific spot for the technique

---

28 While the focus of our research is on continental EU law, this problem applies just as well to common law. One example is the US, where the Federal Rules on Evidence were amended to reflect that for *"electronically stored information, "original" means any printout--or other output readable by sight--if it accurately reflects the information. An "original" of a photograph includes the negative or a print from it."* Fed. R. Evid. 1001(d).

29 Utah Digital Signature Act, Utah Code §46-3-101 – 504.

30 Gesetz vom 13. Juni 1997 zur Regelung der Rahmenbedingungen für Informations- und Kommunikationsdienste (Informations- und Kommunikationsdienste-Gesetz – IuKDG), *BGBl. I* 28 July 1997, 1872–6.

31 Legge n. 59 15 marzo 1997 Delega al Governo per il conferimento di funzioni e compiti alle regioni ed enti locali, per la riforma della Pubblica Amministrazione e per la semplificazione amministrativa, *Gazzetta Ufficiale* n. 63 of 17 March 1997.

32 Directive 1999/93/EC of the European Parliament and of the Council of 13 December 1999 on a Community framework for electronic signatures, *OJ* L 13 of 19 January 2000, 12–20. This directive has been replaced by: Regulation (EU) No 910/2014 of the European Parliament and of the Council of 23 July 2014 on electronic identification and trust services for electronic transactions in the internal market and repealing Directive 1999/93/EC, *OJ* L 257 of 28 August 2014, 73–114.

of the digital signature as its qualified electronic signature.[33] Under the new rules, electronic signatures cannot be denied effectiveness and admissibility as evidence solely on the grounds of them being a signature in electronic form or for not being a qualified electronic signature.[34] National courts, however, retain the competence to accept such electronic signatures as valid in terms of evidence or not.[35] Member States can thus decide when to allow electronic signatures, but where they are allowed, their effectiveness cannot be denied.[36]

26. Another initiative taken by the European legislator was aimed at electronic commerce, including the use of electronic contracts. In 2000, the EU adopted the so-called E-commerce Directive – or: Directive on Electronic Commerce – for the purposes of further developing the internal market in terms of the establishment of service providers, commercial communications, electronic contracts, the liability of intermediaries, codes of conduct, out-of-court dispute settlements, court actions and cooperation between Member States.[37] The reason for this was that the lack of specific legislation aimed at facilitating the emergence and development of electronic commerce was found to lead to a lack of legal certainty and to mistrust.[38] Apart from including provisions aimed at various matters, such as unsolicited commercial communications and the liability of intermediary service providers, this directive also includes provisions aimed at facilitating the conclusion of contracts by electronic means.[39] More in particular, it is stated that Member States must allow contracts to be concluded by electronic means, meaning that such contracts cannot be denied legal effectiveness and validity solely because of their having been concluded by electronic means.[40] The

---

33 Dumortier, J. (2004) "Legal status of qualified electronic signatures in Europe", in Paulus, S., Pohlmann, N. and H. Reimer (eds), *ISSE 2004-Securing Electronic Business Processes*, Wiesbaden: Springer Vieweg, 281–289.

34 Article 5(2) Directive 1999/93/EC.

35 This follows from recital 21 to Directive 1999/93/EC, which states that national law must decide upon when to accept electronic signatures and electronic documents and that "*this Directive is without prejudice to the power of a national court to make a ruling regarding conformity with the requirements of this Directive and does not affect national rules regarding the unfettered judicial consideration of evidence*". See: Dumortier, J., Vandezande, N. (2014) "Legal evidence in a digital context: will signatures disappear?", in: Savin, A., Trzaskowski, J. (eds.), *Research Handbook on EU Internet Law*, Cheltenham: Edward Elgar, 435–436.

36 Note that the use of electronic contracts has been strongly enforced by article 9 of Directive 2000/31/EC, thus restricting the freedom of Member States to decide when to allow electronic signatures and electronic contracts.

37 Article 1 Directive 2000/31/EC of the European Parliament and of the Council of 8 June 2000 on certain legal aspects of information society services, in particular electronic commerce, in the Internal Market ('Directive on electronic commerce'), *OJ* L 178 of 17 July 2000, 1–16.

38 Van Eecke, P. (2003) "Hoofdstuk I. Artikelsgewijze bespreking van de wetten elektronische handel", in: Van Eecke, P., Dumortier, J. (eds.), *Elektronische Handel – Commentaar bij de wetten van 11 maart 2003*, Brugge: die Keure, 12–13.

39 More in particular: article 9 Directive 2000/31/EC.

40 Article 9(1) Directive 2000/31/EC. Note, however, that article 9(2) Directive 2000/31/EC does include a list of exceptions. For instance, Member States may require that the transfer of rights relating to real estate must be concluded on paper and not by electronic means.

way in which this directive influenced Belgian civil law will be discussed further on in chapter III.

27. While the legislator's efforts in facilitating the digitalization process can certainly be applauded, it must be borne in mind that these initiatives also demonstrate a clear preference for a particular policy option. Rather than seeing electronic information as a fundamental paradigm shift worthy of its own unique rules – as paper-based information has – the legislator has chosen to merely 'upgrade' the scope of existing rules to extend to electronic information. As will become clear later on in this work, this has not always proven to be an entirely successful approach.

CHAPTER III
ORIGINALITY IN CIVIL LAW

1. EVIDENCE IN THE BELGIAN CIVIL CODE

28. In this section, the current Belgian civil law framework regarding the probative value of information will be analyzed, with a particular focus on the traditional laws of evidence directed at paper-based procedures. From this analysis, the precise place of the originality requirement in this branch of law will become clear. To limit and demarcate the scope of this analysis, the focus will be put solely on the rules that are applicable to evidence in matters of civil law.[41] As a result, specific probative rules that are applicable in other domains – such as criminal law or commercial law – will principally not be included in the present analysis. However, there are cases in which the probative rules in civil law are to be read in conjunction with rules deriving from other domains. For instance, in certain matters the rules on evidence in civil law are complemented by rules emanating from judicial law.[42] Conversely, other domains may refer to the rules of evidence in civil law, for instance when a merchant has to prove an obligation against a non-merchant.[43] As a result, it is important to clearly assess the nature of the matter that needs to be proven, as well as the capacity of the parties involved.[44]

---

41 More specifically, the provisions analyzed here are applicable to matters regarding property and agreements. Matters concerning familial situations – such as marriage – fall under the scope of different rules. See also: Mougenot, D. (2002) *Droit des obligations: la preuve*, Brussel: Larcier, 63. While, for brevity's sake, this section will extensively refer to civil law, it should be clear that this only pertains to matters regarding property and agreements within civil law.

42 Minjauw, H., Vandendriessche, J. (2008) "Titel VI. Het bewijsrecht in burgerlijke zaken", in: Roodhooft, R. (ed.), *Bestendig Handboek Verbintenissenrecht*, Mechelen: Kluwer, VI.1–2a. See also articles 870 – 1016*bis* Belgian Judicial Code, which regulate the procedural conduct such as the presentation of evidence, the collaboration between parties in the procedure and the role of the judge.

43 While a non-merchant may rely on the more liberal rules on evidence in commercial transactions when proving against a merchant, the merchant will be bound by the rules on evidence in civil matters against non-merchants. Cass. 18 January 1990, *jure.juridat.just.fgov.be*; Minjauw, H., Vandendriessche, J. (2008) "Titel VI. Het bewijsrecht in burgerlijke zaken", in: Roodhooft, R. (ed.), *Bestendig Handboek Verbintenissenrecht*, Mechelen: Kluwer, VI.1–3.

44 For instance, as commercial law applies to acts of commerce, two non-merchants may rely on the rules of evidence under commercial law when they need to prove an act of commerce between them. Or a merchant could be bound by the rules of evidence under civil law if the act that requires proof did not constitute an act of commerce. Minjauw, H., Vandendriessche,

29. Belgian civil law is enshrined in the Belgian Civil Code, which is in essence still the same code that was introduced under Napoleon Bonaparte when Belgium was part of the First French Republic in 1804.[45] While the Napoleonic Code[46] has been heavily amended over the years, certain sections – such as that concerning the rules on evidence – have barely been changed, if at all, throughout the years.[47] As a result, it is clear that the principles regarding evidence in civil law were not originally drafted with the intent to accommodate electronic information.

1.1. EVIDENCE

30. Evidence can be regarded as the substantiation of a legal claim.[48] The rules on evidence are, then, the legal principles that govern the process of providing evidence. Important to know here is that the reality of matters, as it happened in actuality, may not be the same as the reality established by proof.[49] As a result, evidence serves to present a sufficiently convincing case that does not necessarily represent the actual truth, but rather a 'legal truth'.[50] It is therefore up to the judge presiding over the case to assess whether or not there are still any profound reasons to doubt the credibility of the evidence presented to him and to base his decisions on a likelihood bordering on certainty.[51]

J. (2008) "Titel VI. Het bewijsrecht in burgerlijke zaken", in: Roodhooft, R. (ed.), *Bestendig Handboek Verbintenissenrecht*, Mechelen: Kluwer, VI.1-3-4.

45 The Code entered into force on 21 March 1804, just before the French Empire was proclaimed with the crowning of Napoleon I on 18 May 1804.

46 Official title: Code civil des français. X (1804) *Code civil des français. Édition originale et seule officielle.* Paris: Imp. de la République.

47 More precisely: there are only eight notable alterations to the articles referring to the rules on evidence:
- A 2003 addition to article 1317.
- A 2009 addition to article 1317, itself amended in 2017.
- A 2016 amendment and addition to article 1317.
- A 1967 amendment to article 1319.
- A 2000 addition to article 1322.
- A 2016 addition to article 1334.
- Several amendments of the monetary sum included in articles 1341–1345, most recently in 2000.
- The 1967 abolishment of article 1351.

These alterations will be further explored elsewhere in this work.

48 De Page, H. (1967) *Traité élémentaire de droit civil Belge, Tome Troisième (Les Obligations)*, Brussel: Bruylant, 693; Wagner, K. (2009) "Actualia burgerlijk bewijsrecht", *P&B*, 157; Mourlon Beernaert, F. (2006) "Partie VI. Le droit de la preuve – Introduction", in: X, *Obligations. Traité théorique et pratique*, Brussel: Kluwer, VI.1.1 – 2; Mougenot, D. (2002) *Droit des obligations: la preuve*, Brussel: Larcier, 63.

49 Minjauw, H., Vandendriessche, J. (2008) "Titel VI. Het bewijsrecht in burgerlijke zaken", in: Roodhooft, R. (ed.), *Bestendig Handboek Verbintenissenrecht*, Mechelen: Kluwer, VI.1-4.

50 Wagner, K. (2009) "Actualia burgerlijk bewijsrecht", *P&B*, 153–154; Mougenot, D. (2002) *Droit des obligations: la preuve*, Brussel: Larcier, 80–81.

51 Cornelis, L. (2000) *Algemene theorie van de verbintenis*, Antwerpen: Intersentia, 204; Minjauw, H., Vandendriessche, J. (2008) "Titel VI. Het bewijsrecht in burgerlijke zaken",

31. One of the most important matters in evidence is to establish who needs to provide proof of what. In general, the party making a claim will have to put forward the evidence required to substantiate that claim, known as the principle of *actori incumbit probatio.*[52] Alternatively, the party who wishes to make an objection or to invoke an exception will have to provide proof to substantiate that position, also known as *reus excipiendo fit actor.*[53]

32. A second important notion is to know what needs to be proven. In principle, this concerns all facts relevant for the judge to make his decision with sufficient certainty.[54] Here, four types of facts can be distinguished.[55]

General facts are facts of no legal relevance, but that may relate to the case in a certain way. For instance, in the case of a traffic accident, the weather and road conditions at the time of the accident may be taken into account in the decision.[56]

Legal facts are facts that do have legal relevance, without requiring the intent of parties to give rise to legal consequences. This may include a party's age in case of dealing with minors, the passing of a term limit, or even the commitment of criminal or tortuous acts.[57]

Legal acts are those acts performed by parties with the clear intent to establish legal consequences, such as the signing of a contract or the redaction of a will.[58]

Legal rules are considered to be known by the court and, therefore, do not need to be proven, according to the principle of *ius novit curia.*[59]

---

in: Roodhooft, R. (ed.), *Bestendig Handboek Verbintenissenrecht*, Mechelen: Kluwer, VI.1-4; Wagner, K. (2009) "Actualia burgerlijk bewijsrecht", *P&B*, 153-154. Similarly, when a certain matter cannot be sufficiently proven, it does not mean that this matter did not effectively happen or exist; it only means that that matter cannot be taken into consideration by the court. Cornelis, L. (2000) *Algemene theorie van de verbintenis*, Antwerpen: Intersentia, 204; De Page, H. (1967) *Traité élémentaire de droit civil Belge, Tome Troisième (Les Obligations)*, Brussel: Bruylant, 695.

52 In Belgian civil evidence law, this principle can be found in article 1315, first paragraph Belgian Civil Code. This principle is also found in article 870 Belgian Judicial Code. See also: Minjauw, H., Vandendriessche, J. (2008) "Titel VI. Het bewijsrecht in burgerlijke zaken", in: Roodhooft, R. (ed.), *Bestendig Handboek Verbintenissenrecht*, Mechelen: Kluwer, VI.2-2; Wagner, K. (2009) "Actualia burgerlijk bewijsrecht", *P&B*, 157; Mougenot, D. (2002) *Droit des obligations: la preuve*, Brussel: Larcier, 92.

53 This is found in the second paragraph of article 1315 Belgian Civil Code.

54 Cornelis, L. (2000) *Algemene theorie van de verbintenis*, Antwerpen: Intersentia, 207.

55 Mourlon Beernaert, F. (2006) "Partie VI. Le droit de la preuve - Objet de la preuve", in: X, *Obligations. Traité théorique et pratique*, Brussel: Kluwer, VI.1.2 - 2; Mougenot, D. (2002) *Droit des obligations: la preuve*, Brussel: Larcier, 84-85.

56 Minjauw, H., Vandendriessche, J. (2008) "Titel VI. Het bewijsrecht in burgerlijke zaken", in: Roodhooft, R. (ed.), *Bestendig Handboek Verbintenissenrecht*, Mechelen: Kluwer, VI.1-5.

57 *Id.*

58 Important to note here is that these first three types are in fact related to each other. For instance, each legal fact is a specific type of regular fact and each legal act is a specific type of legal fact.

59 Cornelis, L. (2000) *Algemene theorie van de verbintenis*, Antwerpen: Intersentia, 207-208; Dumortier, J. (2010) *ICT-Recht*, Leuven: Acco, 128; Wagner, K. (2009) "Actualia burgerlijk

Furthermore, parties will only need to provide evidence for disputed facts.[60] If one party puts forward a fact and the other party does not dispute it, then the judge presiding over the case may accept it as an assumption.[61] However, that second party may still decide to dispute the fact later on, thus putting the onus of proof on the party putting forward the now disputed fact.[62]

1.2. ADMISSIBILITY

33. As already hinted at previously, there is no single universally accepted set of rules regarding evidence. Despite the rising importance of intergovernmental and supranational organs such as the European Union, probative matters remain a matter of national law primarily.[63] One of the main distinctions between different sets of rules is the distinction between open and regulated systems of evidence.[64] In an open probative system, all lawfully obtained evidence can be presented to the court for its discretionary consideration.[65] Examples of such open probative system are criminal law and commercial law. Under a regulated system, there is a clear set of rules that determines precisely which types of evidence – and under which requirements and restrictions – are allowed to be presented to the court, as well as rules governing the competence of the judge to decide upon the probative value of

bewijsrecht", *P&B*, 162; Mourlon Beernaert, F. (2006) "Partie VI. Le droit de la preuve – Objet de la preuve", in: X, *Obligations. Traité théorique et pratique*, Brussel: Kluwer, VI.1.2 – 5.

60 Minjauw, H., Vandendriessche, J. (2008) "Titel VI. Het bewijsrecht in burgerlijke zaken", in: Roodhooft, R. (ed.), *Bestendig Handboek Verbintenissenrecht*, Mechelen: Kluwer, VI.1–6; Mourlon Beernaert, F. (2006) "Partie VI. Le droit de la preuve – Objet de la preuve", in: X, *Obligations. Traité théorique et pratique*, Brussel: Kluwer, VI.1.2 – 2–3; Mougenot, D. (2002) *Droit des obligations: la preuve*, Brussel: Larcier, 85.

61 Cass. 25 October 1979, *jure.juridat.just.fgov.be*.

62 Cass. 25 October 1979, *jure.juridat.just.fgov.be*; Cass. 1 March 1973, *jure.juridat.just.fgov.be*. A more difficult situation presents itself when a negative fact is disputed. While the judge cannot relieve a party of the duty to prove a negative fact, it is common to attempt to prove a positive fact that rules out the disputed negative fact. Cass. 16 December 2004, *jure.juridat.just.fgov.be*. It can also be argued that the judge can decide more easily on shifting the burden of proof when a negative fact needs to be proven, Cornelis, L. (2000) *Algemene theorie van de verbintenis*, Antwerpen: Intersentia, 213; Wagner, K. (2009) "Actualia burgerlijk bewijsrecht", *P&B*, 160; Mourlon Beernaert, F. (2006) "Partie VI. Le droit de la preuve – Objet de la preuve", in: X, *Obligations. Traité théorique et pratique*, Brussel: Kluwer, VI.1.2 – 3–4.

63 Divergences can be found even within national law. Criminal law, for instance, is generally known to have a different set of rules relating to evidence than civil law. In commercial matters, fiscal matters or social matters, different rules may also apply.

64 Dumortier, J. (2010) *ICT-Recht*, Leuven: Acco, 127–128; Cornelis, L. (2000) *Algemene theorie van de verbintenis*, Antwerpen: Intersentia, 216; Mougenot, D. (2002) *Droit des obligations: la preuve*, Brussel: Larcier, 65.

65 Van Gerven, W., Covemaker, S. (2006) *Verbintenissenrecht*, Leuven: Acco, 653; Mourlon Beernaert, F. (2006) "Partie VI. Le droit de la preuve – Introduction", in: X, *Obligations. Traité théorique et pratique*, Brussel: Kluwer, VI.1.1 – 3.

such evidence.[66] The rules on evidence in Belgian civil law are a clear example of a regulated system of evidence, as will become clear later on.[67] The difference between an open and a regulated system of evidence is, however, not absolute. In open systems, there will also always be at least some rules on admissibility.[68] Likewise, regulated systems of evidence may also display certain elements that are rather open.[69]

34. The reason why the Belgian rules on evidence in civil law are generally considered as a regulated system of evidence is that there are clear and well-defined rules on which types of evidence are allowed in which case, how the burden of proof is distributed and even on the value of each type of evidence as well as the hierarchical relationship between them.[70] The Belgian Civil Code provides a list of types of evidence that are allowed.[71] As far as the hierarchy of these types of evidence is concerned, there is a clear correlation between the place in the evidentiary hierarchy of a particular type of evidence and the margin of appreciation left to the judge. More clearly regulated evidence will leave less appreciation to the judge and will, thus, be ranked higher up the hierarchy. In general, the following hierarchy is followed[72]:

Irrefutable evidence: such as the decisive oath and the judicial confession.

Evidence with a statutorily defined probative value: such as public and private instruments, statutory presumptions and extra-judicial confessions. If the court finds that the defined requirements for these types of evidence are met, it must accord the defined probative value to such evidence. The opposing party can still deliver evidence against these types of evidence, thus rendering them refutable.

Free evidence: such as writings other than public or private instruments, witnesses and factual presumptions. Here, the judge can accord the probative value he sees fit.

---

66 Dumortier, J. (2010) *ICT-Recht*, Leuven: Acco, 127–128.

67 It should, however, be noted that there are exceptions in which evidence in civil matters can be rather open. A number of such exceptions will be discussed further on.

68 Van Gerven, W., Covemaker, S. (2006) *Verbintenissenrecht*, Leuven: Acco, 653 and 657.

69 In the case of Belgian civil law, the presumptions can be considered as an open type of evidence, as will become clear later on.

70 De Page, H. (1967) *Traité élémentaire de droit civil Belge, Tome Troisième (Les Obligations)*, Brussel: Bruylant, 695–698; Lamensch, M. (2006) "La règle de la primauté de la preuve écrite: une application delicate", *TBBR*, 49; Mougenot, D. (2002) *Droit des obligations: la preuve*, Brussel: Larcier, 66.

71 Article 1316 Belgian Civil Code. Note that judicial law adds a number of types of evidence that can be used:
- Expert analysis (article 962 *et seq.* Belgian Judicial Code)
- Party interrogation (article 982 *et seq.* Belgian Judicial Code)
- Bailiff's findings (article 516 Belgian Judicial Code)
- Investigation on location (article 1007 Belgian Judicial Code).

72 Dumortier, J. (2010) *ICT-Recht*, Leuven: Acco, 128.

It should, however, be noted that most principles of Belgian civil evidence law are not considered to be of public order, meaning that parties can choose to deviate from these principles and establish their own set of probative rules.[73]

35. While the principally exhaustive list of admissible types of evidence and the hierarchy between them already indicates a preference for evidence in writing, this is further exacerbated by the principles put forward by article 1341 Belgian Civil Code. This article holds that: "*A notary or private instrument must be drafted for all matters exceeding the sum or value of EUR 375, even regarding voluntary bailment; proof by witnesses is not allowed against and above the content of the instruments, nor regarding what is alleged before, during or after the drafting of such instruments, even when it concerns a sum or value of less than EUR 375. This does not detract from what is stipulated in the laws regarding commerce.*"[74] What is stipulated here has two important implications. First, when the matter that requires proof exceeds EUR 375[75], only evidence in writing provided by a notary or private instrument, a deed, is allowed. This means that other types of evidence, such as witnesses and presumptions, are not allowed here.[76, 77] Second, when a deed is present, evidence contrary to or above what is

73 Mourlon Beernaert, F. (2006) "Partie VI. Le droit de la preuve – Introduction", in: X, *Obligations. Traité théorique et pratique*, Brussel: Kluwer, VI.1.1 – 6–7; Mougenot, D. (2002) *Droit des obligations: la preuve*, Brussel: Larcier, 68–69.

74 Translation provided by author; no official translation available.

75 Note that this is one of the few matters that has been changed since the original Code Napoleon of 1804. The original code concerned 150 French francs. Prior to the introduction of the euro, this had been raised up to 15,000 Belgian francs, which was converted into the current amount of EUR 375. Mougenot, D. (2002) *Droit des obligations: la preuve*, Brussel: Larcier, 112. Some countries have raised this threshold higher, perhaps in response to changes in purchasing power due to inflation. Luxembourg, for instance, has raised the bar to EUR 2,500. Article 79 Règlement grand-ducal of 1 August 2008 concernement le basculement en euro le 1er janvier 2002, *Mémorial A n° 117* of 18 September 2001. France has raised the bar to EUR 1,500. Article 1 Décret n°80–533 of 15 July 1980 pris pour l'application de l'article 1341 du code civil, modifié par article 56 Décret n°2004–836 of 20 August 2004, *JORF* 22 August 2004. The obvious result of this is that Luxembourg and France have a much broader scope of agreements where written evidence is not prescribed.

76 Even though presumptions are not explicitly mentioned, there is a consensus in legal literature that presumptions are also covered by the exclusion of article 1341 Belgian Civil Code. Van Gerven, W., Covemaker, S. (2006) *Verbintenissenrecht*, Leuven: Acco, 682 and 685; Minjauw, H., Vandendriessche, J. (2008) "Titel VI. Het bewijsrecht in burgerlijke zaken", in: Roodhooft, R. (ed.), *Bestendig Handboek Verbintenissenrecht*, Mechelen: Kluwer, VI.3–5. The reason for this is article 1353 Belgian Civil Code, which holds that non-legal presumptions can only be allowed in cases where evidence by witnesses is allowed. As a result, it can reasonably be argued that presumptions are not allowed when evidence by witnesses is not allowed.

77 Note, however, that in principle confessions and oaths are still allowed. However, as these types of evidence require the cooperation of the adverse party, they cannot be procured solely by the claimant himself. Mourlon Beernaert, F., Gaudy, A. (2006) "Partie VI. Le droit de la preuve – La prééminence de la preuve écrite", in: X, *Obligations. Traité théorique et pratique*, Brussel: Kluwer, VI.4.1 – 4.

alleged in that instrument can only be provided by another deed, regardless of the value of the matter. The consequence of this is a clear preference for evidence in writing provided by notary or private instrument.[78] Other types of evidence – such as witnesses and presumptions – are considered as fallback when no evidence in writing can be produced.[79] It also provides an illustration of how legal and factual reality may differ: if an agreement exceeds the value of EUR 375, but is not backed by a written instrument, then it will be difficult to provide proof of that agreement. While the agreement exists and is valid, it cannot be considered as such in establishing the legal truth.[80] The historical reason for this preference for evidence in writing is rather straightforward: the economics of procedure.[81] Examining evidence in writing is considered to be simpler, faster and more reliable than hearing witnesses.[82] Evidence in writing is also generally drafted at a time at which there was not yet an ongoing or suspected conflict-being *in tempore non suspecto* – and is therefore considered more trustworthy.[83] Similarly, presumptions are considered to offer less certainty regarding what needs to be proven.[84]

36. The evidence that parties wish to present to the court must, of course, also be lawful, meaning that it has been lawfully obtained and that its presentation would be allowed.[85] Evidence of which the presentation breaches a duty of confidentiality, that was forged or that is contrary to the public order and good decency is considered to be unlawful.[86] If the evidence in itself is valid

---

78 Like most principles discussed here, this article is not considered to be mandatory or of public order. In other words, parties can agree to deviate from it. Cass. 21 December 1999, *jure.juridat.just.fgov.be*.

79 Minjauw, H., Vandendriessche, J. (2008) "Titel VI. Het bewijsrecht in burgerlijke zaken", in: Roodhooft, R. (ed.), *Bestendig Handboek Verbintenissenrecht*, Mechelen: Kluwer, VI.3–5.

80 Minjauw, H., Vandendriessche, J. (2008) "Titel VI. Het bewijsrecht in burgerlijke zaken", in: Roodhooft, R. (ed.), *Bestendig Handboek Verbintenissenrecht*, Mechelen: Kluwer, VI.3–6; Mourlon Beernaert, F., Gaudy, A. (2006) "Partie VI. Le droit de la preuve – La prééminence de la preuve écrite", in: X, *Obligations. Traité théorique et pratique*, Brussel: Kluwer, VI.4.1 – 2.

81 Mougenot traces these principles back to the 15th century. Mougenot, D. (2002) *Droit des obligations: la preuve*, Brussel: Larcier, 108. See also: Mourlon Beernaert, F. (2006) "Partie VI. Le droit de la preuve – Introduction", in: X, *Obligations. Traité théorique et pratique*, Brussel: Kluwer, VI.1.1 – 3–4.

82 Mougenot, D. (2002) *Droit des obligations: la preuve*, Brussel: Larcier, 108; Van Gerven, W., Covemaker, S. (2006) *Verbintenissenrecht*, Leuven: Acco, 653–654.

83 Minjauw, H., Vandendriessche, J. (2008) "Titel VI. Het bewijsrecht in burgerlijke zaken", in: Roodhooft, R. (ed.), *Bestendig Handboek Verbintenissenrecht*, Mechelen: Kluwer, VI.1–5.

84 De Page, H. (1967) *Traité élémentaire de droit civil Belge, Tome Troisième (Les Obligations)*, Brussel: Bruylant, 722.

85 Van Gerven, W., Covemaker, S. (2006) *Verbintenissenrecht*, Leuven: Acco, 657; Allemeersch, B., Schollen, P. (2002) "Behoorlijk bewijs in burgerlijke zaken. Over de geoorloofdheidvereiste in het burgerlijk bewijsrecht", *RW*, 41; Van Kildonck, K. (2010) "Privacy Werknemers. Onrechtmatig verkregen bewijs op het werk", *NJW*, 180.

86 Allemeersch, B., Schollen, P. (2002) "Behoorlijk bewijs in burgerlijke zaken. Over de geoorloofdheidvereiste in het burgerlijk bewijsrecht", *RW*, 41.

and lawful, but if it was obtained in a manner that breaches the law, then the evidence is considered to have been unlawfully obtained.[87] Such is the case, for instance, if the evidence was obtained through theft, fraud, extortion or by breaching private communications. In such cases, it is generally up to the court to judge the severity of the unlawfulness – taking into account the different interests at stake, as well as the rights possibly violated by unlawfully obtaining said evidence – and whether or not the evidence so obtained can still be used.[88] The Belgian Supreme Court has decided on this matter that unlawfully obtained evidence may only be refused if it violates a rule that is prescribed under the penalty of nullity, when the evidence is tainted by a vice that diminishes its reliability, or when its admission would jeopardize the right to a fair trial.[89] The presiding judge will need to take into account the formal nature of the irregularity, the effect of the irregularity on the rights affected by the violation, whether or not the violation was committed intentionally, whether the severity of the violation supersedes the irregularity committed, whether the unlawfully obtained evidence only concerns a material element in the violation and whether the irregularity preceding or accompanying the establishment of the violation is disproportionate to the severity of the violation.[90] As a result, while evidence must principally be obtained lawfully, courts do have a degree of discretionary power to judge its admissibility.

1.3. EXCEPTIONS TO THE PRECEDENCE OF WRITTEN EVIDENCE

37. While the rules on evidence in the Belgian Civil Code display a clear preference for evidence in writing, there are a few important exceptions to this principle. One of the most important exceptions concerns the different types of facts that need to be proven. As discussed previously, rules of law do not need to be proven. This leaves the parties in a dispute to prove regular facts, legal facts and legal acts. In legal literature, there is a clear majority of authors that argues that article 1341 of the Belgian Civil Code only applies to legal acts.[91] While a different approach may be argued for[92], the distinction made between acts and facts is

---

87 *Ibid.*, 50.

88 *Ibid.*, 51–57.

89 Cass. 10 March 2008, *jure.juridat.just.fgov.be*.

90 *Id.*

91 Van Gerven, W., Covemaker, S. (2006) *Verbintenissenrecht*, Leuven: Acco, 656; Minjauw, H., Vandendriessche, J. (2008) "Titel VI. Het bewijsrecht in burgerlijke zaken", in: Roodhooft, R. (ed.), *Bestendig Handboek Verbintenissenrecht*, Mechelen: Kluwer, VI.1–5 and VI.3–6b; Cornelis, L. (2000) *Algemene theorie van de verbintenis*, Antwerpen: Intersentia, 244.

92 For instance, the Belgian Supreme Court has once ruled that the rules on evidence in the Belgian Civil Code apply to all legal facts, which thus also covers legal acts as these are a specific type of legal facts. Cass. 4 November 1926, *Pas.* 1927, 84. See also: De Page, H. (1967)

generally considered as valid.[93] This would mean that facts – both regular facts and legal facts – are in principle not covered by the limitation of article 1341 of the Belgian Civil Code and can therefore be proven by all means.[94, 95] While generally accepted as valid, it should, however, be reminded that this exception is by no means absolute and should therefore not simply be taken at face value.[96] The requirement to produce evidence in writing can also serve to encourage parties to carefully consider their commitments and to reduce the risk of misunderstandings.[97]

38. A second important exception to the rule of article 1341 Belgian Civil Code concerns third parties. Such third parties are principally not party to the matter under dispute and can, therefore, be considered as not having had the possibility to procure evidence in writing.[98] As a result, it can be argued that the position of the third party toward the parties to the dispute concerns proof of legal facts, which – according to the exception discussed in the previous paragraph – can be provided by all means.[99] This means that third parties in a conflict can use

Traité élémentaire de droit civil Belge, Tome Troisième (Les Obligations), Brussel: Bruylant, 705 et seq. Note, however, that De Page does not fully oppose the idea of making a distinction between cases where article 1341 Belgian Civil Code does apply and where it does not apply, as explained in footnote 93.

93 Mougenot, D. (2002) *Droit des obligations: la preuve*, Brussel: Larcier, 109. Also note that the Belgian Civil Code generally does not explicitly restrict the proof of all legal facts, but only of legal acts. Moreover, it can be argued that precisely the performance of a legal act lends itself to the drafting of a written agreement, which corresponds to the *ratio legis* of article 1341 Belgian Civil Code. Minjauw, H., Vandendriessche, J. (2008) "Titel VI. Het bewijsrecht in burgerlijke zaken", in: Roodhooft, R. (ed.), *Bestendig Handboek Verbintenissenrecht*, Mechelen: Kluwer, VI.3–6b. Following this *ratio legis*, it could be argued that article 1341 Belgian Civil Code should not apply when there is an absolute impossibility to provide evidence in writing *in tempore non suspecto*. Such could be considered to apply in most examples of legal facts, as they are generally characterized by their lack of intent to cause legal consequences. De Page, H. (1967) *Traité élémentaire de droit civil Belge, Tome Troisième (Les Obligations),* Brussel: Bruylant, 704–706.

94 Thereby forming an example of how a regulated system can also contain elements of an open system of evidence.

95 Cornelis has argued that the constitutional elements of an agreement – being concurrence, capacity, object and cause – are legal facts and can thus be proven by all means. However, proof of these individual elements does not constitute proof of the agreement itself, which is still considered as proof of a legal act bound to the applicability of article 1341 Belgian Civil Code. Cornelis, L., Goethals, P. (2000) "Contractuele aspecten van e-commerce", in: X, *De elektronische handel*, Antwerpen: Kluwer, 1–49.

96 For instance, certain legal facts – such as birth and death – do require an instrument in writing. Likewise, there are special provisions that do allow proof by witnesses or presumptions for legal acts, for instance in a lease. Minjauw, H., Vandendriessche, J. (2008) "Titel VI. Het bewijsrecht in burgerlijke zaken", in: Roodhooft, R. (ed.), *Bestendig Handboek Verbintenissenrecht*, Mechelen: Kluwer, VI.3–7.

97 Van Gerven, W., Covemaker, S. (2006) *Verbintenissenrecht*, Leuven: Acco, 653–654.

98 Minjauw, H., Vandendriessche, J. (2008) "Titel VI. Het bewijsrecht in burgerlijke zaken", in: Roodhooft, R. (ed.), *Bestendig Handboek Verbintenissenrecht*, Mechelen: Kluwer, VI.3–6a; Mougenot, D. (2002) *Droit des obligations: la preuve*, Brussel: Larcier, 118–119.

99 Cornelis, L. (2000) *Algemene theorie van de verbintenis*, Antwerpen: Intersentia, 244; Mourlon Beernaert, F., Gaudy, A. (2006) "Partie VI. Le droit de la preuve – La prééminence de la preuve écrite", in: X, *Obligations. Traité théorique et pratique*, Brussel: Kluwer, VI.4.1 – 5.

all means to provide evidence against and above the value of what is stipulated in an instrument in writing between the parties to the conflict. However, when a party to the conflict wants to provide proof of the legal acts in the dispute against the third party, the principles of article 1341 Belgian Civil Code will apply.[100] A different situation arises when a third party can procure evidence in writing, in which case parties to the conflict can provide evidence to the contrary by witnesses or presumptions – thus not applying the rule of article 1341 Belgian Civil Code.[101]

1.4. EVIDENCE IN WRITING

39. As found in the previous sections, the Belgian Civil Code has a clear preference for evidence in writing. The most important type of evidence in writing are instruments, either private between parties or by a notary, deeds. Such instruments are generally drafted to document the legal acts of parties and to detail their obligations toward one another and to later serve as evidence if a dispute would arise regarding the existence or scope of their obligations.[102] While the term 'instruments' is often used synonymously with the notion of 'evidence in writing', it should be noted that instruments are only one particular type of evidence in writing.[103] As such, they are accorded a specific probative value that other types of evidence in writing may not possess. This terminological confusion should, therefore, be avoided. Other types of evidence in writing include the beginning of evidence in writing, copies, account books, registers, correspondence, etc.

1.4.1. Private instruments

40. Private instruments are documents drafted between a creditor and debtor, without intervention by a public official such as a notary, signed by both parties and in which they acknowledge certain obligations or legal facts, thus constituting a legal act.[104] If there are no mutual obligations, then the instrument

[100] R.v.St. nr. 13.270, Rijksdienst voor de Sociale Verzekering der Zelfstandigen – Tops, 10 december 1968, *Arresten en Adviezen van de Raad van State 1968*, 962–965; Minjauw, H., Vandendriessche, J. (2008) "Titel VI. Het bewijsrecht in burgerlijke zaken", in: Roodhooft, R. (ed.), *Bestendig Handboek Verbintenissenrecht*, Mechelen: Kluwer, VI.3–6b.

[101] Cass. 25 mei 1992, *jure.juridat.just.fgov.be.*

[102] Van Gerven, W., Covemaker, S. (2006) *Verbintenissenrecht*, Leuven: Acco, 670.

[103] Minjauw, H., Vandendriessche, J. (2008) "Titel VI. Het bewijsrecht in burgerlijke zaken", in: Roodhooft, R. (ed.), *Bestendig Handboek Verbintenissenrecht*, Mechelen: Kluwer, VI.3–18.

[104] Van Gerven, W., Covemaker, S. (2006) *Verbintenissenrecht*, Leuven: Acco, 675; Minjauw, H., Vandendriessche, J. (2008) "Titel VI. Het bewijsrecht in burgerlijke zaken", in: Roodhooft, R. (ed.), *Bestendig Handboek Verbintenissenrecht*, Mechelen: Kluwer, VI.3–21; Dumortier, J. (2010) *ICT-Recht*, Leuven: Acco, 128.

may also be signed solely by the debtor acknowledging his obligations.[105] Such instrument is to be drafted *in tempore non suspecto* to serve as evidence in the event of later dispute.[106]

1.4.1.1. Properties

41. First of all, the document must contain the full extent of the legal acts it is documenting.[107] Where legal acts are absent, or if the legal acts are not sufficiently comprehensibly documented, the document will in principle not be qualified as an instrument.[108] Furthermore, the legal acts must constitute the disposal of the document. Mere mentions of facts can, at most, be considered as a beginning of evidence in writing, unless their mentioning is directly related to the disposal.[109]

42. Second, the document must be appropriated by the person against whom it is invoked. This means that there must be a clear intentional element within that person to confirm his acceptance of the document's content.[110] Generally, it is accepted that such appropriation occurs through the third property element: the signature.

43. Third, the document must be signed by the party against whom it is invoked as evidence.[111] As noted, this signature is accepted as the appropriation of the document by the signatory.[112] The signature also serves to identify the

---

105 Cornelis, L. (2000) *Algemene theorie van de verbintenis*, Antwerpen: Intersentia, 221. Note that for probative purposes it is sufficient for a party to possess an instrument signed by the party against whom it is invoked. Cass. 17 June 1981, *jure.juridat.just.fgov.be.*

106 Lamensch, M. (2006) "La règle de la primauté de la preuve écrite: une application delicate", *TBBR*, 47.

107 De Page, H. (1967) *Traité élémentaire de droit civil Belge, Tome Troisième (Les Obligations)*, Brussel: Bruylant, 788–790.

108 But it could still be qualified as a beginning of evidence in writing, as will be discussed further on. Note also that the judge has some leeway to interpret the document if the legal acts it contains are not sufficiently clear. Some level of vagueness or ambiguity could, therefore, still allow the qualification of a document as an instrument, if the judge finds that he can determine the parties' intent.

109 Article 1320 Belgian Civil Code. However, this may not mean much in practice as a judge is more likely to accord a higher probative value to facts in writing – even if it technically does not constitute an instrument – than to mere presumptions. Cornelis, L. (2000) *Algemene theorie van de verbintenis*, Antwerpen: Intersentia, 218.

110 Van Eecke, P. (2004) *Naar een juridische status voor de elektronische handtekening: Een rol voor de handtekening in de informatiemaatschappij?*, PhD thesis KU Leuven – Faculty of Law, 324.

111 Cornelis, L. (2000) *Algemene theorie van de verbintenis*, Antwerpen: Intersentia, 221.

112 De Page, H. (1967) *Traité élémentaire de droit civil Belge, Tome Troisième (Les Obligations)*, Brussel: Bruylant, 756 and 795; Van Gerven, W., Covemaker, S. (2006) *Verbintenissenrecht*, Leuven: Acco, 671; Minjauw, H., Vandendriessche, J. (2008) "Titel VI. Het bewijsrecht in burgerlijke zaken", in: Roodhooft, R. (ed.), *Bestendig Handboek Verbintenissenrecht*,

signatory.[113] In principle, the signature can also be considered as a means to safeguard the document integrity of, meaning that the document is finalized and cannot be altered at a later stage.[114] The signature can also fulfill a symbolic purpose, giving the signatory a moment to reflect on his intentions and is also, generally, an occasion on which to bring the different parties together.[115] Under Belgian jurisprudence, a signature is recognized as a handwritten mark generally used by the signatory to reveal his identity to others.[116] More specifically, jurisprudence and legal doctrine have established a number of criteria with which a valid signature should comply.[117] A signature should be placed by hand.[118] It should consist of characters.[119] It must be placed at the bottom of

---

Mechelen: Kluwer, VI.3–18; Van Eecke, P. (2004) *Naar een juridische status voor de elektronische handtekening: Een rol voor de handtekening in de informatiemaatschappij?*, PhD thesis KU Leuven – Faculty of Law, 346; Van Baeveghem, B. (2006) "De paraaf: "Slip of the pen" of geldige handtekening?", *Tijdschrift voor Belgisch Burgerlijk Recht (TBBR)*, 596.

113 Van Eecke, P. (2004) *Naar een juridische status voor de elektronische handtekening: Een rol voor de handtekening in de informatiemaatschappij?*, PhD thesis KU Leuven – Faculty of Law, 322. When identification – establishing a person's identity – is used, it should be noted that implicitly also authentication – verifying whether a person is really who he purports to be – is meant. For instance, a signature can identify the alleged signatory, but it will also have to be assessed whether the person creating the signature is also the person to whom this signature belongs. In keeping with the terminology used, the following sections will mainly reference identification, while thus implicitly also meaning authentication.

114 Van Eecke, P. (2004) *Naar een juridische status voor de elektronische handtekening: Een rol voor de handtekening in de informatiemaatschappij?*, PhD thesis KU Leuven – Faculty of Law, 326–327. The value of this principle should, however, not be overestimated. While a signature can give some indication of whether or not the document has been altered or tampered with, it cannot physically nor technically prevent such tampering.

115 Van Eecke, P. (2004) *Naar een juridische status voor de elektronische handtekening: Een rol voor de handtekening in de informatiemaatschappij?*, PhD thesis KU Leuven – Faculty of Law, 249–250.

116 Cass. 2 October 1964, *jure.juridat.just.fgov.be*; Cornelis, L. (2000) *Algemene theorie van de verbintenis*, Antwerpen: Intersentia, 221. Van Baeveghem, B. (2006) "De paraaf: "Slip of the pen" of geldige handtekening?", *Tijdschrift voor Belgisch Burgerlijk Recht (TBBR)*, 597; Wéry, P., Gobert, D., Kerzmann, L. (2003) "La preuve", in: Coipel, M., Wéry, P., Durant, I., Cruquenaire, A., *Guide juridique de l'entreprise*, Brussel: Kluwer, 50.

117 See: Van Eecke, P. (2009) "De elektronische handtekening in het recht", *Tijdschrift voor Belgisch Handelsrecht*, 326 *et seq*; Mougenot, D. (2002) *Droit des obligations: la preuve*, Brussel: Larcier, 164.

118 *Ibid.*, 326–327; De Corte, R. (2001) "Elektronische handtekening en identificatie in de virtuele wereld", *P&B*, 220. Only in rare cases, such as for instance when signing bearer bonds in corporate law, can a handwritten signature be replaced by a stamp. Article 466 Belgian Corporate Law Code. While evidence in commercial matters is generally considered as less regulated than under civil law, also here it has been accepted that a signature should be placed by hand: Cass. 26 February 1993, *jure.juridat.just.fgov.be*. Historically, the requirement of a handwritten signature can be considered as a means to justify the physical presence of the signatory at the moment of signing, to emphasize the ritualistic nature of the signing and to ensure the appropriation. Van Eecke, P. (2004) *Naar een juridische status voor de elektronische handtekening: Een rol voor de handtekening in de informatiemaatschappij?*, PhD thesis KU Leuven – Faculty of Law, 162–163.

119 Thereby rendering invalid drawings, symbols or a simple 'x'. Cass. 14 November 1901, *Pas.* 1902, I, 37–38. This requirement aims to serve the identifying properties of the signature. Van

a document containing legally relevant information.[120] The signature must be placed directly on the document.[121] The signature must be materialized.[122] The name of the signatory must be contained in the signature.[123] The signature must be legible.[124] It must be a creative expression.[125] It must be placed by the signatory.[126] There must be formal continuity.[127] It is clear that the requirements imposed on signatures by jurisprudence and doctrine are fairly adverse to the use of modern technologies. Electronic signatures raise, for instance, questions regarding how such a signature can be placed by hand on a document. Specific legislative measures were adopted to facilitate the use of electronic signatures. These will be discussed further below. Apart from the external qualities of the signature, it is clear that there must also be an internal element, namely the intention of the signatory to affix his signature to the document, thereby

---

Eecke, P. (2004) *Naar een juridische status voor de elektronische handtekening: Een rol voor de handtekening in de informatiemaatschappij?*, PhD thesis KU Leuven – Faculty of Law, 170–171.

120 De Page, H. (1967) *Traité élémentaire de droit civil Belge, Tome Troisième (Les Obligations)*, Brussel: Bruylant, 796. It should be noted that jurisprudence does demonstrate some leniency by allowing marginal signatures. Van Eecke, P. (2009) "De elektronische handtekening in het recht", *T.B.H.*, 327.

121 This requirement is mainly to render invalid signatures printed by a copy, fax, or other of such means. Cass. 28 June 1982, *jure.juridat.just.fgov.be*. Here, jurisprudence also shows certain leniency by accepting that a document to which a signature was not directly affixed – for instance a copy – can still constitute a valid instrument even though the signature in itself is invalid. Van Eecke, P. (2004) *Naar een juridische status voor de elektronische handtekening: Een rol voor de handtekening in de informatiemaatschappij?*, PhD thesis KU Leuven – Faculty of Law, 185. This demonstrates a more functional approach to the figure of the signature than a strictly formal approach.

122 Meaning that the signature must be given a stable form. Van Eecke, P. (2009) "De elektronische handtekening in het recht", *T.B.H.*, 327.

123 This requirement follows from the acceptance of the signature as serving identification of the signatory. Mere characters or even initials can therefore principally not suffice. Van Eecke, P. (2009) "De elektronische handtekening in het recht", *T.B.H.*, 328. Van Baeveghem, B. (2006) "De paraaf: "Slip of the pen" of geldige handtekening?", *Tijdschrift voor Belgisch Burgerlijk Recht (TBBR)*, 597; Wéry, P., Gobert, D., Kerzmann, L. (2003) "La preuve", in: Coipel, M., Wéry, P., Durant, I., Cruquenaire, A., *Guide juridique de l'entreprise*, Brussel: Kluwer, 51.

124 Van Eecke, P. (2009) "De elektronische handtekening in het recht", *T.B.H.*, 328. This requirement also references the identifying properties of the signature. Note that an illegible signature can still be accepted if identification of the signatory can be established through other means, for instance by accompanying the signature with the full name of the signatory.

125 While the signature must legibly contain the name of the signatory, it must also demonstrate a personal expression to distinguish it from a mere notation of that person's name. This creative expression was originally considered a constitutive element of the signature. Later jurisprudence, however, relaxed this criterion, finding that writing a name with the intention of placing a signature can also be accepted as a signature. Cass. 13 June 1986, *jure.juridat.just.fgov.be*. Van Eecke, P. (2004) *Naar een juridische status voor de elektronische handtekening: Een rol voor de handtekening in de informatiemaatschappij?*, PhD thesis KU Leuven – Faculty of Law, 218–220.

126 In other words, a person's signature cannot be placed by a third party. Van Eecke, P. (2009) "De elektronische handtekening in het recht", *T.B.H.*, 329.

127 Meaning that the signature should display the same external qualities and should not be altered over time. Here, leniency can also be found in jurisprudence. Van Eecke, P. (2004) *Naar een juridische status voor de elektronische handtekening: Een rol voor de handtekening in de informatiemaatschappij?*, PhD thesis KU Leuven – Faculty of Law, 228–229.

accepting the legal consequences emanating from such act. This is referred to as the *animus signandi*.[128] It is this intentional element that can be considered as the appropriation, as discussed previously.[129]

44. As already noted in discussing the signature, the integrity of the document must be ensured. This means that a signed document can only constitute an instrument if its contents have not been altered since the moment of signing – and thus has been appropriated by the signatory. Any later alterations would invalidate that appropriation and, therefore, deny the document the qualification of an instrument. While the signature – typically placed at the end of the document – can offer some protection of the document's integrity, it is clear that this cannot fully guarantee such integrity. In case of later alterations, parties could agree to put their initials next to any such alterations.[130] This would limit the likelihood of disputes concerning the docmuent's lack of integrity due to such alterations.[131]

1.4.1.2. Formalities

45. In principle, there are no requirements of formality to a private instrument.[132] However, when there are mutual obligations contained in the instrument, there are a few specific formalities that must be followed.[133] In such event, there must be as many copies of the original document as there are parties with a discernible interest.[134] Each of these originals must also mention how many originals were drafted.[135] This provision is aimed at creating equality between parties, ensuring that each has the ability to provide proof of their

---

128 Van Eecke, P. (2009) "De elektronische handtekening in het recht", *T.B.H.*, 329. Van Baeveghem, B. (2006) "De paraaf: "Slip of the pen" of geldige handtekening?", *Tijdschrift voor Belgisch Burgerlijk Recht (TBBR)*, 5.

129 Van Eecke, P. (2009) "De elektronische handtekening in het recht", *T.B.H.*, 330.

130 Minjauw, H., Vandendriessche, J. (2008) "Titel VI. Het bewijsrecht in burgerlijke zaken", in: Roodhooft, R. (ed.), *Bestendig Handboek Verbintenissenrecht*, Mechelen: Kluwer, VI.3-21-22.

131 *Id.*

132 Minjauw, H., Vandendriessche, J. (2008) "Titel VI. Het bewijsrecht in burgerlijke zaken", in: Roodhooft, R. (ed.), *Bestendig Handboek Verbintenissenrecht*, Mechelen: Kluwer, VI.3-21.

133 Article 1325 Belgian Civil Code. Since in practice most agreements will contain mutual obligations, this article can be considered more to be describing the general rule, rather than the exception. Mougenot, D. (2002) *Droit des obligations: la preuve*, Brussel: Larcier, 206.

134 Article 1325 Belgian Civil Code. Minjauw, H., Vandendriessche, J. (2008) "Titel VI. Het bewijsrecht in burgerlijke zaken", in: Roodhooft, R. (ed.), *Bestendig Handboek Verbintenissenrecht*, Mechelen: Kluwer, VI.3-24. Parties with the same interest can hold one copy. Note that while using the term 'copy', it is the goal of this provision to ensure that each party has possession over an original version of the document – meaning a version of the document to which all opposing parties have directly affixed their signature – identical to the originals held by other parties. As will be further discussed below, the distinction between originals and copies is highly important from a probative point of view.

135 Article 1325 Belgian Civil Code. However, the absence of this notice cannot be used in a claim for nullity by the party who has already fulfilled the obligations formulated in the document concerning himself.

mutual agreements to be used as evidence against one another.[136] Moreover, the requirement to have multiple originals of the document, held by different parties, can also be found to support proof of integrity of the document as it makes later tampering more difficult.[137] Non-abidance by these rules will result in the relative nullity of the document, meaning that the parties can decide to still accept it as valid.[138] Moreover, even in case of a dispute, the agreement between the parties in itself is still valid, but the document describing the agreement cannot be qualified as an instrument.[139]

46. The Civil Code contains another deviation from the principal lack of formality requirements, namely when the document concerns a unilateral promise of payment.[140] Such documents should principally be fully handwritten by the signatory, or at least contain the sum of the promise written out in full in letters and the signature preceded by a handwritten declaration of 'good for' or 'approved for'.[141] If the sum is mentioned within the document but deviates from the sum written after the 'good for' or 'approved for' declaration, only the lowest sum will be considered.[142] Under article 1325 Belgian Civil Code, non-abidance by this principle will result in the relative nullity of the document, barring its qualification as an instrument.

1.4.1.3. Probative value

47. When a document between parties complies with the aforementioned formal requirements and displays the properties discussed prior to that, it can be

---

136 Van Gerven, W., Covemaker, S. (2006) *Verbintenissenrecht*, Leuven: Acco, 670; Minjauw, H., Vandendriessche, J. (2008) "Titel VI. Het bewijsrecht in burgerlijke zaken", in: Roodhooft, R. (ed.), *Bestendig Handboek Verbintenissenrecht*, Mechelen: Kluwer, VI.3–24; Mougenot, D. (2002) *Droit des obligations: la preuve*, Brussel: Larcier, 207.

137 De Page, H. (1967) *Traité élémentaire de droit civil Belge, Tome Troisième (Les Obligations)*, Brussel: Bruylant, 823. This would mean that if there are discrepancies between different originals of the same document – unless very minor, such as a different date or place of signature – the probative value of the document could be considered to be tainted, thereby disqualifying the document from consideration as an instrument. Minjauw, H., Vandendriessche, J. (2008) "Titel VI. Het bewijsrecht in burgerlijke zaken", in: Roodhooft, R. (ed.), *Bestendig Handboek Verbintenissenrecht*, Mechelen: Kluwer, VI.3–27.

138 Mourlon Beernaert, F., Gaudy, A. (2006) "Partie VI. Le droit de la preuve – La preuve littérale", in: X, *Obligations. Traité théorique et pratique*, Brussel: Kluwer, VI.4.2 – 22.

139 De Page, H. (1967) *Traité élémentaire de droit civil Belge, Tome Troisième (Les Obligations)*, Brussel: Bruylant, 831; Minjauw, H., Vandendriessche, J. (2008) "Titel VI. Het bewijsrecht in burgerlijke zaken", in: Roodhooft, R. (ed.), *Bestendig Handboek Verbintenissenrecht*, Mechelen: Kluwer, VI.3–28; Wéry, P., Gobert, D., Kerzmann, L. (2003) "La preuve", in: Coipel, M., Wéry, P., Durant, I., Cruquenaire, A., *Guide juridique de l'entreprise*, Brussel: Kluwer, 55.

140 Article 1326 Belgian Civil Code.

141 *Id.* Note that this article also lists a number of exceptions, for merchants for instance. This requirement was meant to decrease the likelihood of fraud in numbers or blank signatures. Minjauw, H., Vandendriessche, J. (2008) "Titel VI. Het bewijsrecht in burgerlijke zaken", in: Roodhooft, R. (ed.), *Bestendig Handboek Verbintenissenrecht*, Mechelen: Kluwer, VI.3–29.

142 Article 1327 Belgian Civil Code. Unless it can be proven where the mistake lies.

qualified as a private instrument, thus being accorded the probative value usually assigned to such evidence. While proof can still be provided against a private instrument, it must be reminded that article 1341 Belgian Civil Code restricts such counterproof to another instrument or an oath or confession.[143] The fact that an instrument is automatically accepted as evidence – unless challenged on grounds of its formal validity – does not mean that its contents must be accepted 'as is'.[144] When the wording of the text does not allow for a clear assessment of the legal acts agreed upon by the parties, it is up to the judge to interpret the instrument in order to establish the mutual intentions of the parties, rather than keeping to the literal meaning of the words in the text.[145] Specific measures may be ordered by the court to assist in this interpretation.[146]

48. When a document is accepted as a private instrument and the person against whom it is invoked is recognized – or is legally held as recognized – it has the same probative value between the parties and their legal successors as a public notary deed.[147] The core element of a private instrument is the presence of a valid signature. The signature on a document must therefore be outright recognized or accepted by the party against whom the document is invoked.[148] If a signature is refuted, an investigation will have to establish the veracity of the signature.[149]

49. As noted previously, the legal acts concluded between parties are considered as legal facts toward third parties who are not party to the agreement.[150] While a private instrument can be invoked as proof of the factual existence of the agreement against third parties, these third parties are in principle not covered

143 Minjauw, H., Vandendriessche, J. (2008) "Titel VI. Het bewijsrecht in burgerlijke zaken", in: Roodhooft, R. (ed.), *Bestendig Handboek Verbintenissenrecht*, Mechelen: Kluwer, VI.3-35.

144 *Ibid.*, VI.3-6.

145 Article 1156 Belgian Civil Code. This interpretation, however, may not go the extent of being irreconcilable to the text. Van Gerven, W., Covemaker, S. (2006) *Verbintenissenrecht*, Leuven: Acco, 673. Note also that a clearly drafted text should not require interpretation. Van Baeveghem, B. (2006) "De paraaf: "Slip of the pen" of geldige handtekening?", *Tijdschrift voor Belgisch Burgerlijk Recht (TBBR)*, 596-597.

146 Minjauw, H., Vandendriessche, J. (2008) "Titel VI. Het bewijsrecht in burgerlijke zaken", in: Roodhooft, R. (ed.), *Bestendig Handboek Verbintenissenrecht*, Mechelen: Kluwer, VI.3-6.

147 Article 1322 Belgian Civil Code.

148 Article 1323 Belgian Civil Code. The legal successors of that party can suffice with claiming not to know that person's signature.

149 Article 1324 Belgian Civil Code. This procedure is outlined in articles 883-894 Belgian Judicial Code. Cornelis, L. (2000) *Algemene theorie van de verbintenis*, Antwerpen: Intersentia, 222. The Belgian Supreme Court has ruled that the judge can also order such investigation and that he can even rule on the validity of the signature without such investigation on grounds of sufficient certainty provided by the facts of the case. Cass. 7 March 2002, *jure.juridat.just.fgov.be*.

150 Minjauw, H., Vandendriessche, J. (2008) "Titel VI. Het bewijsrecht in burgerlijke zaken", in: Roodhooft, R. (ed.), *Bestendig Handboek Verbintenissenrecht*, Mechelen: Kluwer, VI.3-6a.

by the rules of article 1341 Belgian Civil Code and can, therefore, provide counterproof by any means.[151] Regarding the date of the private instrument, it is stipulated that this is only opposable to third parties at the date the instrument has been registered, at the date of the death of one of the signatories, or at the date the contents of the instrument were integrated into a public instrument.[152]

1.4.2. Public instruments

50. Public instruments, or deeds, differ from private instruments mainly due to their reliance on a public official, generally being a notary.[153] In order to be recognized as a public instrument, a document must comply with a number of formal requirements.

1.4.2.1. Formalities

51. A public instrument not only requires the intervention of a public official, this public official must also act within the scope of his authority and within the boundaries of his jurisdiction.[154] Notaries are furthermore bound to not act against public order, decency and mandatory law.[155] Public instruments are strictly regulated in terms of content and format.[156] These formal requirements are essential. If a document does not correspond with the prescribed format,

---

151 *Ibid.*, VI.3–41; Van Gerven, W., Covemaker, S. (2006) *Verbintenissenrecht*, Leuven: Acco, 675.

152 Article 1328 Belgian Civil Code. This provision aims to prevent pre- or post-dating of private instruments. Minjauw, H., Vandendriessche, J. (2008) "Titel VI. Het bewijsrecht in burgerlijke zaken", in: Roodhooft, R. (ed.), *Bestendig Handboek Verbintenissenrecht*, Mechelen: Kluwer, VI.3–41; Cornelis, L. (2000) *Algemene theorie van de verbintenis*, Antwerpen: Intersentia, 222.

153 Article 1317 Belgian Civil Code describes this as an "*instrument drafted in the legally defined format done before a public official who is thereto authorized at the place where it is drafted.*" Other examples of public officials are bailiffs, court clerks and officials of public registers. Minjauw, H., Vandendriessche, J. (2008) "Titel VI. Het bewijsrecht in burgerlijke zaken", in: Roodhooft, R. (ed.), *Bestendig Handboek Verbintenissenrecht*, Mechelen: Kluwer, VI.3–19–20; Wéry, P., Gobert, D., Kerzmann, L. (2003) "La preuve", in: Coipel, M., Wéry, P., Durant, I., Cruquenaire, A., *Guide juridique de l'entreprise*, Brussel: Kluwer, 43; Mougenot, D. (2002) *Droit des obligations: la preuve*, Brussel: Larcier, 149.

154 For instance, only a notary can preside over an instrument arranging the transfer of ownership over real estate. A notary can only validly preside over such instrument within the boundaries of his judicial territory. Articles 1 and 5–6 Belgian Act on the Profession of Notary, 16 March 1803 (25 ventôse XI). Mougenot, D. (2002) *Droit des obligations: la preuve*, Brussel: Larcier, 152.

155 However, they are still bound *ratione loci*. Minjauw, H., Vandendriessche, J. (2008) "Titel VI. Het bewijsrecht in burgerlijke zaken", in: Roodhooft, R. (ed.), *Bestendig Handboek Verbintenissenrecht*, Mechelen: Kluwer, VI.3–19–20.

156 *Id.* For instance, instruments done before a notary must include the name and location of the presiding notary, the names, professions and locations of the parties and must write dates and sums in full in letters. How the instrument must be written and signed is also regulated, as well as how additions and corrections must be executed. The specific rules on these matters can be found in the Civil Code, the Act on the Profession of Notary and other specific acts.

or was drafted by an official without the required competence and capacity, the document will not be accepted as a public instrument.[157] If properly signed by the parties, such document could, however, still be accepted as a private instrument.[158]

1.4.2.2. Probative value

52. Public instruments provide complete evidence of the legal acts between the parties that they describe.[159] However, a distinction can be made between the different statements that instrument contains.[160] Authentic statements are facts stated by the presiding public official, acting within the scope of his authority and jurisdiction.[161] These statements are considered to be authentic in the sense that they are presumed to be valid due to the trust placed in the person from whom they are issued.[162] Such statements reflect what the public official has been able to witness and to verify in person, such as the names of the parties.[163] Due to the nature of his profession, such statements by a public official are considered as irrefutable by counterproof, unless they are challenged on the grounds of fraud or forgery.[164] Apart from authentic statements, a public instrument can contain statements that could not be directly verified by the public official. Such statements are not covered by the automatic presumption of accuracy flowing from the position of the public official and are, therefore, accorded the same value as any statement in a private instrument.[165]

---

157 Article 1318 Belgian Civil Code.

158 *Id.* Where such would be possible. Mougenot, D. (2002) *Droit des obligations: la preuve*, Brussel: Larcier, 153.

159 Article 1319 Belgian Civil Code. Note, however, that this formulation is not fully correct. The instrument does not provide complete evidence given that it is possible to provide proof counter to the instrument. Mougenot, D. (2002) *Droit des obligations: la preuve*, Brussel: Larcier, 154.

160 Mourlon Beernaert, F., Gaudy, A. (2006) "Partie VI. Le droit de la preuve – La preuve littérale", in: X, *Obligations. Traité théorique et pratique*, Brussel: Kluwer, VI.4.2 – 13.

161 Van Gerven, W., Covemaker, S. (2006) *Verbintenissenrecht*, Leuven: Acco, 672; Minjauw, H., Vandendriessche, J. (2008) "Titel VI. Het bewijsrecht in burgerlijke zaken", in: Roodhooft, R. (ed.), *Bestendig Handboek Verbintenissenrecht*, Mechelen: Kluwer, VI.3–36.

162 Note the contrast with the notion of authenticity in, for instance, signatures, where authenticity refers to the origin or author of the signature.

163 Minjauw, H., Vandendriessche, J. (2008) "Titel VI. Het bewijsrecht in burgerlijke zaken", in: Roodhooft, R. (ed.), *Bestendig Handboek Verbintenissenrecht*, Mechelen: Kluwer, VI.3–36.

164 Article 1319 Belgian Civil Code; Minjauw, H., Vandendriessche, J. (2008) "Titel VI. Het bewijsrecht in burgerlijke zaken", in: Roodhooft, R. (ed.), *Bestendig Handboek Verbintenissenrecht*, Mechelen: Kluwer, VI.3–37.

165 Minjauw, H., Vandendriessche, J. (2008) "Titel VI. Het bewijsrecht in burgerlijke zaken", in: Roodhooft, R. (ed.), *Bestendig Handboek Verbintenissenrecht*, Mechelen: Kluwer, VI.3–38. Note that this does require a close reading of the disputed public instrument. A public official can, for instance, authentically verify that parties have made a certain statement. However, if he could not verify the contents of that statement, those are considered to be non-authentic. Mougenot, D. (2002) *Droit des obligations: la preuve*, Brussel: Larcier, 156.

53. The trust in authentic statements in a public instrument is extended toward third parties, meaning that they also cannot provide counterproof unless they challenge the instrument on the basis of fraud or forgery.[166] Similarly, non-authentic statements are also considered to have the same value as statements in private instruments toward third parties, meaning that they can provide counterproof by all means.[167]

1.4.3. Beginning of evidence in writing

54. As referenced previously, there are cases in which a document that does not fully comply with the requirements, to be accepted as an instrument, could be considered as a 'beginning of evidence in writing'. Such beginning of evidence in writing is defined as being *"any written instrument emanating from against whom it is invoked – or by his representative – and which can make the alleged fact probable"*.[168] Note that the term 'instrument' is chosen, somewhat unfortunately, given that any kind of written document can be taken into consideration.[169] Moreover, beginning of evidence in writing is generally considered to constitute incomplete evidence, given that this type of evidence is often considered to be a fallback for when a document cannot be considered as an actual private or public instrument, thus requiring supplementation by other means of evidence, such as witnesses or presumptions.[170]

1.4.3.1. Properties

55. While beginning of evidence in writing can be considered as a less strictly regulated type of evidence than instruments, any potential evidence does need to display certain properties in order to be accepted as beginning of evidence in writing.

56. First, any beginning of evidence in writing must be a written instrument. Despite the use of this term, any type of document in writing can be

---

166 Minjauw, H., Vandendriessche, J. (2008) "Titel VI. Het bewijsrecht in burgerlijke zaken", in: Roodhooft, R. (ed.), *Bestendig Handboek Verbintenissenrecht*, Mechelen: Kluwer, VI.3-37.

167 *Ibid.*, VI.3-38-39.

168 Article 1347 Belgian Civil Code. Literally, this article states that the instrument must emanate from against whom the action is brought. Jurisprudence has shown that this should be interpreted as meaning that the instrument must emanate from against whom it – and its alleged facts – is invoked. Cass. 29 September 1955, *Arr. Cass.* 1955, 53-55.

169 Cornelis, L. (2000) *Algemene theorie van de verbintenis*, Antwerpen: Intersentia, 222-223; Minjauw, H., Vandendriessche, J. (2008) "Titel VI. Het bewijsrecht in burgerlijke zaken", in: Roodhooft, R. (ed.), *Bestendig Handboek Verbintenissenrecht*, Mechelen: Kluwer, VI.3-9; Van Gerven, W., Covemaker, S. (2006) *Verbintenissenrecht*, Leuven: Acco, 683; De Page, H. (1967) *Traité élémentaire de droit civil Belge, Tome Troisième (Les Obligations)*, Brussel: Bruylant, 909; Mougenot, D. (2002) *Droit des obligations: la preuve*, Brussel: Larcier, 128-129.

170 De Page, H. (1967) *Traité élémentaire de droit civil Belge, Tome Troisième (Les Obligations)*, Brussel: Bruylant, 911.

considered.[171] There is no need for this document to be handwritten, nor for it to be signed or to be original.[172]

57. Second, the document that is invoked as beginning of evidence in writing must emanate from the party against whom it is invoked.[173] For instance, a document that is written but not signed by a debtor can be invoked by the creditor as beginning of evidence in writing.[174] This property can also be broadly interpreted as it has been accepted that also documents by a third party can be considered as beginning of evidence in writing, as long as they are appropriated by the party against whom they are invoked.[175] Appropriation is, therefore, a necessity for potential evidence to be accepted as beginning of evidence in writing.[176] While a signature can be considered as a good sign of appropriation, it is not an absolute requirement.[177] Appropriation under beginning of evidence in writing can, therefore, be established by all means, be it explicitly or implicitly.[178]

58. As discussed previously, evidence serves to help the court to establish the legal truth by rendering the allegations made by parties probable or rather likely bordering on certainty. As a result, documents invoked as beginning of evidence in writing must also be able to convince the court, making facts probable and not

171 Cornelis, L. (2000) *Algemene theorie van de verbintenis*, Antwerpen: Intersentia, 222–223; Minjauw, H., Vandendriessche, J. (2008) "Titel VI. Het bewijsrecht in burgerlijke zaken", in: Roodhooft, R. (ed.), *Bestendig Handboek Verbintenissenrecht*, Mechelen: Kluwer, VI.3–9; Mourlon Beernaert, F., Gaudy, A. (2006) "Partie VI. Le droit de la preuve – La prééminence de la preuve écrite", in: X, *Obligations. Traité théorique et pratique*, Brussel: Kluwer, VI.4.1 – 8.

172 *Id.* Stenographic notes and cheques have been accepted as beginning of evidence in writing. However, the Ghent Appellate Court has ruled that the transcript of a conversation does not constitute beginning of evidence in writing. Ghent, 21 November 2002, *NJW 2003*, nr. 33, 634, note by Brewaeys, E.

173 Article 1347 Belgian Civil Code.

174 In this example, as well as in cases in which the requirements formulated under articles 1325 and 1326 Belgian Civil Code were not complied with, the document cannot be accepted as an instrument, but could serve as beginning of evidence in writing.

175 Cornelis, L. (2000) *Algemene theorie van de verbintenis*, Antwerpen: Intersentia, 223; Mougenot, D. (2002) *Droit des obligations: la preuve*, Brussel: Larcier, 130; Minjauw, H., Vandendriessche, J. (2008) "Titel VI. Het bewijsrecht in burgerlijke zaken", in: Roodhooft, R. (ed.), *Bestendig Handboek Verbintenissenrecht*, Mechelen: Kluwer, VI.3–10; Mourlon Beernaert, F., Gaudy, A. (2006) "Partie VI. Le droit de la preuve – La prééminence de la preuve écrite", in: X, *Obligations. Traité théorique et pratique*, Brussel: Kluwer, VI.4.1 – 8.

176 *Id.*

177 Minjauw, H., Vandendriessche, J. (2008) "Titel VI. Het bewijsrecht in burgerlijke zaken", in: Roodhooft, R. (ed.), *Bestendig Handboek Verbintenissenrecht*, Mechelen: Kluwer, VI.3–11. For instance, accounting documents, scrap notes, agendas and bank statements can be considered as beginning of evidence in writing without being signed.

178 See footnote 177. For instance, if a debtor presents a document to his creditor for the purposes of obtaining that person's signature, the debtor can be considered to have appropriated the instrument, even if he did not sign it himself. Minjauw, H., Vandendriessche, J. (2008) "Titel VI. Het bewijsrecht in burgerlijke zaken", in: Roodhooft, R. (ed.), *Bestendig Handboek Verbintenissenrecht*, Mechelen: Kluwer, VI.3–11.

just possible.[179] It is up to the judge to decide upon the probability of documents produced as beginning of evidence in writing, as long as he does not contradict the notion of probability.[180] The document put forward as potential beginning of evidence in writing does, however, not need to give full and indisputable certainty regarding the alleged facts.[181] On the contrary, beginning of evidence in writing will often refer to a related fact.[182]

1.4.3.2. Probative value

59. As noted previously, beginning of evidence in writing constitutes incomplete evidence and cannot serve as sufficient proof of the alleged facts on its own.[183] Therefore, beginning of evidence in writing must be supplemented by other means of evidence.[184] Once a document put forward as beginning of evidence in writing has been sufficiently supplemented by other means of evidence that help making the alleged fact probable enough for the court to rule in favor of its judicial certainty, it is granted full probative value.[185] This need to supplement beginning of evidence in writing forms an important exception to the scope of article 1341 Belgian Civil Code, as it allows the use of witness statements and presumptions.[186] The reason for this deviation is that the requirements contained in article 1347 Belgian Civil Code – such as the need to produce a written document and the probability requirement – ensure that there is already a certain substantiation of the claim made by the invoking party,

179 Minjauw, H., Vandendriessche, J. (2008) "Titel VI. Het bewijsrecht in burgerlijke zaken", in: Roodhooft, R. (ed.), *Bestendig Handboek Verbintenissenrecht*, Mechelen: Kluwer, VI.3–11; Cornelis, L. (2000) *Algemene theorie van de verbintenis*, Antwerpen: Intersentia, 223; Mourlon Beernaert, F., Gaudy, A. (2006) "Partie VI. Le droit de la preuve – La prééminence de la preuve écrite", in: X, *Obligations. Traité théorique et pratique*, Brussel: Kluwer, VI.4.1 – 8–9.

180 Cass. 30 April 1982, *jure.juridat.just.fgov.be/view_decision?justel=N-19820430-5&idxc_id=148596&lang=nl.*

181 Minjauw, H., Vandendriessche, J. (2008) "Titel VI. Het bewijsrecht in burgerlijke zaken", in: Roodhooft, R. (ed.), *Bestendig Handboek Verbintenissenrecht*, Mechelen: Kluwer, VI.3–11; Cornelis, L. (2000) *Algemene theorie van de verbintenis*, Antwerpen: Intersentia, 223.

182 This, in turn, can be related back to the status of beginning of evidence in writing as incomplete evidence that requires supplementation with other evidence. Minjauw, H., Vandendriessche, J. (2008) "Titel VI. Het bewijsrecht in burgerlijke zaken", in: Roodhooft, R. (ed.), *Bestendig Handboek Verbintenissenrecht*, Mechelen: Kluwer, VI.3–11; Cornelis, L. (2000) *Algemene theorie van de verbintenis*, Antwerpen: Intersentia, 223.

183 Minjauw, H., Vandendriessche, J. (2008) "Titel VI. Het bewijsrecht in burgerlijke zaken", in: Roodhooft, R. (ed.), *Bestendig Handboek Verbintenissenrecht*, Mechelen: Kluwer, VI.3–8–9; Cornelis, L. (2000) *Algemene theorie van de verbintenis*, Antwerpen: Intersentia, 223.

184 *Id.*

185 Putting the beginning of evidence in writing – with supplemental evidence – at the same level as a private or public instrument. Stijns, S. (2009) *Leerboek Verbintenissenrecht Boek 2*, Brugge: die Keure, 182.

186 Van Gerven, W., Covemaker, S. (2006) *Verbintenissenrecht*, Leuven: Acco, 683; De Page, H. (1967) *Traité élémentaire de droit civil Belge, Tome Troisième (Les Obligations)*, Brussel: Bruylant, 920.

thereby lowering the risk normally associated with witness statements and presumptions.[187]

1.4.4. Other types of evidence in writing

60. The Belgian Civil Code also recognizes a number of other types of evidence in writing, even though these types are generally accorded a lower probative value.[188]

1.4.4.1. Copies and transcripts

61. Articles 1334 to 1336 Belgian Civil Code refer to transcripts of titles. In these provisions, 'title' is meant to refer to an original of a document.[189] The main difference between transcripts and copies on the one hand and originals on the other is the required presence of a signature on originals, whereas such signature – or at least a valid signature – is absent on transcripts and copies.[190] The difference between transcripts and copies is that transcripts are principally handwritten, while copies are machine-produced.[191] Content-wise, both transcripts and copies are literal reproductions of the original.[192] In both cases, the absence of a valid signature is the reason why these documents are denied the full probative value accorded to instruments.[193]

---

187 De Page, H. (1967) *Traité élémentaire de droit civil Belge, Tome Troisième (Les Obligations)*, Brussel: Bruylant, 910–911.

188 Cornelis, L. (2000) *Algemene theorie van de verbintenis*, Antwerpen: Intersentia, 224.

189 For instance, referring to the originals held by each of the parties with a distinct interest in the case of mutual agreements, as required by article 1325 Belgian Civil Code.

190 Mougenot, D. (2002) *Droit des obligations: la preuve*, Brussel: Larcier, 248; De Page, H. (1967) *Traité élémentaire de droit civil Belge, Tome Troisième (Les Obligations)*, Brussel: Bruylant, 856; Gobert, D., Montero, E. (2001) "L'ouverture de la preuve littérale aux écrits sous forme électronique", *J.T.*, 127; Mourlon Beernaert, F., Gaudy, A. (2006) "Partie VI. Le droit de la preuve – La preuve littérale", in: X, *Obligations. Traité théorique et pratique*, Brussel: Kluwer, VI.4.2 – 7–8. While, if a signed original is copied, the copy will contain a full and accurate reproduction of the original signature, it is still considered to be a copy and is thus in the strict sense not accepted as a valid signature. However, as noted in footnote 121, there is some leniency to this found in case law.

191 Minjauw, H., Vandendriessche, J. (2008) "Titel VI. Het bewijsrecht in burgerlijke zaken", in: Roodhooft, R. (ed.), *Bestendig Handboek Verbintenissenrecht*, Mechelen: Kluwer, VI.3–89. While the Belgian Civil Code only mentions the handwritten transcripts, it has been accepted that these provisions can also apply to photocopies and other methods of modern-day text reproduction. Van Gerven, W., Covemaker, S. (2006) *Verbintenissenrecht*, Leuven: Acco, 679.

192 Van Gerven, W., Covemaker, S. (2006) *Verbintenissenrecht*, Leuven: Acco, 679.

193 If a party would place a handwritten signature on a copy, this copy would become an original. Minjauw, H., Vandendriessche, J. (2008) "Titel VI. Het bewijsrecht in burgerlijke zaken", in: Roodhooft, R. (ed.), *Bestendig Handboek Verbintenissenrecht*, Mechelen: Kluwer, VI.3–89; Cornelis, L. (2000) *Algemene theorie van de verbintenis*, Antwerpen: Intersentia, 225; Wagner, K. (2008) "Recente ontwikkelingen met betrekking tot het bewijs in burgerlijke zaken", in: Serrus, D. (ed.), *Actualia Gerechtelijk Recht*, Gent: Larcier, 181.

62. According to article 1334 Belgian Civil Code, transcripts can only provide evidence of what is included in the title – this being the original document – insofar as the title still exists. If the validity of a transcript is disputed or doubted, parties can always demand that the title be produced.[194] As a result, transcripts principally do not have the same probative value as the related instrument, but only serve as reference to the original and only insofar as their conformity with that original is not disputed.[195] If the original cannot be produced, the disputed transcript or copy can at most be considered to be a presumption or beginning of evidence in writing.[196]

63. Transcripts of public instruments can still be accorded certain value if the original has ceased to exist.[197] For instance, executable transcripts[198] of the minutes of the public instrument, court-ordered transcripts produced in the presence of parties and transcripts produced in the presence and with mutual consent of the parties can be considered as having the same probative value as their originals.[199] Public officials can also provide certified copies without being ordered to do so by the court or parties, whereby the trust in the position of the public official is used as attestation of the conformity of that certified copy with the original. Such copies are accorded probative value if the original is lost and if they are older than 30 years.[200] Other copies of public instruments are not accorded the same probative value as the original and their conformity can, therefore, be disputed.[201] The recording of a public instrument into public

---

194 Article 1334 Belgian Civil Code.

195 Minjauw, H., Vandendriessche, J. (2008) "Titel VI. Het bewijsrecht in burgerlijke zaken", in: Roodhooft, R. (ed.), *Bestendig Handboek Verbintenissenrecht*, Mechelen: Kluwer, VI.3-90. However, if the conformity of the transcript or copy with the original is not disputed, its contents are accepted as proof of the original. Cornelis, L. (2000) *Algemene theorie van de verbintenis*, Antwerpen: Intersentia, 225; Mougenot, D. (2002) *Droit des obligations: la preuve*, Brussel: Larcier, 249.

196 Cornelis, L. (2000) *Algemene theorie van de verbintenis*, Antwerpen: Intersentia, 225; Mons 27 February 2007, note by Mougenot, D. (2007) "Le statut probatoire de la photocopie: nuageux avec éclaircies", *TBBR*, 468-475; Wagner, K. (2008) "Recente ontwikkelingen met betrekking tot het bewijs in burgerlijke zaken", in: Serrus, D. (ed.), *Actualia Gerechtelijk Recht*, Gent: Larcier, 183. Contra: Minjauw, H., Vandendriessche, J. (2008) "Titel VI. Het bewijsrecht in burgerlijke zaken", in: Roodhooft, R. (ed.), *Bestendig Handboek Verbintenissenrecht*, Mechelen: Kluwer, VI.3-90; Mougenot, D. (2002) *Droit des obligations: la preuve*, Brussel: Larcier, 249.

197 While article 1334 Belgian Civil Code is considered to apply to transcripts of both private and public instruments, articles 1335 and 1336 Belgian Civil Code are considered to only apply to public instruments. Minjauw, H., Vandendriessche, J. (2008) "Titel VI. Het bewijsrecht in burgerlijke zaken", in: Roodhooft, R. (ed.), *Bestendig Handboek Verbintenissenrecht*, Mechelen: Kluwer, VI.3-90.

198 Dutch: *'grosse'*.

199 Article 1335, 1° Belgian Civil Code.

200 Article 1335, 2° Belgian Civil Code. If they are less than 30 years old, they are at most considered as beginning of evidence in writing.

201 Article 1335, 3° Belgian Civil Code. Minjauw, H., Vandendriessche, J. (2008) "Titel VI. Het bewijsrecht in burgerlijke zaken", in: Roodhooft, R. (ed.), *Bestendig Handboek Verbintenissenrecht*, Mechelen: Kluwer, VI.3-90.

registers can at most – and only when certain conditions are fulfilled – serve as the beginning of evidence in writing.[202]

64. The probative value of transcripts and copies can be considered as being limited. In principle, most copies and transcripts will not be accorded probative value on their own, and even if they are accepted as evidence, the judge will need to decide upon the weight they will be accorded.[203] Only when both parties accept – or rather decline to dispute – a copy or transcript, will it be accepted as providing evidence of the contents of the original. Despite the technological advancements in document reproduction – whereby techniques are available to reliably produce a fully accurate representation of the original – the lack of an original signature will result in such limitation of the probative value of the copy.[204]

1.4.4.2. Account books

65. Account books need to be kept by merchants for accounting purposes.[205] They cannot be used against non-merchants, save for what is determined regarding the oath.[206] They can, however, be used as evidence against the merchant, although the person invoking this as evidence cannot separate from them what contradicts his allegation.[207] They can also be used by merchants against merchants if the dispute concerns a commercial matter and if the books

202 Article 1336 Belgian Civil Code.

203 Minjauw, H., Vandendriessche, J. (2008) "Titel VI. Het bewijsrecht in burgerlijke zaken", in: Roodhooft, R. (ed.), *Bestendig Handboek Verbintenissenrecht*, Mechelen: Kluwer, VI.3–89.

204 *Ibid.*, 91. Note however that there are specific regulations in certain matters that describe the procedures and requirements to produce copies that are accorded the same value as originals. Minjauw, H., Vandendriessche, J. (2008) "Titel VI. Het bewijsrecht in burgerlijke zaken", in: Roodhooft, R. (ed.), *Bestendig Handboek Verbintenissenrecht*, Mechelen: Kluwer, VI.3–92.

205 Minjauw, H., Vandendriessche, J. (2008) "Titel VI. Het bewijsrecht in burgerlijke zaken", in: Roodhooft, R. (ed.), *Bestendig Handboek Verbintenissenrecht*, Mechelen: Kluwer, VI.3–84. See also articles 20–24 Belgian Commercial Code.

206 Article 1329 Belgian Civil Code. Mougenot, D. (2002) *Droit des obligations: la preuve*, Brussel: Larcier, 267. Despite the limitations of article 1329 Belgian Civil Code, there are still situations in which the merchant could use his regularly maintained account books as evidence against non-merchants. The requirement of the account books being regularly maintained stems from article 20 Belgian Commercial Code. Note also that account books can only be accepted as evidence if they are not disputed by the non-merchant parties. However, the judge is free to decide upon the admissibility of such evidence, even between merchants. Minjauw, H., Vandendriessche, J. (2008) "Titel VI. Het bewijsrecht in burgerlijke zaken", in: Roodhooft, R. (ed.), *Bestendig Handboek Verbintenissenrecht*, Mechelen: Kluwer, VI.3–85. Moreover, the account books will need to be supplemented with an oath in order to provide complete evidence. Whereby article 1329 Belgian Civil Code must be read in conjunction with article 1367 Belgian Civil Code. Minjauw, H., Vandendriessche, J. (2008) "Titel VI. Het bewijsrecht in burgerlijke zaken", in: Roodhooft, R. (ed.), *Bestendig Handboek Verbintenissenrecht*, Mechelen: Kluwer, VI.3–86.

207 Article 1330 Belgian Civil Code.

are regularly maintained.[208] Given the lack of evidentiary hierarchy under commercial law, the judge will be free to evaluate the value of these books.[209]

1.4.4.3. Domestic papers and registers

66. Domestic papers and registers are documentation kept by non-merchants including notes, agenda's, receipts, etc.[210] As these papers and notes are not regulated in any form – unlike the merchant's account books – and are made unilaterally, they cannot provide assurance regarding the validity of their contents.[211] Therefore, such papers and registers cannot be accepted as evidence in favor of the person who invokes them.[212]

1.4.4.4. Notes upon title

67. Sometimes, the margin, bottom or back of a title – being an original – can contain notes by one of the parties. Such notes are generally not signed and are, therefore, not to be considered as amendments or corrections to the title that are accepted by all parties.[213] Such notes can be considered to provide evidence of the release of the debtor.[214] Notes by a creditor can also be used against him if made on the title held by the debtor.[215]

1.4.4.5. Correspondence

68. In principle, correspondence could be considered as a private instrument, if it complies with the specific properties thereof.[216] This means that there must be

---

208 Article 20 Belgian Commercial Code. When account books are used by a non-merchant against a merchant, their probative value is put on par with an extrajudicial confession. Cornelis, L. (2000) *Algemene theorie van de verbintenis*, Antwerpen: Intersentia, 227; Minjauw, H., Vandendriessche, J. (2008) "Titel VI. Het bewijsrecht in burgerlijke zaken", in: Roodhooft, R. (ed.), *Bestendig Handboek Verbintenissenrecht*, Mechelen: Kluwer, VI.3–85; De Page, H. (1967) *Traité élémentaire de droit civil Belge, Tome Troisième (Les Obligations)*, Brussel: Bruylant, 849–851.

209 Minjauw, H., Vandendriessche, J. (2008) "Titel VI. Het bewijsrecht in burgerlijke zaken", in: Roodhooft, R. (ed.), *Bestendig Handboek Verbintenissenrecht*, Mechelen: Kluwer, VI.3–86.

210 *Ibid.*, 87.

211 De Page, H. (1967) *Traité élémentaire de droit civil Belge, Tome Troisième (Les Obligations)*, Brussel: Bruylant, 851–852.

212 Article 1331 Belgian Civil Code. However, under certain circumstances they could still be accepted as a presumption in cases where evidence by presumptions is allowed. Minjauw, H., Vandendriessche, J. (2008) "Titel VI. Het bewijsrecht in burgerlijke zaken", in: Roodhooft, R. (ed.), *Bestendig Handboek Verbintenissenrecht*, Mechelen: Kluwer, VI.3–87–88; De Page, H. (1967) *Traité élémentaire de droit civil Belge, Tome Troisième (Les Obligations)*, Brussel: Bruylant, 852; Van Gerven, W., Covemaker, S. (2006) *Verbintenissenrecht*, Leuven: Acco, 680.

213 Minjauw, H., Vandendriessche, J. (2008) "Titel VI. Het bewijsrecht in burgerlijke zaken", in: Roodhooft, R. (ed.), *Bestendig Handboek Verbintenissenrecht*, Mechelen: Kluwer, VI.3–88.

214 Article 1332, first line Belgian Civil Code.

215 Article 1332, second line Belgian Civil Code.

216 Minjauw, H., Vandendriessche, J. (2008) "Titel VI. Het bewijsrecht in burgerlijke zaken", in: Roodhooft, R. (ed.), *Bestendig Handboek Verbintenissenrecht*, Mechelen: Kluwer, VI.3–95–96; De

a document that contains at least one legal act, which is appropriated and signed by the parties.[217] The probative value of correspondence as a private instrument will depend on whether or not the correspondence is able to accurately and precisely document the parties' intentions.[218] If correspondence cannot be accepted as a private instrument, due to the absence of a valid signature for instance, it could still be presented as beginning of evidence in writing, if the conditions required thereby – being a written document emanating from the person against whom it is invoked or appropriated by that person and rendering the alleged fact probable – are met.[219] If the qualification of correspondence as beginning of evidence in writing fails, then qualifying it as an extrajudicial confession or as a factual presumption could still be attempted.[220]

1.4.4.6. Others

69. The Belgian Civil Code also refers to a number of other types of evidence, such as tallies. Notches on a tally stick corresponding to counter-notches provide evidence between parties used to establish deliveries between them in that way.[221] Instruments of recognition and confirmation are instruments drafted to recognize or to confirm previous agreements.[222] As with transcripts, they are not accorded a significant probative value and the original can still be required.[223] An act of confirmation can be used to correct the relative nullity of the original, albeit under strict conditions.[224]

Page, H. (1967) *Traité élémentaire de droit civil Belge, Tome Troisième (Les Obligations)*, Brussel: Bruylant, 868; Mougenot, D. (2002) *Droit des obligations: la preuve*, Brussel: Larcier, 243–244.

217 See section 1.4.1. When mutual agreements are included in the correspondence, the formalities of article 1325 Belgian Civil Code must in principle be complied with. However, out of practical concerns, it has been accepted that correspondence cannot comply with all of these formalities, such as the requirement to produce as many originals as there are parties who have a discernable interest. Minjauw, H., Vandendriessche, J. (2008) "Titel VI. Het bewijsrecht in burgerlijke zaken", in: Roodhooft, R. (ed.), *Bestendig Handboek Verbintenissenrecht*, Mechelen: Kluwer, VI.3–96; Mougenot, D. (2002) *Droit des obligations: la preuve*, Brussel: Larcier, 245. Article 1326 Belgian Civil Code regarding the unilateral promises of payment remains applicable.

218 If such intentions are clear and the other properties and formalities are complied with, correspondence can be accepted as a private instrument, thus being accorded the accompanying probative value. Minjauw, H., Vandendriessche, J. (2008) "Titel VI. Het bewijsrecht in burgerlijke zaken", in: Roodhooft, R. (ed.), *Bestendig Handboek Verbintenissenrecht*, Mechelen: Kluwer, VI.3–96; Mougenot, D. (2002) *Droit des obligations: la preuve*, Brussel: Larcier, 244–245. As noted previously, the judge has the competence to interpret the document to discover those intentions, following article 1156 Belgian Civil Code.

219 Cornelis, L. (2000) *Algemene theorie van de verbintenis*, Antwerpen: Intersentia, 223. See section 1.4.3.

220 These types of evidence are discussed further on, in sections 1.5.3 and 1.5.2 respectively.

221 Article 1333 Belgian Civil Code.

222 Minjauw, H., Vandendriessche, J. (2008) "Titel VI. Het bewijsrecht in burgerlijke zaken", in: Roodhooft, R. (ed.), *Bestendig Handboek Verbintenissenrecht*, Mechelen: Kluwer, VI.3–92.

223 Article 1337 Belgian Civil Code.

224 Articles 1338–1340 Belgian Civil Code.

1.5. NON-WRITTEN EVIDENCE

70. Despite the clear preference of the rules of Belgian civil law for evidence in writing, there are also specific rules addressing particular types of non-written evidence.

1.5.1. Witness statements

71. Witness statements are statements made under oath before court by persons claiming to have directly observed acts or events or that have indirectly gained knowledge about such acts or events.[225] As discussed previously, the rules set by article 1341 Belgian Civil Code always allow for evidence to be provided in writing, by oaths or by confessions, but it limits the use of evidence by witness statements and presumptions. Therefore, evidence provided by witness statements is often only allowed as supplementary evidence – for instance supplementing beginning of evidence in writing – and is not accorded a high probative value and is, thus, left up to the discretion of the judge.[226] When witness statements are admissible, the judge retains the right to decide whether or not this type of evidence can serve the case at hand, provided that he does not deny a party's right to invoke such evidence.[227] As witness statements do not have a predefined probative value of their own, the judge remains free to decide upon that value.[228] The judge may decide to follow some statements made by the witnesses and to refute others as insufficiently credible, or may decide to follow one witness even when his statement is contradicted by other witnesses.[229]

---

225 Minjauw, H., Vandendriessche, J. (2008) "Titel VI. Het bewijsrecht in burgerlijke zaken", in: Roodhooft, R. (ed.), *Bestendig Handboek Verbintenissenrecht*, Mechelen: Kluwer, VI.3–47; Cornelis, L. (2000) *Algemene theorie van de verbintenis*, Antwerpen: Intersentia, 227; Van Gerven, W., Covemaker, S. (2006) *Verbintenissenrecht*, Leuven: Acco, 681.

226 Minjauw, H., Vandendriessche, J. (2008) "Titel VI. Het bewijsrecht in burgerlijke zaken", in: Roodhooft, R. (ed.), *Bestendig Handboek Verbintenissenrecht*, Mechelen: Kluwer, VI.3–46–47.

227 Minjauw, H., Vandendriessche, J. (2008) "Titel VI. Het bewijsrecht in burgerlijke zaken", in: Roodhooft, R. (ed.), *Bestendig Handboek Verbintenissenrecht*, Mechelen: Kluwer, VI.3–49; Cornelis, L. (2000) *Algemene theorie van de verbintenis*, Antwerpen: Intersentia, 228.

228 Minjauw, H., Vandendriessche, J. (2008) "Titel VI. Het bewijsrecht in burgerlijke zaken", in: Roodhooft, R. (ed.), *Bestendig Handboek Verbintenissenrecht*, Mechelen: Kluwer, VI.3–50; Van Gerven, W., Covemaker, S. (2006) *Verbintenissenrecht*, Leuven: Acco, 681–682; Cornelis, L. (2000) *Algemene theorie van de verbintenis*, Antwerpen: Intersentia, 229; Stijns, S. (2009) *Leerboek Verbintenissenrecht Boek 2*, Brugge: die Keure, 175; Mougenot, D. (2002) *Droit des obligations: la preuve*, Brussel: Larcier, 280–281.

229 Minjauw, H., Vandendriessche, J. (2008) "Titel VI. Het bewijsrecht in burgerlijke zaken", in: Roodhooft, R. (ed.), *Bestendig Handboek Verbintenissenrecht*, Mechelen: Kluwer, VI.3–50. The reason for this limitation of admissibility and probative value of witness statements is that they depend on the witness' perception and recollection, which may be incorrect.

1.5.2. Presumptions

72. Presumptions are conclusions drawn by law or by a judge from a known fact to decide upon an unknown fact.[230] This entails a certain reasoning, whereby an established fact is used to deduct from it another fact which has not been proven yet.[231] It allows the court to decide with a probability bordering upon certainty that certain legal facts have occurred, in turn leading to conclusions regarding the existence of legal obligations.[232]

1.5.2.1. Statutory presumptions

73. Statutory presumptions are presumptions that by specific legal provisions have been drawn from certain acts or facts.[233] Their admissibility follows from their very existence, as their admissibility is prescribed by law.[234] The probative value of statutory presumptions is also clearly regulated by Belgian civil evidence law.[235] Statutory presumptions relieve the party to whose benefit they are concluded from any burden of proof.[236] Whether the opposing party can produce counterproof depends on the refutability of the statutory presumptions.[237] Refutable statutory presumptions – *iuris tantum* – are considered valid, unless the opposing party can prove otherwise.[238] Irrefutable statutory presumptions – *iuris et de iure* – do not allow counterproof, except by oath or confession.[239]

---

230 Article 1349 Belgian Civil Code. Mourlon Beernaert, F., Gaudy, A. (2006) "Partie VI. Le droit de la preuve – La preuve par présomption", in: X, *Obligations. Traité théorique et pratique*, Brussel: Kluwer, VI.4.4 – 1; Mougenot, D. (2002) *Droit des obligations: la preuve*, Brussel: Larcier, 282.

231 Stijns, S. (2009) *Leerboek Verbintenissenrecht Boek 2*, Brugge: die Keure, 175; Minjauw, H., Vandendriessche, J. (2008) "Titel VI. Het bewijsrecht in burgerlijke zaken", in: Roodhooft, R. (ed.), *Bestendig Handboek Verbintenissenrecht*, Mechelen: Kluwer, VI.3–50.

232 Stijns, S. (2009) *Leerboek Verbintenissenrecht Boek 2*, Brugge: die Keure, 175–176.

233 Article 1350 Belgian Civil Code. Article 1351 was removed in 1967, making this one of the few cases where the original text of the Code Napoleon was amended.

234 Minjauw, H., Vandendriessche, J. (2008) "Titel VI. Het bewijsrecht in burgerlijke zaken", in: Roodhooft, R. (ed.), *Bestendig Handboek Verbintenissenrecht*, Mechelen: Kluwer, VI.3–53.

235 Article 1352 Belgian Civil Code.

236 Article 1352, first line Belgian Civil Code.

237 Minjauw, H., Vandendriessche, J. (2008) "Titel VI. Het bewijsrecht in burgerlijke zaken", in: Roodhooft, R. (ed.), *Bestendig Handboek Verbintenissenrecht*, Mechelen: Kluwer, VI.3–51; Stijns, S. (2009) *Leerboek Verbintenissenrecht Boek 2*, Brugge: die Keure, 176.

238 Such counterproof can be delivered by all means. Cornelis, L. (2000) *Algemene theorie van de verbintenis*, Antwerpen: Intersentia, 231; Minjauw, H., Vandendriessche, J. (2008) "Titel VI. Het bewijsrecht in burgerlijke zaken", in: Roodhooft, R. (ed.), *Bestendig Handboek Verbintenissenrecht*, Mechelen: Kluwer, VI.3–51; Stijns, S. (2009) *Leerboek Verbintenissenrecht Boek 2*, Brugge: die Keure, 176; Mourlon Beernaert, F., Gaudy, A. (2006) "Partie VI. Le droit de la preuve – La preuve par présomption", in: X, *Obligations. Traité théorique et pratique*, Brussel: Kluwer, VI.4.4 – 2.

239 Cornelis, L. (2000) *Algemene theorie van de verbintenis*, Antwerpen: Intersentia, 231; Minjauw, H., Vandendriessche, J. (2008) "Titel VI. Het bewijsrecht in burgerlijke zaken", in: Roodhooft, R. (ed.), *Bestendig Handboek Verbintenissenrecht*, Mechelen: Kluwer, VI.3–52; S.

1.5.2.2. Factual presumptions

74. When a presumption is not prescribed by law and is, thus, left to the discretion of the judge, it concerns a factual presumption.[240] Despite being a fairly open category of evidence, factual presumptions must comply with a number of requirements. First, the facts underlying the reasoning of the factual presumption must be clearly established, meaning that uncertain or probable facts cannot serve.[241] Second, the conclusion – being the presumption – drawn from the established fact must be plausible and justifiable. This means that the presumption does not need to be an inevitable conclusion given the facts, but only a possible conclusion.[242] However, such conclusion should still be possible, given the facts, and thus not be unrelated or unjustifiable.[243] In other words, there must be a clear correlation between the established facts and the conclusion drawn therefrom.[244] Third, the presumptions considered by the judge must be weighty, certain and concordant.[245] However, despite the fact that it is in principle up to the court to deduct a presumption from established facts, it is often the parties who present presumptions of their own in the hopes of enhancing their case's credibility.[246]

75. Evidence by factual presumptions is principally only allowed where evidence by witness statements is considered admissible, unless when acting against an act of fraud or deception.[247] Both types of evidence are seemingly

---

Stijns (2009) *Leerboek Verbintenissenrecht Boek 2*, Brugge: die Keure, 176; Mourlon Beernaert, F., Gaudy, A. (2006) "Partie VI. Le droit de la preuve – La preuve par présomption", in: X, *Obligations. Traité théorique et pratique*, Brussel: Kluwer, VI.4.4 – 2.

240 Article 1353 Belgian Civil Code.

241 Cass. 19 May 1983, *jure.juridat.just.fgov.be*; Minjauw, H., Vandendriessche, J. (2008) "Titel VI. Het bewijsrecht in burgerlijke zaken", in: Roodhooft, R. (ed.), *Bestendig Handboek Verbintenissenrecht*, Mechelen: Kluwer, VI.3–55; Van Gerven, W., Covemaker, S. (2006) *Verbintenissenrecht*, Leuven: Acco, 685.

242 Note that this is the position of the Belgian Supreme Court. Lower courts do tend to require an absolute certainty. Minjauw, H., Vandendriessche, J. (2008) "Titel VI. Het bewijsrecht in burgerlijke zaken", in: Roodhooft, R. (ed.), *Bestendig Handboek Verbintenissenrecht*, Mechelen: Kluwer, VI.3–56–58; Cass. 18 April 2008, *jure.juridat.just.fgov.be*; Stijns, S. (2009) *Leerboek Verbintenissenrecht Boek 2*, Brugge: die Keure, 176.

243 Cass. 20 December 2007, *jure.juridat.just.fgov.be*; Minjauw, H., Vandendriessche, J. (2008) "Titel VI. Het bewijsrecht in burgerlijke zaken", in: Roodhooft, R. (ed.), *Bestendig Handboek Verbintenissenrecht*, Mechelen: Kluwer, VI.3–56.

244 Cornelis, L. (2000) *Algemene theorie van de verbintenis*, Antwerpen: Intersentia, 232; Minjauw, H., Vandendriessche, J. (2008) "Titel VI. Het bewijsrecht in burgerlijke zaken", in: Roodhooft, R. (ed.), *Bestendig Handboek Verbintenissenrecht*, Mechelen: Kluwer, VI.3–56.

245 Article 1353 Belgian Civil Code; Minjauw, H., Vandendriessche, J. (2008) "Titel VI. Het bewijsrecht in burgerlijke zaken", in: Roodhooft, R. (ed.), *Bestendig Handboek Verbintenissenrecht*, Mechelen: Kluwer, VI.3–55; Cornelis, L. (2000) *Algemene theorie van de verbintenis*, Antwerpen: Intersentia, 232.

246 Cornelis, L. (2000) *Algemene theorie van de verbintenis*, Antwerpen: Intersentia, 229–230.

247 Article 1353 Belgian Civil Code.

afforded the same weight in the probative hierarchy following from the provisions of the Belgian Civil Code. This means that factual presumptions do not have a predefined probative value, leaving the decision upon their value up to the judge.[248] Consequently, counterproof can be delivered by all means.[249]

1.5.3. Other types of non-written evidence

76. Next to witness statements and presumptions, the Belgian Civil Code lists a few more types of non-written evidence. This mainly concerns oaths and confessions, as well as a provision aimed at the cases where no written evidence could be produced. As these types of evidence have no direct relation to this research, they will not be discussed further.

2. THE ORIGINALITY REQUIREMENT IN BELGIAN CIVIL LAW

77. The previous section provided an overview of the classic rules on evidence in Belgian civil law. Here, conclusions will be drawn from this overview with regard to the notion of originality.

78. From the previous overview, it has become clear that the rules on evidence under Belgian civil law show a distinct preference for evidence in writing. The main provision on admissibility, article 1341 Belgian Civil Code, explicitly aims to prohibit the use of certain types of evidence that are often considered to be less trustworthy, namely witness statements and presumptions. In terms of legal certainty, there are only a few types of evidence other than public and private instruments that can provide the parties with almost absolute certainty regarding their admissibility and their probative value. Many other types of evidence possess only incomplete or no probative value, leaving the final decision on the value of such evidence up to the judge.

79. For the purposes of these rules on evidence, instruments can be defined as documents that contain information about legal acts between the parties and which are signed and appropriated by those parties. When a document does not possess the properties or formalities to be considered as an instrument, it could still – under certain conditions – be considered as a beginning of evidence in writing, a form of incomplete evidence. When the qualification of evidence as

---

248 Minjauw, H., Vandendriessche, J. (2008) "Titel VI. Het bewijsrecht in burgerlijke zaken", in: Roodhooft, R. (ed.), *Bestendig Handboek Verbintenissenrecht*, Mechelen: Kluwer, VI.3–54; Van Gerven, W., Covemaker, S. (2006) *Verbintenissenrecht*, Leuven: Acco, 685.

249 Cornelis, L. (2000) *Algemene theorie van de verbintenis*, Antwerpen: Intersentia, 233.

beginning of evidence in writing fails, there will be a factual presumption at most.

80. The main finding here is that within the general preference for evidence in writing, the Belgian Civil Code accords a higher probative value to writings that display a higher degree of reliability. The most important element in providing guarantees toward such reliability is the signature. It is here that the importance of originality can be situated. Despite technological evolutions, thanks to which a perfect and reliable identical reproduction of a document can be produced, the lack of a handwritten signature on that copy will still principally disqualify it from being considered as an original instrument.[250] The sanction for failing to provide a valid signature will, therefore, involve the barring of the document from qualification as an original instrument, thereby assigning it a qualification of beginning of evidence in writing at most. As a result, it will be an important element of the analysis in the sections that follow to see how electronic information can cope with this signature requirement, lest its probative value become stranded at the lower levels of the evidentiary hierarchy.

81. Another finding that relates to the originality requirement is the idea that providing evidence always entails a reliance on certain presumptions of truth. As noted, the rules on evidence do not focus on establishing the factual truth, but rather a legal truth. When evidence is sufficiently reliable, it can be presumed to establish such legal truth. These presumptions are present at all layers of the rules on evidence. As it is practically unfeasible to conduct a full and thorough examination of each and every document produced as evidence, the examination of certain criteria – mainly being the fulfillment of a number of formalities and verifying whether or not a valid signature is present – will determine the value of such document. Here, it can be held that the presence of a valid signature on a document leads to the presumption of its trustworthiness and thus to its qualification as an original instrument. As already touched upon when exploring the notion of originality itself, the originality requirement in Belgian civil law can therefore be fulfilled by adhering to formalities.

---

[250] Demoulin, M., Soyez, S. (2012) "L'authenticité, de l'original papier à la copie numérique – Les enjeux juridiques et archivistiques de la numérisation", in: Duranti, L., Schaeffer, E. (eds) *The Memory of the World in the Digital Age: Digitization and Preservation*, Conference proceedings of UNESCO: Vancouver, 26–28 September 2013, 747; Gobert, D., Montero, E. (2000) "La signature dans les contrats et les paiements électroniques: l'approche fonctionelle", in: Montero, E. (ed.) *Commerce électronique: le temps des certitudes*, Brussels: Bruylant, 62. Note, however, some deviations in case law, as noted under footnote 121.

3. DIGITALIZATION IN THE BELGIAN CIVIL CODE

82. This section will analyze how the Belgian legislator has implemented the digitalization process in Belgian civil law. In doing so, it assesses how electronic information can be presented as evidence under matters of Belgian civil law. An immediate and obvious finding here is that the Belgian Civil Code does not contain separate rules relating to the procurement of electronic information as evidence under civil proceedings. This already leads to our first finding, namely that the existing rules regarding the classic types of evidence will also have to be applied to the new types of evidence created by electronic information. Initially, there were only two cases, article 1317 and article 1322, where the Belgian Civil Code was amended to allow for the application of these rules to matters concerning electronic information. The Belgian legislator has adopted three legal acts to facilitate this process. In this section, those three acts will first be analyzed. Here, it will become clear that the figure of the electronic signature has been introduced to act as the electronic counterpart of the handwritten signature. Given its importance, this figure will need to be further analyzed. Next, how the existing rules on civil law evidence can be applied to matters of electronic information will be analyzed.

3.1. ACT OF 20 OCTOBER 2000

83. On 20 October 2000, the Belgian legislator adopted an act concerning the introduction of the electronic signature in judicial proceedings.[251] This brief act makes two important additions to the existing rules of the Belgian Civil Code: the electronic signature and the notification.[252] As discussed previously, the signature can be considered as the most important element under the rules of Belgian civil evidence law. It is the presence or absence of a valid signature that will determine the admissibility and probative value of the evidence presented during civil proceedings to a great extent. However, as the signature is typically defined as a handwritten mark applied directly to a document, it is clear that this figure cannot be applied to electronic information.[253] Being dynamic and not fixed to a particular medium, electronic information is, by its nature, not adapted to accommodate the formalities expected from a signature. Only if the

---

251 Act of 20 October 2000 introducing the use of means of telecommunication and of the electronic signature in judicial and extrajudicial proceedings, *Belgian State Gazette* 22 December 2000.

252 It also contained a number of provisions amending the Belgian Judicial Code. These provisions were later removed again.

253 Storme, M.E. (2001) "De invoering van de elektronische handtekening in ons bewijsrecht", *RW*, 1514.

electronic information would be made static and fixed to a medium – *i.e.* printed onto paper – would the application of a signature become possible. As noted previously, an EU directive was adopted that introduced the notion of electronic signatures.[254] Under Belgian law, this has resulted in the addition of a second paragraph to article 1322 Belgian Civil Code by the Act of 20 October 2000. This paragraph states: *"For the application of this article, a whole of electronic data that can be attributed to a particular person and that can demonstrate the integrity of the contents of the instrument can be considered to comply with the requirements of a signature."*[255]As a result, electronic information can also be considered to be signed if there is electronic data that can establish the authorship of that 'signature', if that author cannot repudiate his authorship – thereby also establishing the author's intention to appropriate the contents of the signed electronic information – and if that data can establish the integrity of the contents of the signed electronic information. In principle, such signed electronic information could be qualified as a private instrument.[256]

84. The broad formulation of the new article 1322 does not include any specific formalities. However, the electronic signature must display certain properties. First, the signature must be a collection of electronic data. This can be very broadly interpreted.[257] Second, that electronic data must be able to be attributed to a particular person. While it is not explicitly stated that such person must be identified, it is clear that such identification can follow from the fact that the person must be *particular*.[258] In the preparatory works, explicit reference is also given to identification and attribution as being main characteristics of a signature that should be transposed to the electronic version of a signature.[259] Therefore, as with a handwritten signature, the placement of a signature by electronic data is also presumed to constitute the appropriation of the content of the signed information by the signatory.[260] Third, in order for the electronic data to be considered as a signature, it must demonstrate the integrity of the signed information. As discussed previously, a signature is generally accepted to provide proof that the signed document has not been tampered with since the

254 Directive 1999/93/EC of the European Parliament and of the Council of 13 December 1999 on a Community framework for electronic signatures, *Official Journal* L 013 of 19 January 2000, 12–20. This directive will be further discussed under section 3.2.1.

255 Article 2 Act of 20 October 2000. Author's own translation.

256 Note that, by inserting this addition into article 1322, the legislator has made it clear that this rule is only intended for application to private instruments. Other provisions, for instance requiring a certain type of will to be handwritten (article 970 Belgian Civil Code), can therefore not benefit from this addition. Van Eecke, P. (2009) "De elektronische handtekening in het recht", *T.B.H.*, 340.

257 Van Eecke, P. (2009) "De elektronische handtekening in het recht", *T.B.H.*, 338.

258 *Id.*

259 Amendment 12 to the proposal to introduce new means of telecommunication in the judicial and extrajudicial procedures, *Parl. St. Kamer* 1999–2000, 0038/6, 11.

260 *Id.*

moment of signing.[261] To ensure that this important property of the signature is maintained, the legislator has chosen to explicate it in its addition to article 1322 Belgian Civil Code.[262]

85. An immediate concern that can be raised with the introduction of a signature by electronic means is whether this provision can suffice to fulfill all of the requirements to have electronic information be qualified as, for instance, a private instrument. After all, apart from being duly signed, instruments are considered to be documents in writing. Can electronic information, dynamic in nature and not bound to a particular medium, be considered as written documents as understood in the Belgian Civil Code? This question can be answered positively. Legal doctrine has established that there is no requirement that such documents in writing need to be handwritten, thereby allowing for the use of modern techniques.[263] In order for information to be accepted as writing, it is sufficient that it is expressed in a language, using understandable signs, and given some durability.[264] This has later been recognized by the legislator.[265]

86. The original Civil Code contained a provision concerning notification. This provision was removed in 1949.[266] The Act of 20 October 2000 restores this provision in a modified format, allowing for notification to be made by electronic means. The article is constituted very broadly, allowing that written notification can be made by all means that result in a written notification at the end of the recipient.[267] Despite allowing for such notification to be made by a broad range

---

261 Van Eecke, P. (2004) *Naar een juridische status voor de elektronische handtekening: Een rol voor de handtekening in de informatiemaatschappij?*, PhD thesis KU Leuven - Faculty of Law, 326–327.

262 Amendment 12 to the proposal to introduce new means of telecommunication in the judicial and extrajudicial procedures, *Parl. St. Kamer* 1999–2000, 0038/6, 11.

263 Van Eecke, P. (2009) "De elektronische handtekening in het recht", *T.B.H.*, 333; De Page, H. (1967) *Traité élémentaire de droit civil Belge, Tome Troisième (Les Obligations),* Brussel: Bruylant, 794–795; Wéry, P., Gobert, D., Kerzmann, L. (2003) "La preuve", in: Coipel, M., Wéry, P., Durant, I., Cruquenaire, A., *Guide juridique de l'entreprise*, Brussel: Kluwer, 47–48; Mourlon Beernaert, F., Gaudy, A. (2006) "Partie VI. Le droit de la preuve - La preuve littérale", in: X, *Obligations. Traité théorique et pratique*, Brussel: Kluwer, VI.4.2 - 3. This was also remarked in the legislative preparations to the Act of 20 October 2000: Amendment 12 to the proposal to introduce new means of telecommunication in the judicial and extrajudicial procedures, *Parl. St. Kamer* 1999–2000, 0038/6, 11.

264 Van Eecke, P. (2009) "De elektronische handtekening in het recht", *T.B.H.*, 333; Van Gerven, W., Covemaker, S. (2006) *Verbintenissenrecht*, Leuven: Acco, 696; Storme, M.E. (2001) "De invoering van de elektronische handtekening in ons bewijsrecht", *RW*, 1514–1515; Mougenot, D. (2002) *Droit des obligations: la preuve*, Brussel: Larcier, 139–140.

265 Under the Act of 11 March 2003 concerning certain legal aspects of services of the information society, *Belgian State Gazette* 17 March 2003. This Act will be further discussed under section 3.3.

266 As noted in article 3 Act of 20 October 2000.

267 Article 3 Act of 20 October 2000. More in particular, the article references telegrams, telex, telefax, electronic mail or any other form of telecommunication means.

of means, it is held that the recipient can request a signed notification, thus again reaffirming the importance of the signature. While this provision does not directly relate to the rules of evidence of the Belgian Civil Code, it is a clear attempt by the legislator to allow for the use of modern means of communication to be used in matters between parties.[268]

87. The Act of 20 October 2000 is of invaluable importance to the implementation of electronic information into the hierarchy of evidence under Belgian civil law.[269] Because of its provisions, duly signed electronic information can now be accepted as valid evidence, and even be qualified as a private instrument, thereby being awarded the high probative value associated with that type of evidence.[270] It is also important to note that the addition to article 1322 does not directly introduce the notion of the electronic signature or a particular technique to create such signatures, but only broadens the existing notion of the signature.[271] The legislative preparations for the Act of 20 October 2000 make it very clear that it was the intention of the legislator to formulate the addition to article 1322 as broadly as possible, in order to ensure its technological neutrality.[272] One result of this broad notion is that a signature made by electronic means is not automatically accepted as being equal to a handwritten signature. Given the formulation of article 1322 Belgian Civil Code, it will be up to the judge to verify whether or not the electronic data presented to him complies with the identification, non-repudiation and integrity requirements of that article.[273] While it could be argued that the broad concept of article 1322

268 Caboor, P. (2001) "De wet van 20 oktober 2000 tot invoering van het gebruik van telecommunicatiemiddelen en van de elektronische handtekening in de gerechtelijke en de buitengerechtelijke procedure: een eerste verkenning", *A.J.T.*, 639.

269 It can also be argued that this provision provides some relief to the classic duality maintained between original and copy. By allowing the signing of electronic information – thus allowing electronic information to fulfill the same integrity requirements as desired from paper documents – such signed electronic information can now be considered as an original and no longer as merely a copy. Amendment 12 to the proposal to introduce new means of telecommunication in the judicial and extrajudicial procedures, *Parl. St. Kamer* 1999–2000, 0038/6, 11–12; Van Eecke, P. (2009) "De elektronische handtekening in het recht", *T.B.H.*, 339.

270 Storme, M.E. (2001) "De invoering van de elektronische handtekening in ons bewijsrecht", *RW*, 1514; Van Eecke, P. (2009) "De elektronische handtekening in het recht", *T.B.H.*, 337–338.

271 Van Eecke, P. (2009) "De elektronische handtekening in het recht", *T.B.H.*, 337.

272 "*The formulation of the proposed article is not limited to the procedure of the "digital" signature, in order to allow for the development of new techniques. In doing so, the risk that the Civil Code will have to be amended repeatedly is avoided.*" (Original text: De omschrijving van het voorgestelde artikel is echter niet beperkt tot het procédé van de "digitale" handtekening om nieuwe technieken de kans te geven zich te ontwikkelen. Tevens wordt hierdoor het risico vermeden dat het Burgerlijk Wetboek te pas en te onpas moet worden gewijzigd.). Amendment 12 to the proposal to introduce new means of telecommunication in the judicial and extrajudicial procedures, *Parl. St. Kamer* 1999–2000, 0038/6, 11.

273 Van Eecke, P. (2009) "De elektronische handtekening in het recht", *T.B.H.*, 339; Storme, M.E. (2001) "De invoering van de elektronische handtekening in ons bewijsrecht", *RW*, 1520; Wéry, P., Gobert, D., Kerzmann, L. (2003) "La preuve", in: Coipel, M., Wéry, P., Durant, I., Cruquenaire, A., *Guide juridique de l'entreprise*, Brussel: Kluwer, 62.

Belgian Civil Code, by relying on the appreciation of the judge, cannot provide legal certainty regarding whether or not electronic data presented as a signature will be accepted as being an actual signature, such judiciary appreciation was also already present for handwritten signatures.[274] Another consequence of this broad notion is that no specific formalities were introduced, leaving the acceptance of electronic data presented as a signature up to the deduction of three properties from that data. While these properties – identification, non-repudiation and integrity – were already important elements for the validation of handwritten signatures, their inclusion under the broad notion of article 1322 allows for the acceptance of very different techniques to satisfy the classic signature requirement.[275]

3.2. ACT OF 9 JULY 2001

88. With the Act of 20 October 2000, the Belgian legislator broadened the exstant notion of the signature to allow for signatures to be created by electronic means. Later, on 9 July 2001, the Act on electronic signatures was adopted.[276, 277] The latter act is the Belgian implementation of the European Directive on electronic signatures.[278] While it may be perceived that the legislator first broadened the notion of signatures and only later thought about introducing electronic signatures, this is not correct.[279] In fact, the legislative proposal

274 Caboor argues that, by not providing for a clear legal rule, article 1322 Belgian Civil Code leaves this matter entirely up to the judge and thus fails to deliver legal certainty. Caboor, P. (2001) "De wet van 20 oktober 2000 tot invoering van het gebruik van telecommunicatiemiddelen en van de elektronische handtekening in de gerechtelijke en de buitengerechtelijke procedure: een eerste verkenning", *A.J.T.*, 638. Mougenot uses similar arguments: Mougenot, D. (2002) *Droit des obligations: la preuve*, Brussel: Larcier, 194–195. However, Van Eecke and the Belgian legislator have argued that this is no different from the existing appreciation margin by the judge. Van Eecke, P. (2009) "De elektronische handtekening in het recht", *T.B.H.*, 339; Amendment 12 to the proposal to introduce new means of telecommunication in the judicial and extrajudicial procedures, *Parl. St. Kamer* 1999–2000, 0038/6, 12.

275 Amendment 12 to the proposal to introduce new means of telecommunication in the judicial and extrajudicial procedures, *Parl. St. Kamer* 1999–2000, 0038/6, 11.

276 Act of 9 July 2001 concerning the determination of certain rules regarding the legal framework for electronic signatures, electronic certified mail and certification services, *Belgian State Gazette* 29 September 2001.

277 In recent years, the Belgian legislator has undertaken an effort in codifying different legislative acts on economic matters into a Code of Economic Law. While the Act of 9 July 2001 was, at first, not included in that Code, it was clear that there was always an intention to do so. See footnote 473.

278 Directive 1999/93/EC of the European Parliament and of the Council of 13 December 1999 on a Community framework for electronic signatures, *Official Journal* L 013 of 19 January 2000, 12–20.

279 Van Eecke, P. (2004) *Naar een juridische status voor de elektronische handtekening: Een rol voor de handtekening in de informatiemaatschappij?*, PhD thesis KU Leuven – Faculty of Law, 592.

leading to the Act of 9 July 2001 was already under parliamentary discussion at the same time as the proposal eventually leading to the Act of 20 October 2000.[280] More importantly, the provision broadening the notion of a signature – the addition to article 1322 Belgian Civil Code – was not originally part of that proposal and was only introduced when, during the discussions on the proposal regarding electronic signatures, it was found that first an amendment to the Belgian Civil Code was needed in order for such techniques to be allowed under Belgian civil evidence law.[281]

3.2.1. The electronic signature

89. As discussed previously, the broadening of the notion of a signature established by article 1322 Belgian Civil Code opens a wide range of possibilities to create signatures by electronic means. In principle, a picture of a handwritten signature or even the signature typically found at the bottom of an e-mail could be considered as signatures under that provision, but that the judge would have to decide whether or not those signatures could sufficiently demonstrate the three properties expected from such signatures – identification, non-repudiation and integrity.

90. Moreover, the aforementioned EU directive established three distinct types of electronic signatures. The most developed type, the qualified electronic signature, is granted automatic equivalence to a handwritten signature.[282] While the directive does establish a non-discrimination principle – prohibiting Member States from denying validity to an electronic signature solely on the basis of it being in an electronic form or for not being a qualified electronic signature[283] – the acceptance of the other two types of electronic signatures is mostly left open to the discretion of the Member States. As a result, it is clear that the directive cannot be understood as imposing the use of electronic signatures in all instances where a handwritten signature is required.[284]

---

280 The former was introduced on 16 December 1999, the latter on 4 August 1999. Note, however, that both proposals were already discussed within the government during the previous parliamentary session. Proposal introducing new means of telecommunication in the judicial and extrajudicial procedures, *Parl. St. Kamer* 1997–1998, 1501/1; Proposal concerning the working of certification services regarding the use of electronic signatures, *Parl. St. Kamer* 1999–2000, 0322/1, 5.

281 Amendment 12 to the proposal to introduce new means of telecommunication in the judicial and extrajudicial procedures, *Parl. St. Kamer* 1999–2000, 0038/6; Proposal concerning the working of certification services regarding the use of electronic signatures, *Parl. St. Kamer* 1999–2000, 0322/1.

282 Article 5(1) Directive 1999/93/EC.

283 See also: Mougenot, D. (2002) *Droit des obligations: la preuve*, Brussel: Larcier, 182.

284 J. Dumortier (2004) "Legal Status of Qualified Electronic Signatures in Europe", in: Paulus, S., Pohlmann, N., Reimer, H. (ed.), *ISSE 2004-Securing Electronic Business Processes*, Wiesbaden: Vieweg, 281–289.

91. In its most basic form, Directive 1999/93/EC defines an electronic signature as "data in electronic form which are attached to or logically associated with other electronic data and which serve as a method of authentication".[285] The directive does not clarify how the different elements of this provision should be interpreted. In general, it can be held that the requirement of attachment or logical association should be interpreted as meaning that there should be a clear physical or logical bond between the data serving as a signature and the electronic information intended to be signed.[286] Authentication, in turn, should be considered as establishing the non-refutable origin and the integrity of the signed electronic information.[287] In keeping this definition as broad as possible, it is clear that the EU aimed for this to apply to all kinds of signatures by electronic means. While this definition does resemble what has been stipulated in the addition to article 1322 Belgian Civil Code, article 1322 should not be considered as the transposition of this provision of the directive.[288] Following the non-discrimination rule included in the directive, such common electronic signature cannot be denied legal validity solely on the basis of it being a signature in electronic form or for not being a qualified electronic signature.[289] However, the judge to which evidence signed with an electronic signature is presented remains free to decide whether or not that signature fulfills all of the requirements – the attachment or logical association and the authentication – in order for it to be accepted as such.[290]

92. The second type of electronic signature introduced under Directive 1999/93/EC is the advanced electronic signature. This type is defined as "*an electronic signature which meets the following requirements: (a) it is uniquely linked to the signatory; (b) it is capable of identifying the signatory; (c) it is created using means*

285 Art. 2(1) Directive 1999/93/EC.

286 Van Eecke, P. (2009) "De elektronische handtekening in het recht", *T.B.H.*, 342.

287 *Id.* While it has been argued that the integrity of the electronic information does not necessarily need to follow from the signature technique used, and that other techniques could be applied to preserve the integrity of the information, this appears to be a minority opinion not shared in legal doctrine generally. Wéry, P., Gobert, D., Kerzmann, L. (2003) "La preuve", in: Coipel, M., Wéry, P., Durant, I., Cruquenaire, A., *Guide juridique de l'entreprise*, Brussel: Kluwer, 53.

288 Van Eecke, P. (2009) "De elektronische handtekening in het recht", *T.B.H.*, 343. For instance, by introducing a potential equivalence between handwritten signatures and signatures in electronic form, article 1322 Belgian Civil Code relates more to article 5(1) Directive 1999/93/EC. Article 5 (2) Directive 1999/93/EC, of which the addition to article 1322 Belgian Civil Code supposedly is the transposition, only establishes a non-discrimination principle. Van Eecke, P. (2004) *Naar een juridische status voor de elektronische handtekening: Een rol voor de handtekening in de informatiemaatschappij?*, PhD thesis KU Leuven – Faculty of Law, 623.

289 Article 5 (2) Directive 1999/93/EC.

290 Van Eecke, P. (2009) "De elektronische handtekening in het recht", *T.B.H.*, 342; Vandenabeele, V. (2002) "De elektronische handtekening: rechten en plichten van de certificatiedienstverlener, de certificaathouder en de vertrouwende derde", *TBBR*, 611; Mougenot, D. (2002) *Droit des obligations: la preuve*, Brussel: Larcier, 188–189.

that the signatory can maintain under his sole control; and (d) it is linked to the data to which it relates in such a manner that any subsequent change of the data is detectable".[291] The main difference between the common and the advanced electronic signature is that the principles of identification, non-repudiation and integrity are clearly defined for the advanced electronic signature.[292] While the directive does not explicitly define how these requirements should be met, it is clear that the technique of the digital signature is the preferred method here, as well as the only method accepted at present.[293] The recognition of the advanced electronic signature is principally the same as that of the common electronic signature: on the basis of the non-discrimination rule, it cannot be denied validity solely on the basis of it being an electronic signature or for it not being a qualified electronic signature, yet it is not granted automatic equivalence to handwritten signatures.[294] However, as the technique of the digital signature is aimed at more clearly and more trustworthily establishing the origin and non-repudiation of the signature, as well as the integrity of the electronic information to which it is transfixed, it can be expected that the advanced electronic signature will be more easily recognized and accepted by a judge.[295]

93. The digital signature is not a signature in its own right, but rather a cryptographic technique used to create electronic signatures.[296] This technique combines two cryptographic methods, namely asymmetric cryptography using a Public Key Infrastructure (PKI) and a hash function.[297] Before being able to generate signatures, each party operating within such scheme is issued a key pair, consisting out of a private key and a public key.[298] These keys correspond

---

291 Article 2(2) Directive 1999/93/EC.

292 Van Eecke, P. (2009) "De elektronische handtekening in het recht", *T.B.H.*, 343.

293 *Ibid.*, 343; Storme, M.E. (2001) "De invoering van de elektronische handtekening in ons bewijsrecht", *RW*, 1516; Dumortier, J., Van Den Eynde, S. (2001) "De juridische erkenning van de elektronische handtekening", *Computerrecht*, 185–194; De Corte, R. (2001) "Elektronische handtekening en identificatie in de virtuele wereld", *P&B*, 225.

294 Van Eecke, P. (2009) "De elektronische handtekening in het recht", *T.B.H.*, 343.

295 *Ibid.*, 344.

296 As a result, the terms 'electronic signature' and 'digital signature' are not interchangeable. All signatures created using the digital signature technique are electronic signatures, but not all electronic signatures are created using the digital signature technique.

297 Dumortier, J. (2010) *ICT-Recht*, Leuven: Acco, 140–143; Storme, M.E. (2001) "De invoering van de elektronische handtekening in ons bewijsrecht", *RW*, 1515–1516; Van Eecke, P. (2009) "De elektronische handtekening in het recht", *T.B.H.*, 335–336; Dumortier, J., Van Den Eynde, S. (2001) "De juridische erkenning van de elektronische handtekening", *Computerrecht*, 185–194; De Corte, R. (2001) "Elektronische handtekening en identificatie in de virtuele wereld", *P&B*, 221–224; Vandenabeele, V. (2002) "De elektronische handtekening: rechten en plichten van de certificatiedienstverlener, de certificaathouder en de vertrouwende derde", *TBBR*, 610; Mougenot, D. (2002) *Droit des obligations: la preuve*, Brussel: Larcier, 174–176.

298 In symmetric cryptography, only one key is used to both encrypt and decrypt information. The obvious weakness of such a scheme is that the person encrypting information will have to transfer the key to the recipient, thereby exposing it to interception or abuse.

with each other in the sense that whatever is encrypted using the private key can only be decrypted using the corresponding public key. Moreover, the relation between the public and private key is so complex that it is impossible to deduct the private key from the public key.[299] When generating a signature to be affixed to certain electronic information, there will first be a hash algorithm used to calculate the unique hash value of the electronic information to which the signature will be affixed.[300] Such hash value is unique in the sense that if even one single bit of that information is changed, a new hash calculation will result in a different hash value. Next, the PKI is used, whereby the signatory's private key is used to encrypt the hash value. The result, the digital signature, is attached to the electronic information. The party receiving that electronic information will then be able to verify the signature by decrypting the encoded hash value using the signatory's public key. He will then calculate the hash value of the electronic information he has received and compare it to the decoded hash value. If these values are the same, the information has not been altered between the moment of signing and the moment it is verified. The digital signature is then considered to be valid and verified. The process of creating and verifying digital signatures has become easy and user-friendly with the development of several devices and applications capable of performing these tasks.[301] In principle, this technique – as used in the advanced electronic signature – can provide certain guarantees regarding identification, non-repudiation and integrity. The use of asymmetric cryptography already ensures non-repudiation: what can be decrypted by a certain public key could only have been encrypted using the corresponding private key.[302] The use of the hash function demonstrates whether or not the signed electronic information has been altered since the moment of

---

299 Van Eecke, P. (2009) "De elektronische handtekening in het recht", *T.B.H.*, 335; Vandenabeele, V. (2002) "De elektronische handtekening: rechten en plichten van de certificatiedienstverlener, de certificaathouder en de vertrouwende derde", *TBBR*, 610. The two main weaknesses in asymmetric cryptography are, therefore, loss of the private key by the owner or cracking of the algorithm. To protect against the latter, keys are generally given a larger bit length, making them harder to crack. In the Belgian electronic identity card, for instance, key lengths of 1024 and 2048 bit are used. De Cock, D., Wolf, C., Preneel, B. (2006) "The Belgian Electronic Identity Card (Overview)", in: Dittmann, J. (ed.), *Sicherheit 2005, Sicherheit – Schutz und Zuverlässigkeit, Beiträge der 3rd Jahrestagung des Fachbereichs Sicherheit der Gesellschaft für Informatik e.v. (GI), Lecture Notes in Informatics (LNI) LNI P-77*, Bonner Köllen Verlag, 298–301. As a result, it is recommendable to ensure broad publication of public keys, in order to ensure that recipients of encrypted information can access the public key required to decrypt that information. This can be done, for instance, in public X.500 directories. ITU-T (2008) "Recommendation X.500", *itu.int*.

300 Using, for instance, the Secure Hash Algorithm (SHA), established by the US National Institute for Standards and Technology (NIST). NIST (2012) "Secure Hash Standard (SHS)", *FIPS PUB 180-4*.

301 In principle, every computer, tablet or phone could be used for this process. The private key of a PKI key pair is generally stored on a safe token, such as a smart card or a USB-stick.

302 One possible exception is the unauthorized use of that private key by someone else than the owner, for instance when that key has been stolen. Storme, M.E. (2001) "De invoering van de elektronische handtekening in ons bewijsrecht", *RW*, 1518; Vandenabeele, V. (2002)

signing.[303] The only point where this technique could be argued to fall short is in identifying the signatory, as in principle the digital signature technique in itself does not guarantee the person to whom a key pair belongs.[304]

94. The use of certificates was introduced to counter the ownership problem of the keys used in the digital signature technique. Here, a Trusted Third Party (TTP) is assigned the role of Certificate Authority (CA), which means that this party will certify that a certain key pair belongs to a particular person.[305] Given the importance of this task, the role of CA is often left to public sector bodies. In Belgium, for instance, the Belgian State serves as the root CA that certifies ownership of all the signature certificates included in the Belgium electronic identity card.[306] This notion of certification has also been included under the scope of Directive 1999/93/EC.[307] Moreover, the directive includes specific requirements for the 'qualified' version of certificates[308], CAs[309] and secure-signature-creation devices.[310] If an electronic signature is created using a secure-signature-creation device and is attested by a qualified certificate – which by definition is issued by a qualified CA – the signature is considered to be a qualified electronic signature, the third type of electronic signature proclaimed by the directive.[311] The most important consequence of the qualification of an electronic signature as a qualified electronic signature is that it is automatically considered to be equal to a handwritten signature and is, thus, admissible in court proceedings.[312] The reason for this is that this figure is considered to completely and reliably fulfill the requirements of identification – by using qualified certificates in the PKI – non-repudiation – by using a certified asymmetric cryptography key pair – and integrity – due to the hash function. While the equivalence that could follow from article 1322 Belgian Civil Code was limited to the scope of that article itself, the acceptance of the qualified electronic signature is in principle unrestricted.[313] When used in the context of

"De elektronische handtekening: rechten en plichten van de certificatiedienstverlener, de certificaathouder en de vertrouwende derde", *TBBR*, 610.

303 Vandenabeele, V. (2002) "De elektronische handtekening: rechten en plichten van de certificatiedienstverlener, de certificaathouder en de vertrouwende derde", *TBBR*, 610.

304 Van Eecke, P. (2009) "De elektronische handtekening in het recht", *T.B.H.*, 336.

305 *Id.* This CA will keep a list of all valid, expired and revoked certificates, to easily verify their validity. Vandenabeele, V. (2002) "De elektronische handtekening: rechten en plichten van de certificatiedienstverlener, de certificaathouder en de vertrouwende derde", *TBBR*, 612.

306 *Repository.eid.belgium.be/certificates.php?cert=Root&lang=en.*

307 Article 2(9) and (11) Directive 1999/93/EC. Note that the CA is addressed here as 'certification service provider'.

308 Annex I Directive 1999/93/EC.

309 Annex II Directive 1999/93/EC.

310 Annex III Directive 1999/93/EC.

311 Article 5(1) Directive 1999/93/EC.

312 *Id.*

313 Van Eecke, P. (2009) "De elektronische handtekening in het recht", *T.B.H.*, 345.

Belgian civil evidence law, the requirements of article 1322 Belgian Civil Code will be considered to be automatically complied with.[314]

95. One important element of the automated equivalence between qualified electronic signatures and handwritten signatures is precisely its reference to handwritten signatures. First, it means that the qualified electronic signature fully derives its probative value from that of the handwritten signature.[315] If, for instance, a handwritten signature is not deemed sufficient for something to be accepted as evidence, neither will the qualified electronic signature. Moreover, it is clear that the validity of handwritten signatures is fully determined by national law.[316] As a result, by depending on national provisions concerning handwritten signatures, the precise status of a qualified electronic signature may be rather different between EU Member States, potentially leading to interoperability issues.[317]

3.2.2. Belgian implementation and future developments

96. The previous section referenced the principles found in Directive 1999/93/EC primarily. On this section, how these principles were transposed into Belgian law in the Act of 9 July 2001 on electronic signatures will be analyzed. In general, it can be found that this Act is a fairly faithful, almost literal, transposition of the directive. There are, however, some exceptions.

97. First, it appears that there is some terminological inconsistency due to the deviation of the Dutch – and Estonian – version of the directive from other language versions.[318] With the Belgian Act – both in its Dutch and French versions – being based on the French version of the directive, there is now an inconsistency between the Dutch version of the Belgian Act and the Dutch version of the EU Directive. However, as the legislator did not have the

---

314 This was also the clear intention of the legislator: Amendment 12 to the proposal to introduce new means of telecommunication in the judicial and extrajudicial procedures, *Parl. St. Kamer* 1999–2000, 0038/6, 2–3. Note, however, that such does not derogate from rules explicitly demanding a handwritten text and signature, such as concerning the holographic will of article 970 Belgian Civil Code.

315 Dumortier, J. (2004) "Legal Status of Qualified Electronic Signatures in Europe", in: Paulus, S., Pohlmann, N., Reimer, H. (ed.), *ISSE 2004-Securing Electronic Business Processes*, Wiesbaden: Vieweg, 281–289.

316 Recital 20 Directive 1999/93/EC.

317 Dumortier, J. (2004) "Legal Status of Qualified Electronic Signatures in Europe", in: Paulus, S., Pohlmann, N., Reimer, H. (ed.), *ISSE 2004-Securing Electronic Business Processes*, Wiesbaden: Vieweg, 281–289.

318 The Dutch and Estonian version refer in article 2(1) to 'electronic data' (Dutch: *elektronische gegevens*; Estonian: *elektroonilised andmed*), whereas all other language versions refer to 'data in electronic form' (*e.g.* French: *donnée sous forme électronique*; German: *Daten in elektronischer Form*; Spanish: *datos en forma electronica*).

intention to deviate, these inconsistencies should be ignored and interpreted as intended.[319]

98. Second, the duality between article 1322 Belgian Civil Code and the Act on electronic signatures demonstrates a misunderstanding in transposing the directive. As noted previously, the Belgian legislator meant to transpose the non-discrimination principle of article 5(2) of the directive into article 1322 Belgian Civil Code, but has not done this correctly.[320] The Act of 9 July 2001 somewhat corrects this mistake by including both the equivalency rule of article 5(1) Directive 1999/93/EC and the non-discrimination rule of the directive's article 5(2).[321] As a result of the equivalency rule, a qualified electronic signature affixed to electronic information will automatically result in the validity of that signature and, thus, will principally lead to the acceptance of that electronic information as a private instrument.[322] However, under this equivalency rule, the other provisions of the Belgian Civil Code are also explicitly mentioned to still apply.[323] For instance, the signatory can deny his signature under article 1323 Belgian Civil Code.[324]

99. This leads to a third point, the division of liability between CA and the certificate holder. In general, the Act of 9 July 2001 almost literally transposes

---

319 Van Eecke, P. (2009) "De elektronische handtekening in het recht", *T.B.H.*, 342. Note also that the Dutch version of the directive does use the term 'data in electronic form' (Dutch: *gegevens in elektronische vorm*) in its article 5(1). This confirms the assumption that the deviation in article 2(1) is merely a translation error and not meant to create differences in interpretation between both terms.

320 Amendment 12 to the proposal to introduce new means of telecommunication in the judicial and extrajudicial procedures, *Parl. St. Kamer* 1999–2000, 0038/6, 9–10; Van Eecke, P. (2009) "De elektronische handtekening in het recht", *T.B.H.*, 343. Mougenot also points out the inconsistencies of this implementation: Mougenot, D. (2002) *Droit des obligations: la preuve*, Brussel: Larcier, 193–194.

321 Respectively in article 4 §4 and §5 of the Act of 9 July 2001.

322 If the other formalities for the qualification as a private instrument are complied with. Storme, M.E. (2001) "De invoering van de elektronische handtekening in ons bewijsrecht", *RW*, 1516; Van Eecke, P. (2004) *Naar een juridische status voor de elektronische handtekening: Een rol voor de handtekening in de informatiemaatschappij?*, PhD thesis KU Leuven – Faculty of Law, 642–643. The requirements of identification, non-repudiation and integrity of the addition to article 1322 Belgian Civil Code are therefore assumed to have been complied with. Amendment 12 to the proposal to introduce new means of telecommunication in the judicial and extrajudicial procedures, *Parl. St. Kamer* 1999–2000, 0038/6, 2–3.

323 The equivalency rule is preceded by the notice: "Notwithstanding articles 1323 and following of the Belgian Civil Code" (Dutch: *Onverminderd de artikelen 1323 en volgende van het Burgerlijk Wetboek*).

324 Following the principle of equality, if those rules are applicable to handwritten signatures, they are also applicable to the qualified electronic signatures assimilated with such handwritten signatures. Therefore, this explicit reference can be deemed superfluous. Van Eecke, P. (2004) *Naar een juridische status voor de elektronische handtekening: Een rol voor de handtekening in de informatiemaatschappij?*, PhD thesis KU Leuven – Faculty of Law, 647–648; Mougenot, D. (2002) *Droit des obligations: la preuve*, Brussel: Larcier, 198.

the corresponding article 6 of Directive 1999/93/EC.[325] Principally, the CA is responsible for the contents and the correctness of the certificates it issues.[326] This liability is stricter when qualified certificates are involved, making the CA liable for all damages caused to whom reasonably relied on the certificate, concerning the correctness of its information, its correlation with the signatory's key pair and the proper functioning of that key pair if issued by the same CA.[327] Moreover, the CA is liable for the proper registration of certificate revocations.[328] In both cases, the CA can try to evade liability by proving that he did not act negligently.[329] The CA can also limit his liability by explicitly stating limitations to the use of the certificates or limitations to the maximum value of that use in the user agreements.[330] The responsibility for the confidentiality of the certificates is put at the certificate holder.[331] In the case of unauthorized use – for instance when a third party gains access to the signatory's password or PIN code and uses the certificates – the certificate holder will have to bear the consequences of any signatures placed.[332] However, he can still try to evade this by proving that he had already started the revocation procedure before the certificates were used. Following the application of article 1323 Belgian Civil Code, he can also try to deny that he placed that signature.[333]

---

325 Note that these principles apply to qualified certificates and qualified CAs. When 'normal' certificates are issued by non-qualified CAs, the principles of general contract law will apply between the parties. Vandenabeele, V. (2002) "De elektronische handtekening: rechten en plichten van de certificatiedienstverlener, de certificaathouder en de vertrouwende derde", *TBBR*, 609.

326 Van Eecke, P. (2004) *Naar een juridische status voor de elektronische handtekening: Een rol voor de handtekening in de informatiemaatschappij?*, PhD thesis KU Leuven – Faculty of Law, 648.

327 Article 14 §1 Act of 9 July 2001; Vandenabeele, V. (2002) "De elektronische handtekening: rechten en plichten van de certificatiedienstverlener, de certificaathouder en de vertrouwende derde", *TBBR*, 613.

328 Article 14 §2 Act of 9 July 2001.

329 Article 14 §1 and §2 Act of 9 July 2001.

330 Article 14 §3 and §4 Act of 9 July 2001. For instance, the CA for the Belgian electronic identity card, Certipost, has limited its liability to EUR 2.500 per transaction. Certipost (2009) "Certification Practice Statement Citizen CA – Verklaring met betrekking tot de certificatiepraktijk", *repository.eid.belgium.be*, 45. See also: Vandenabeele, V. (2002) "De elektronische handtekening: rechten en plichten van de certificatiedienstverlener, de certificaathouder en de vertrouwende derde", *TBBR*, 614–615.

331 Article 19 §1 Act of 9 July 2001. Vandenabeele, V. (2002) "De elektronische handtekening: rechten en plichten van de certificatiedienstverlener, de certificaathouder en de vertrouwende derde", *TBBR*, 613.

332 Van Eecke, P. (2004) *Naar een juridische status voor de elektronische handtekening: Een rol voor de handtekening in de informatiemaatschappij?*, PhD thesis KU Leuven – Faculty of Law, 649; Storme, M.E. (2001) "De invoering van de elektronische handtekening in ons bewijsrecht", *RW*, 1518.

333 *Id.*

100. One notable development in Belgian law relating to electronic signatures is the conception of the hybrid signature.[334] This figure can be found to solve one of the remaining problems concerning the interchangeability between handwritten and electronic signatures. If, for instance, a paper document with a handwritten signature is digitalized by means of scanning technology, the result will be electronic information. The digitalized handwritten signature could potentially be considered as an electronic signature in the sense of article 1322 Belgian Civil Code, even though it is subject to the judge's appreciation thereof.[335] However, when signed electronic information is materialized, by printing that information to paper for instance, what the status will be of the printed electronic signature is less clear. This was found to be a particular problem for public sector bodies – such as municipalities – that issue paper copies and extracts of electronic information.[336] A legislative proposal to solve this matter has led to the Act of 15 February 2012, which holds that "*the signature of the certificate holder can be materialized in an equivalent complying with the requirements of article 2, second member, 2°*", which was added into the Act of 9 July 2001 under article 4 as §6.[337] This means that an electronic signature can now be materialized, insofar as it complies with the requirements of the advanced electronic signature[338], which in turn means that the materialized electronic signature must be uniquely linked to the signatory, allow for the identification of the signatory, be created by means under the sole control of the signatory and provide proof of the integrity of the electronic information to which it is affixed.[339] Following these requirements, electronic signatures can be materialized without losing their probative value.

3.2.3. eIDAS Regulation

101. As with any directive, Directive 1999/93/EC was marked for review.[340] While the directive has been slightly amended over the years[341], no extensive

334 Minjauw, H., Vandendriessche, J. (2012) "Titel VI. Het bewijsrecht in burgerlijke zaken", in: Roodhooft, R. (ed.), *Bestendig Handboek Verbintenissenrecht*, Mechelen: Kluwer, VI.3–19.

335 As this scanned signature now constitutes electronic information, it will have to be assessed in how far it can provide proof of identification, non-repudiation and integrity.

336 Proposal for an Act amending the Act of 9 July 2001 concerning the determination of certain rules regarding the legal framework for electronic signatures, electronic certified mail and certification services, *Parl. St. Kamer* 2010–2011, 1450/1, 3–4.

337 Act of 15 February 2012 amending the Act of 9 July 2001 concerning the determination of certain rules regarding the legal framework for electronic signatures, electronic certified mail and certification services, *Belgian State Gazette* 7 March 2012.

338 Article 2, second member, 2° of the Act of 9 July 2001 refers to the advanced electronic signature.

339 Proposal for an Act amending the Act of 9 July 2001 concerning the determination of certain rules regarding the legal framework for electronic signatures, electronic certified mail and certification services, *Parl. St. Kamer* 2010–2011, 1450/1, 4.

340 This was to be completed by 19 July 2003 according to article 12 Directive 1999/93/EC.

341 Regulation (EC) No 1137/2008 of the European Parliament and of the Council of 22 October 2008 adapting a number of instruments subject to the procedure laid down in Article 251 of the Treaty to Council Decision 1999/468/EC, with regard to the regulatory procedure with

revision was proposed before 2012.[342] In 2010, the Digital Agenda, which establishes a strategic plan for the coming decade, explicitly references the existence of barriers to Europe's digital development and proposed legislation on e-signatures (Key Action 3) and the mutual recognition of e-identification and authentication (Key Action 16).[343] To this end, the European Commission in 2012 proposed a regulation on electronic identification and trust services for electronic transactions in the internal market.[344] Apart from revising the existing framework, it also adds the figure of trust services under the same umbrella. Instead of amending the existing directive, Directive 1999/93/EC was proposed to be revoked and replaced by a regulation. In so doing, the Commission aims to provide for better accessibility of cross-border online services by removing existing barriers.[345] This proposal was adopted as Regulation 910/2014.[346]

102. In terms of terminology, the regulation does not introduce major changes to the core elements already found in Directive 1999/93/EC.[347] The main innovation of the regulation is that it also applies to public sector identification schemes – such as the Belgian e-ID.[348] Such identification schemes must now be notified and mutually recognized.[349] The second innovation is that it introduces a range of different trust services.[350]

---

scrutiny – Adaptation to the regulatory procedure with scrutiny – Part One, *OJ* L 311 of 21 November 2008, 1–54.

342 In 2006, the European Commission found that "*the objectives of the Directive have been largely fulfilled and that no clear need for its revision has emerged at this stage*". Report from the Commission to the European Parliament and the Council of 15 March 2006 on the operation of Directive 1999/93/EC on a Community framework for electronic signatures", *COM(2006) 120 final*, 10.

343 Communication from the Commission to the European Parliament, the Council, the European Economic and Social Committee and the Committee of the Regions of 26 August 2010, A Digital Agenda for Europe, *COM(2010) 245 final/2*.

344 Commission proposal for a regulation of the European Parliament and of the Council of 4 June 2012 on electronic identification and trust services for electronic transactions in the internal market, *COM(2012) 238 final* (hereinafter: proposed regulation).

345 Recital 11 Proposed regulation. Amending the existing directive was considered insufficient as "*the freedom given to MS when transposing a Directive (in terms of interpretation and of implementation of the systems) contributed to the current problems of mutual recognition of services and products and of cross-border interoperability*". Commission staff working document of 7 June 2012 impact assessment accompanying the document proposal for a regulation of the European Parliament and of the Council on electronic identification and trust services for electronic transactions in the internal market, *SWD(2012) 135 final*, 40–41.

346 Regulation (EU) No 910/2014 of the European Parliament and of the Council of 23 July 2014 on electronic identification and trust services for electronic transactions in the internal market and repealing Directive 1999/93/EC, *OJ* L 257 of 28 August 2014, 73–114 (hereinafter: eIDAS Regulation). At the moment of writing, this regulation has entered into force.

347 For the definition of an electronic signature, the regulation replaces "*which serve as a method of authentication*" with "*which is used by the signatory to sign*". Article 3(10) Regulation 910/2014.

348 Articles 6-12 Regulation 910/2014.

349 Article 6 Regulation 910/2014.

350 Namely electronic seals, electronic time stamps, electronic registered delivery services, and website authentication.

103. The regulation has entered into force. To secure a smooth transition between the current legal framework set by the directive and its national transpositions and the new legal framework set by the regulation, the regulation provided for a transitory period. During this period, the European Commission still had to adopt secondary legislation. The regulation then repealed the existing Directive 1999/93/EC in July 2016.[351] Due to its nature as an EU Regulation, it also required all inconsistent national legislation on this matter to be repealed or amended. For the particular case at hand, this means that where Belgian national law contradicts the regulation, it should have been amended.

104. The regulation upholds the three-layered structure of electronic signatures and most of the other principles transposed into the Act of 9 July 2001, such as the principle of non-discrimination and the assimilation between qualified electronic signatures and handwritten signatures. As under the directive, the regulation makes no reference to the probative value of handwritten signatures – and thus by extension of electronic signatures – leaving this matter open to national law. The regulation explicitly states in this regard that it "*is for national law to define the legal effect of electronic signatures, except for the requirements provided for in this Regulation according to which a qualified electronic signature should have the equivalent legal effect of a handwritten signature*".[352]

105. The regulation also may prove important to the somewhat deviating signature notion found in article 1322 of the Belgian Civil Code. If this notion were to be construed as purely establishing what can be considered as the legal effect of a signature in an electronic context, it could be held not to contradict the regulation and could therefore remain in force.[353] However, this view has not been shared by everyone.[354] It has, for instance, been remarked that the integrity functionality of the signature notion in article 1322 does not refer to the handwritten signature, but solely to the electronic signature, and should therefore be removed.[355] Moreover, it has been suggested to remove the plethora of different signature notions.[356]

---

351 Per its article 50.

352 Recital 49 Regulation 910/2014.

353 This appears to be the position of the Flemish government, which states that the signature notion of article 1322 Belgian Civil Code remains the main referral point for (electronic) signatures. *bestuurszaken.be/informatiemanagement/digitale-handtekening.*

354 The more general view was that all relevant national legislation would have to be amended to correspond to the regulation. See, for instance: Febelfin (2015) "Samen streven naar digitalisering van de economie", *febelfin.be,* 34–35.

355 Raadgevend Comité voor de Telecommunicatie (2015) "Memorandum aan de Minister bevoegd voor Telecommunicatie en de Digitale Agenda: Een digitale agenda voor België", *rct-cct.be,* 13.

356 *Id.*

106. A final important innovation of the regulation is the non-discrimination principle for electronic documents, which – like electronic signatures – cannot be denied "*legal effect and admissibility as evidence in legal proceedings solely on the grounds that it is in electronic form*".[357] This may warrant a change in the original-copy dichotomy, which until now limited the probative value of electronic copies – meaning those electronic documents that were not electronically signed.

3.3. ACT OF 11 MARCH 2003

107. As noted, also the 2000 E-commerce Directive – or: Directive on Electronic Commerce – is significant in introducing digitalization into Belgian civil law. More in particular, it is stated that Member States must allow contracts to be concluded by electronic means, meaning that such contracts cannot be denied legal effectiveness and validity solely because of their having been concluded by electronic means.[358] This directive was transposed into Belgian law by the E-commerce Act of 11 March 2003.[359, 360]

108. While this act has a broad scope, there are also a number of legal areas that are explicitly excluded from that scope, such as taxation.[361] The services of the information society intended in the scope of this act are defined as "*any service normally provided for remuneration, at a distance, by electronic means and at the individual request of a recipient of services*", which corresponds with the definition found in Article 1(2) of Directive 98/34/EC as amended by Directive 98/48/EC.[362] Such services include, for instance, the selling of

357 Article 46 Regulation 910/2014.

358 Article 9(1) Directive 2000/31/EC. Note, however, that article 9(2) Directive 2000/31/EC does include a list of exceptions. For instance, Member States may require that the transfer of rights relating to real estate must be concluded on paper and not by electronic means.

359 Act of 11 March 2003 concerning certain legal aspects of the services of the information society, *Belgian State Gazette* 17 March 2003. Note that there are in fact two Acts of 11 March 2003 concerning certain legal aspects of the services of the information society. As certain of these aspects required a different legislative procedure, they were regulated in a separate act: Act of 11 March 2003 concerning certain legal aspects of the services of the information society as intended in article 77 of the Constitution, *Belgian State Gazette* 17 March 2003. For the purposes of the research conducted here, only the first and main act will be referenced.

360 As noted previously, a number of legislative acts on economic matters have been codified into a Code of Economic Law. The Act of 11 March 2003 has been implemented into Book XII of this Code. No major changes to the text were introduced when implementing the Act into the Code.

361 Article 3 Act of 11 March 2003, current article XII.1 Code of Economic Law.

362 Article 2(1) Act of 11 March 2003, current article I.18(1) Code of Economic Law; article 2(a) Directive 2000/31/EC; article 1(2) Directive 98/34/EC of the European Parliament and of the Council of 22 June 1998 laying down a procedure for the provision of information in the field of technical standards and regulations and of rules on Information Society services; *Official Journal* L 204 of 21 July 1998, 37.

goods online.[363] While it is held that such services must be provided against remuneration, it is not stipulated that such remuneration must be paid by the recipient of the services.[364] As such, services offered for free to users, but which rely on paid advertisements, are included under the scope of this provision.[365] The notion that the service must be provided at a distance means that the parties are not simultaneously present.[366] By electronic means can be interpreted very broadly, spanning a wide range of services including the provision of access to the Internet, electronic correspondence, hosting, video-on-demand, etc.[367] Such services are to be delivered at the individual request of the recipient, meaning that classic linear services such as television and radio are principally excluded from the scope of this Act.[368] As a full discussion of the broad range of matters covered by the scope of the Act of 11 March 2003 would stray too far from the core topic of this research, only the principles regarding electronic contracts will be further analyzed here.

109. The Belgian Act of 11 March 2003 adopts a strategy of functional equivalence in order to comply with the requirement of Directive 2000/31/EC to allow contracts to be concluded by electronic means.[369] This means that the statutory requirements for the formation of contracts can be complied with by electronic means if the functional qualities of those requirements are met.[370] While the term 'contract' is used, the legislator has clearly aimed for a broad interpretation, by also covering pre-contractual negotiations for instance.[371] The notion of requirements must also be interpreted broadly, spanning all

363 Recital 18 Directive 2000/31/EC.

364 Note also that the employer-employee relationship is not service of the information society. Recital 18 Directive 2000/31/EC. As a result, the rules laid down here regarding contracts by electronic means are not applicable to contracts of employment. Dumortier, J., Dekeyser, H. (2003) "Hoofdstuk V. Ruimen van juridische obstakels bij contracten langs elektronische weg", in: Van Eecke, P., Dumortier, J. (ed.) *Elektronische Handel - Commentaar bij de wetten van 11 maart 2003*, Brugge: die Keure, 164.

365 *Id.*; Van Eecke, P. (2003) "Hoofdstuk I. Artikelsgewijze bespreking van de wetten elektronische handel", in: Van Eecke, P., Dumortier, J. (ed.) *Elektronische Handel - Commentaar bij de wetten van 11 maart 2003*, Brugge: die Keure, 22–23. What is excluded are, for instance, government services such as the issuing of passports and other identity documents, even if citizens must pay for such services.

366 Article 1 (2) Directive 98/34/EC.

367 Proposal to introduce an Act concerning certain legal aspects of the services of the information society, *Parl. St. Kamer* 2002–2003, 2100/1, 14–15.

368 Article 1 (2) Directive 98/34/EC; Van Eecke, P. (2003) "Hoofdstuk I. Artikelsgewijze bespreking van de wetten elektronische handel", in: Van Eecke, P., Dumortier, J. (ed.) *Elektronische Handel - Commentaar bij de wetten van 11 maart 2003*, Brugge: die Keure, 25. Note that new types of services, such as video-on-demand, do fall under the scope of this provision as such services are provided at the specific request of a user.

369 Article 16 Act of 11 March 2003, current article XII.15 Code of Economic Law.

370 Article 16 §1 Act of 11 March 2003, current article XII.15 §2 Code of Economic Law.

371 Proposal to introduce an Act concerning certain legal aspects of the services of the information society, *Parl. St. Kamer* 2002–2003, 2100/1, 41–42.

requirements constituting a valid contract, such as the paper medium, signature, etc.[372] To clarify this, article 16 Act of 11 March 2003 – current article XII.15 Code of Economic Law – specifically addresses a few formal requirements.[373] First, it is held that the requirement to provide a document in writing can be satisfied by means of a series of interpretable signs that are accessible for later consultation, regardless of their medium and the modalities of transmission thereof. While this was already established in jurisprudence and legal doctrine, the legislator decided to lay down this principle explicitly.[374] Second, for the requirement of providing a signature, reference is made to article 1322 Belgian Civil Code and to article 4 §Act of 9 July 2001. From a functional approach, a signature can be considered as providing for the identification of the signatory and as a means of appropriation of the contents of the text by that signatory, which is also included within the addition to article 1322 Belgian Civil Code.[375] When reading article 16 §2 Act of 11 March 2003 – current article XII.15 §2 Code of Economic Law – together with article 1322 Belgian Civil Code, it can be confirmed that the judge keeps the discretionary power to decide whether or not an alleged signature presented to him conforms with the requirements of article 1322 Belgian Civil Code.[376] However, when he finds that such requirements are fulfilled, the alleged signature presented to him will be accepted as a valid electronic signature, equal to a handwritten signature.[377] Important to note here is that this provision does not refer to another quality generally attributed to or expected from signatures, namely providing certainties regarding the integrity of the text to which they are affixed.[378] Third, a written

[372] *Ibid.*, 42; Van Eecke, P. (2003) "Hoofdstuk I. Artikelsgewijze bespreking van de wetten elektronische handel", in: Van Eecke, P., Dumortier, J. (ed.) *Elektronische Handel – Commentaar bij de wetten van 11 maart 2003*, Brugge: die Keure, 39.

[373] Article 16 §2 Act of 11 March 2003, current article XII.15 §2 Code of Economic Law.

[374] Van Eecke, P. (2009) "De elektronische handtekening in het recht", *T.B.H.*, 333–334; Proposal to introduce an Act concerning certain legal aspects of the services of the information society, *Parl. St. Kamer* 2002–2003, 2100/1, 44; Amendment 12 to the proposal to introduce new means of telecommunication in the judicial and extrajudicial procedures, *Parl. St. Kamer* 1999–2000, 0038/6, 11. See also section 3.1.

[375] Van Eecke, P. (2003) "Hoofdstuk I. Artikelsgewijze bespreking van de wetten elektronische handel", in: Van Eecke, P., Dumortier, J. (ed.) *Elektronische Handel – Commentaar bij de wetten van 11 maart 2003*, Brugge: die Keure, 40.

[376] Van Eecke, P. (2009) "De elektronische handtekening in het recht", *T.B.H.*, 339–340.

[377] Where the terminology of article 1322 Belgian Civil Code could raise the impression that the judge could first decide on whether or not the signature is valid – *i.e.* whether it corresponds with the requirements – and then again decide on whether or not to accept that signature, the formulation used under article 16 §2 Act of 11 March 2003 – current article XII.15 §2 Code of Economic Law – renders such interpretation mute. Van Eecke, P. (2009) "De elektronische handtekening in het recht", *T.B.H.*, 339–340.

[378] Thus, where integrity is also required, the provision of article 16 §2 Act of 11 March 2003 – current article XII.15 §2 Code of Economic Law – will not be sufficient. Dumortier, J., Dekeyser, H. (2003) "Hoofdstuk V. Ruimen van juridische obstakels bij contracten langs elektronische weg", in: Van Eecke, P., Dumortier, J. (ed.) *Elektronische Handel – Commentaar bij de wetten van 11 maart 2003*, Brugge: die Keure, 169.

notice emanating from the person who subscribes to the text can be replaced by any procedure that guarantees such an attribution. Given its qualities in terms of identification and authentication, as well as for non-repudiation, the technique of the digital signature used in the advanced and qualified electronic signature can be found to fulfill such tasks.[379]

110. As the functional equivalency rule of article 16 §1 – current article XII.15 §1 Code of Economic Law – has been construed rather broadly and vaguely, the legislator did originally include the possibility to adopt more specific rules aimed at eliminating particular hindrances to the conclusion of contracts by electronic means.[380] Such rules were, however, never adopted. Moreover, certain types of contracts are explicitly removed from the scope of the functional equivalence, such as contracts transferring rights relating to real estate.[381]

111. While the rule of functional equivalence – or even the provisions of the Act of 11 March 2003 and Directive 2000/31/EC in general – may at first sight seem to have a significant impact in promoting and allowing the use of electronic information instead of needing to rely on paper-based procedures, the impact of the provisions analyzed here should not be overestimated. As noted, there are several areas of law that are explicitly excluded from the scope of these provisions.[382] Moreover, only legal hindrances are considered and not practical and technical issues.[383] While it does explicitly provide that electronic information could be considered as writing, it was already pointed out that such was at that point already widely accepted in legal doctrine and jurisprudence.[384] While it does allow for electronic information to be equalized to paper documents, it also does not provide precise criteria and, thus, leaves it up to the

---

379 Van Eecke, P. (2003) "Hoofdstuk I. Artikelsgewijze bespreking van de wetten elektronische handel", in: Van Eecke, P., Dumortier, J. (ed.) *Elektronische Handel – Commentaar bij de wetten van 11 maart 2003*, Brugge: die Keure, 40.

380 Article 16 §3 Act of 11 March 2003, this article was not transposed into the Code of Economic Law. One reason for this dual approach between a general rule and specific deviations was to give the legislator more time to perform the systematic analysis required when transposing Directive 2000/31/EC into Belgian law. Dumortier, J., Dekeyser, H. (2003) "Hoofdstuk V. Ruimen van juridische obstakels bij contracten langs elektronische weg", in: Van Eecke, P., Dumortier, J. (ed.) *Elektronische Handel – Commentaar bij de wetten van 11 maart 2003*, Brugge: die Keure, 159. It should be noted, however, that the legislator to date has not adopted any implementing acts under article 16 §3.

381 Article 17 Act of 11 March 2003, current article XII.16 Code of Economic Law.

382 Noted earlier, for instance, were notary instruments, taxation and employment contracts.

383 For instance, do all parties have access to the technical means – *e.g.* computer and Internet connection – to engage in procedures concerning contracts in electronic format? Dumortier, J., Dekeyser, H. (2003) "Hoofdstuk V. Ruimen van juridische obstakels bij contracten langs elektronische weg", in: Van Eecke, P., Dumortier, J. (ed.) *Elektronische Handel – Commentaar bij de wetten van 11 maart 2003*, Brugge: die Keure, 165.

384 See section 3.1.

judge to decide whether parties can indeed demonstrate sufficient functional equivalence.[385] This can be argued to lead to a lack of legal certainty.[386]

3.4. APPLICATION OF RULES OF EVIDENCE TO ELECTRONIC INFORMATION

112. From the analysis conducted under previous sections, it has become clear that the Belgian legislator has decided not to adopt a separate set of rules dedicated to regulating the probative value of electronic information. Instead, it has been decided that the classic rules of evidence under civil law – aimed at regulating paper-based evidence – must also be applied to electronic information. To facilitate this, three core elements have been provided: allowing electronic information to be accepted as writing, introducing signatures created by electronic means and functional equivalence. In this section, how the application of the existing rules of Belgian civil evidence law to electronic information will influence the probative value of the latter will be analyzed.

3.4.1. Instruments

113. As noted previously, the main requirements for information presented as evidence to be accepted as a private instrument are that such information must constitute a document in writing that documents legal acts and that must be signed with a valid signature.[387] Even though legal doctrine and jurisprudence already accepted that electronic information can constitute writing, the Belgian legislator has explicitly laid down such acceptance into law.[388] Moreover, the introduction of electronic signatures means that electronic information can be

---

385 Dumortier, J., Dekeyser, H. (2003) "Hoofdstuk V. Ruimen van juridische obstakels bij contracten langs elektronische weg", in: Van Eecke, P., J. Dumortier (ed.) *Elektronische Handel - Commentaar bij de wetten van 11 maart 2003*, Brugge: die Keure, 167–168.

386 As was noticed by the Council of State in discussing the legislative proposal: Proposal to introduce an Act concerning certain legal aspects of the services of the information society, *Parl. St. Kamer* 2002–2003, 2100/1, 94; Dumortier, J., Dekeyser, H. (2003) "Hoofdstuk V. Ruimen van juridische obstakels bij contracten langs elektronische weg", in: Van Eecke, P., Dumortier, J. (ed.) *Elektronische Handel - Commentaar bij de wetten van 11 maart 2003*, Brugge: die Keure, 170. However, not all authors share this concern: Montero, E., Demoulin, M. (2004) "La formation du contrat depuis le Code civil de 1804: un régime en mouvement sous une lettre figée", in: Wéry, P. (ed.) *Le droit des obligations contractuelles et le bicentenaire du Code civil*, Bruxelles: La Charte, 43–44. Looking back at over a decade of practice, it must be acknowledged that it does not appear that this principle has resulted in significant problems.

387 See section 1.4.1.

388 Van Eecke, P. (2009) "De elektronische handtekening in het recht", *T.B.H.*, 333–334; article 16 §2 Act of 11 March 2003, current article XII.15 §2 Code of Economic Law. Note that the practical acceptance of electronic information as writing already occurred prior to the introduction of electronic signatures. However, due to the lack of recognition of electronic

signed with a valid signature. As a result, duly signed electronic information can be accepted as a private instrument.[389]

114. This acceptance of duly signed electronic information as a private instrument would have been impossible prior to the introduction of electronic signatures, as only handwritten signatures constituted a valid signature.[390] However, this acceptance does not mean that any duly signed electronic information can or will be accepted as a private instrument. Under the principle of functional equivalence, the other requirements that must be complied with in order to allow the qualification as a private instrument will still apply, be it that they can be complied with by electronic means that satisfy the functional criteria of those requirements.[391] In terms of properties, once electronic information has been accepted as duly signed and in writing, it must still demonstrate its disposal of legal acts.[392] Given the requirements that must be complied with by electronic signatures, the properties of appropriation and integrity can already be considered to be fulfilled by the presence of a valid signature.[393] When mutual agreements are documented, the requirements of article 1325 Belgian Civil Code will principally have to be complied with, meaning that there must be as many originals as there are parties with discernible interest, with mention of the number of originals on each original. In transferring electronic information, when that transferred electronic information is duly signed, the receiving party will also receive electronic information that is validly signed, thus not constituting a duplicate or copy, but an original.[394] When dealing with signed electronic information, moving or duplicating that information from one medium to another does not constitute a loss of originality as the electronic signature is not bound to one particular medium, but to the content of the information.[395] Even if duplicated electronic information could be argued to be a

---

signatures at that time, electronic information could never be validly signed and thus never be accepted as a private instrument.

389 Van Eecke, P. (2009) "De elektronische handtekening in het recht", *T.B.H.*, 339; Storme, M.E. (2001) "De invoering van de elektronische handtekening in ons bewijsrecht", *RW*, 1514; Stijns, S. (2009) *Leerboek Verbintenissenrecht Boek 2*, Brugge: die Keure, 168–170.

390 Steennot, R. (1999) "Juridische problemen in het kader van de elektronische handel", *T.B.H.*, 671; Van Eecke, P. (2009) "De elektronische handtekening in het recht", *T.B.H.*, 339; Storme, M.E. (2001) "De invoering van de elektronische handtekening in ons bewijsrecht", *RW*, 1514.

391 Article 16 §1 Act of 11 March 2003, current article XII.15 §1 Code of Economic Law; Minjauw, H., Vandendriessche, J. (2008) "Titel VI. Het bewijsrecht in burgerlijke zaken", in: Roodhooft, R. (ed.), *Bestendig Handboek Verbintenissenrecht*, Mechelen: Kluwer, VI.3–33.

392 See section 1.4.1.

393 Such was already the case for handwritten signatures.

394 Gobert, D., Montero, E. (2001) "L'ouverture de la preuve littérale aux écrits sous forme électronique", *J.T.*, 127; Mougenot, D. (2002) *Droit des obligations: la preuve*, Brussel: Larcier, 178 & 258.

395 De Groote, B. (2001) "Het bewijs in de elektronische handel – Enkele bedenkingen", *A.J.T.*, 888; Wéry, P., Gobert, D., Kerzmann, L. (2003) "La preuve", in: Coipel, M., Wéry, P., Durant, I., Cruquenaire, A., *Guide juridique de l'entreprise*, Brussel: Kluwer, 67. This was also explicitly

copy, the presence of a valid signature would still make it an original in the sense of article 1325 Belgian Civil Code.[396] Therefore, the provision of article 1325 Belgian Civil Code requiring as many originals as there are parties with a discernible interest – while still possible to comply with – could be argued to be unnecessary when electronic signatures are used.[397] Luckily, jurisprudence has accepted that this principle is not of public order and that parties can therefore – explicitly or implicitly – deviate from it.[398] The principle of functional equivalence is also a remedy for the compliance of electronic information with the requirements regarding unilateral promises of payments or when a sum is expressed in the electronic information[399] As these provisions require handwritten statements, functional equivalence could be utilized to allow for the use of electronic means as long as such means can provide protection against fraud.[400]

115. One question that could be raised concerns the different types of electronic signatures introduced into Belgian law. Does the acceptance of signed electronic information, as a private instrument, require the use of a qualified electronic signature? The answer to this question is negative: all types of electronic

---

stated during the legislative process introducing electronic signatures: Amendment 12 to the proposal to introduce new means of telecommunication in the judicial and extrajudicial procedures, *Parl. St. Kamer* 1999–2000, 0038/6, 9.

396 As a duly signed copy becomes an original. Minjauw, H., Vandendriessche, J. (2008) "Titel VI. Het bewijsrecht in burgerlijke zaken", in: Roodhooft, R. (ed.), *Bestendig Handboek Verbintenissenrecht*, Mechelen: Kluwer, VI.3–89; Cornelis, L. (2000) *Algemene theorie van de verbintenis*, Antwerpen: Intersentia, 225; Wagner, K. (2009) "Actualia burgerlijk bewijsrecht", *P&B*, 160.

397 The goal of this provision was to ensure that each party holds proof of the agreement, making it impossible for one party to alter his original without such alteration being noticeable due to its absence on the other originals. De Boeck, A. (2006) "De bewijskracht van de onderhandse akte: voorzichtige versoepeling van de vormvereisten; op weg naar meer? Enkele bedenkingen bij Cass. 26 april 2001", *Rev. Gén. Droit Civ. Belge*, 348–349. When the technique of the digital signature is used, a party holding electronic information electronically signed by another party cannot alter this information without the private key of the signatory or without invalidating the signature. As a result, any alteration requires the cooperation of both parties, thereby fulfilling the underlying goals of article 1325 Belgian Civil Code. Gobert, D., Montero, E. (2001) "L'ouverture de la preuve littérale aux écrits sous forme électronique", *J.T.*, 128. Moreover, the distinction between copies and originals was based on the presumption that copies would be imperfect replicas of the original. With the current technologies, this is no longer the case. Mougenot, D. (2002) *Droit des obligations: la preuve*, Brussel: Larcier, 258–259.

398 De Boeck, A. (2006) "De bewijskracht van de onderhandse akte: voorzichtige versoepeling van de vormvereisten; op weg naar meer? Enkele bedenkingen bij Cass. 26 april 2001", *Rev. Gén. Droit Civ. Belge*, 348–349.

399 Articles 1326 and 1327 Belgian Civil Code.

400 Fraud being one of the main reasons for the requirements of articles 1326 and 1327 Belgian Civil Code. Minjauw, H., Vandendriessche, J. (2008) "Titel VI. Het bewijsrecht in burgerlijke zaken", in: Roodhooft, R. (ed.), *Bestendig Handboek Verbintenissenrecht*, Mechelen: Kluwer, VI.3–29. Some authors, however, are more careful in allowing the application of functional equivalence in this case: Van Eecke, P. (2009) "De elektronische handtekening in het recht", *T.B.H.*, 341.

signatures could qualify.[401] However, as has become apparent from previous analyses, only the qualified electronic signature will automatically be accepted as equal to a handwritten signature. When using a common electronic signature or even an advanced electronic signature, the addition to article 1322 Belgian Civil Code requires the judge to decide whether or not this signature complies with the requirements of identification, non-repudiation and integrity.[402]

116. While the previous findings only apply to private instruments, similar conclusions can principally be drawn for public instruments since the amendment of article 1317 Belgian Civil Code by the Act of 11 March 2003. Following this amendment, public instruments can be created in dematerialized form, meaning by the use of electronic means and signed by electronic signature.[403] However, this requires a Royal Decree laying down the specific rules thereto, which has not yet been adopted. In 2009, the legislator added that dematerialized notary deeds can be created, and that the Notary Deed Database would serve as the authentic source for the deeds recorded therein.[404] In 2016 and 2017, another round of revisions was made to article 1317 of the Belgian Civil Code, this time providing that dematerialized notary deeds can only be signed with a qualified electronic signature and that the qualification of those signing a dematerialized notary deed should be checked in an authentic database.[405] However, as these provisions have thus far not yet been put into practice, at present only paper documents complying with the specific rules thereto can be considered as public instruments.

3.4.2. Beginning of evidence in writing

117. If electronic information fails to comply with the requirements applicable to instruments, then it could still be accepted as beginning of evidence in

---

401 Such corresponds to the intentions of Directive 1999/93/EC as this directive did not aim to make the use of qualified electronic signatures mandatory in all cases. Recital 21 to Directive 1999/93/EC; Dumortier, J. (2004) "Legal Status of Qualified Electronic Signatures in Europe", in: Paulus, S., Pohlmann, N., Reimer, H. (ed.), *ISSE 2004-Securing Electronic Business Processes*, Wiesbaden: Vieweg, 281–289; Dumortier, J., Vandezande, N. (2012) "Trust in the proposed EU regulation on trust services?", *Computer Law & Security Review*, 571. Note, however, that the legislator has adopted certain provisions requiring the use of a qualified electronic signature in particular situations. Van Eecke, P. (2009) "De elektronische handtekening in het recht", *T.B.H.*, 346–347.

402 Van Eecke, P. (2009) "De elektronische handtekening in het recht", *T.B.H.*, 339.

403 Parliamentary question of 24 February 2001, *www.senate*.be, 5–1485.

404 Article 25 Act of 6 May 2009 holding diverse provisions, *Belgian State Gazette* 19 May 2009.

405 Article 129 Act of 4 May 2016 holding internment and diverse provisions in the field of justice, *Belgian State Gazette* 13 May 2016; article 199 Act of 6 July 2017 holding simplification, harmonization, informatization and modernization of provisions of civil law and of civil procedural law, as well as of the notary and holding diverse provisions concerning justice, *Belgian State Gazette* 24 July 2017.

writing insofar as it concerns "*any written instrument emanating from against whom it is invoked – or by his representative – and which can make the alleged fact probable*".[406] Such was often the case before the introduction of electronic signatures, as the lack of a valid signature automatically disqualified electronic information to be considered as an instrument.[407] Even now, it is clear that only qualified electronic signatures are automatically accepted as being valid and, thus, equivalent to a handwritten signature, leaving other types of electronic signatures – the advanced electronic signature, the common electronic signature and the signatures falling under the broader scope of the addition to article 1322 Belgian Civil Code – subject to the judge's appreciation. As a result, an electronic signature, which is not a qualified electronic signature, could still be denied legal value if the judge finds that it does not provide sufficient proof of identification, non-repudiation and integrity. In such cases, it will have to be analyzed whether or not the electronic information could still qualify as beginning of evidence in writing.

118. Beginning of evidence in writing requires the presence of writing. As noted previously, it has already been accepted that electronic information can satisfy the requirement of writing.[408] Second, the qualification of evidence as beginning of evidence in writing requires that writing to emanate from someone against whom it is invoked. In terms of electronic information, this would mean that the debtor must have authored the electronic information that is invoked against him as beginning of evidence in writing. However, it has been established that this requirement can also be satisfied by appropriation by the party against whom it is invoked.[409] Last, the electronic information must make the alleged fact probable in order to be accepted as beginning of evidence in writing. While that information must not render the alleged fact indisputably certain, it must be made probable and not just possible.[410]

119. The acceptance of electronic information as beginning of evidence in writing would allow such electronic information to bypass the strict rules of article 1341 Belgian Civil Code. However, it must be borne in mind that

---

406 Article 1347 Belgian Civil Code.

407 Steennot, R. (1999) "Juridische problemen in het kader van de elektronische handel", *T.B.H.*, 671; Van Eecke, P. (2009) "De elektronische handtekening in het recht", *T.B.H.*, 339; Storme, M.E. (2001) "De invoering van de elektronische handtekening in ons bewijsrecht", *RW*, 1514.

408 Due to the inclusion of such acceptance under article 16 Act of 11 March 2003 and earlier practical acceptance in jurisprudence and legal doctrine.

409 Cornelis, L. (2000) *Algemene theorie van de verbintenis*, Antwerpen: Intersentia, 223; Minjauw, H., Vandendriessche, J. (2008) "Titel VI. Het bewijsrecht in burgerlijke zaken", in: Roodhooft, R. (ed.), *Bestendig Handboek Verbintenissenrecht*, Mechelen: Kluwer, VI.3–10.

410 See section 1.4.3. Minjauw, H., Vandendriessche, J. (2008) "Titel VI. Het bewijsrecht in burgerlijke zaken", in: Roodhooft, R. (ed.), *Bestendig Handboek Verbintenissenrecht*, Mechelen: Kluwer, VI.3–11; Cornelis, L. (2000) *Algemene theorie van de verbintenis*, Antwerpen: Intersentia, 223.

beginning of evidence in writing is not considered to be full evidence - as instruments are - and thus requires supplementary evidence by any other means.[411] In general, beginning of evidence in writing can be considered as an important category of evidence for the purposes of electronic information, especially if the qualification of the electronic information as an instrument fails due to the lack of a valid signature. Important here is the presence of appropriation, either by authorship or by implicit or explicit appropriation by the party against whom it is invoked.[412]

3.4.3. Presumptions

120. If electronic information cannot be qualified as an instrument, and if the qualification as beginning of evidence in writing also fails, it could still be accepted as a factual presumption, which means it can be accepted as a known fact from which the judge can derive conclusions relating to an unknown fact.[413] However, this qualification as factual presumption is not automatic, there are a number of requirements to be complied with. More particularly, factual presumptions must demonstrate clearly established facts leading to a plausible and justifiable conclusion, whereby the judge only considers weighty, certain and concordant presumptions.[414]

121. The qualification of electronic information as a factual presumption has obvious consequences for its probative value. First, presumptions are only admissible where the restrictions of article 1341 Belgian Civil Code do not apply, or when an exception to those restrictions applies. This limits the admissibility

---

411 Minjauw, H., Vandendriessche, J. (2008) "Titel VI. Het bewijsrecht in burgerlijke zaken", in: Roodhooft, R. (ed.), *Bestendig Handboek Verbintenissenrecht*, Mechelen: Kluwer, VI.3-8-9; Cornelis, L. (2000) *Algemene theorie van de verbintenis*, Antwerpen: Intersentia, 223.

412 For instance, telegrams and telex messages could fail the requirement of appropriation if they do not provide sufficient proof of authorship. In such event, they can be considered as presumptions at most. Minjauw, H., Vandendriessche, J. (2008) "Titel VI. Het bewijsrecht in burgerlijke zaken", in: Roodhooft, R. (ed.), *Bestendig Handboek Verbintenissenrecht*, Mechelen: Kluwer, VI.4-4. However, there are cases where it has been accepted in jurisprudence that such electronic information can provide sufficient proof of authorship, thus allowing the qualification as beginning of evidence in writing. Rb. Turnhout 21 May 1987, *TBBR*, 1989, 171; Mougenot, D. (2002) *Droit des obligations: la preuve*, Brussel: Larcier, 247. This demonstrates the importance of the judge's appreciation of the presence of appropriation. Copies and computer printouts could also be accepted as beginning of evidence in writing, if appropriation is present, along with the requirements of a writing and making the alleged fact probable. Stijns, S. (2009) *Leerboek Verbintenissenrecht Boek 2*, Brugge: die Keure, 182.

413 Minjauw, H., Vandendriessche, J. (2008) "Titel VI. Het bewijsrecht in burgerlijke zaken", in: Roodhooft, R. (ed.), *Bestendig Handboek Verbintenissenrecht*, Mechelen: Kluwer, VI.3-50; L. Cornelis (2000) *Algemene theorie van de verbintenis*, Antwerpen: Intersentia, 229; Stijns, S. (2009) *Leerboek Verbintenissenrecht Boek 2*, Brugge: die Keure, 175.

414 See section 1.5.2.

of electronic information as presumptions. Second, as beginning of evidence in writing, presumptions do not constitute full evidence on their own, thus leaving the decision on their value up to the judge.[415]

3.5. PRACTICAL CASES OF APPLICATION

122. In the previous sections, a theoretical overview was provided on the traditional rules of Belgian civil evidence law and on how these rules can be applied to electronic information. To provide a more practical view, this section will analyze how the rules of Belgian civil evidence law are, in effect, applied to a number of particular types of electronic information.

3.5.1. E-mail

123. Given the importance of e-mail as a communication tool in personal and professional relations, it is evident that statements made in an e-mail message could be interesting for parties to call upon as evidence should a dispute arise between them. As noted previously, in order for information to be accepted as writing, it is sufficient that it is expressed in a language, using understandable signs and given relative durability.[416] An e-mail could be considered to comply with those requirements, thus constituting a writing.[417] This means that an e-mail could be accepted as a private instrument, if it documents document legal acts and is validly signed.

124. A typical phenomenon seen when receiving e-mails is the use of a so-called e-mail signature. In essence, such signature is nothing more than editable text at the bottom of the message providing information about the sender, its affiliation and contact details. As such, it could be considered as a whole of electronic data aimed at identifying the sender and thus constitute a signature within the scope of the broad signature notion of article 1322 Belgian

---

415 Minjauw, H., Vandendriessche, J. (2008) "Titel VI. Het bewijsrecht in burgerlijke zaken", in: Roodhooft, R. (ed.), *Bestendig Handboek Verbintenissenrecht*, Mechelen: Kluwer, VI.3–54.

416 Van Eecke, P. (2009) "De elektronische handtekening in het recht", *T.B.H.*, 333; Storme, M.E. (2001) "De invoering van de elektronische handtekening in ons bewijsrecht", *RW*, 1514–1515.

417 Minjauw, H., Vandendriessche, J. (2008) "Titel VI. Het bewijsrecht in burgerlijke zaken", in: Roodhooft, R. (ed.), *Bestendig Handboek Verbintenissenrecht*, Mechelen: Kluwer, VI.4–6; Ballon, G.L. (2009) "De bewijswaarde van een emailbericht", note to Ghent Appeals Court 10 March 2008, *T.G.R.*, 29; Dumortier, J., Somers, G. (2006) "Het bedrijfsgebruik van elektronische post juridisch doorgelicht", *C.J.*, 2; Mougenot, D. (2002) *Droit des obligations: la preuve*, Brussel: Larcier, 311. Note, however, that some authors are still disputing such qualification: Mourlon Beernaert, F., Gaudy, A. (2006) "Partie VI. Le droit de la preuve – La preuve par présomption", in: X, *Obligations. Traité théorique et pratique*, Brussel: Kluwer, VI.4.4 – 8–9.

Civil Code, if a judge would find that such signature provides sufficient proof of identification, non-repudiation and integrity. This is, however, where such signature is likely to fall short. By nature, an e-mail signature could be placed by anyone, claiming to be whoever they want. There is no way to verify whether the person sending the e-mail is truly who he purports to be in the signature.[418] As a result, a simple e-mail signature is unlikely to be accepted as a valid electronic signature.[419]

125. In order to raise the trustworthiness of an e-mail message, users can decide to affix an electronic signature to that message. Using the technique of the digital signature – thus constituting either an advanced or a qualified electronic signature depending on whether qualified certificates are used – an e-mail could be found to provide sufficient proof of its authorship, the non-repudiation thereof and the integrity of its contents after signing.[420] In such an event, the e-mail could be found to have been validly signed, thereby allowing the qualification thereof as a private instrument.

126. If an e-mail would document legal acts and be validly signed, it could thus be accepted as a private instrument.[421] Where no valid signature is present, the e-mail can be considered as beginning of evidence in writing at most.[422] To allow for this qualification, whether the e-mail originates from or was appropriated by against whom it is invoked and whether it makes the alleged fact probable will have to be assessed.[423] While this also implies a certain form of identification of the e-mail's author – or at least appropriation thereof – the broader scope of beginning of evidence in writing could still allow for this qualification to apply.[424] When the qualification of an e-mail as beginning of evidence in writing fails, it can constitute a factual presumption at most.

---

418 While in principle the e-mail header could provide more information, also this information could be questioned or be tampered with. Moreover, if one of the parties controlled one of the mail servers used, the integrity of the e-mail could be questioned. Ballon, G.L. (2009) "De bewijswaarde van een e-mailbericht", note to Ghent Appeals Court 10 March 2008, *T.G.R.*, 29; Montero, E. (2009), "À propos de la valeur probante des e-mails", note to Ghent Appeals Court 10 March 2008, *D.A.-O.R.*, 317.

419 Van Eecke, P. (2009) "De elektronische handtekening in het recht", *T.B.H.*, 349, with references to jurisprudence on this subject.

420 With automatic acceptance in the case of a qualified electronic signature.

421 Minjauw, H., Vandendriessche, J. (2008) "Titel VI. Het bewijsrecht in burgerlijke zaken", in: Roodhooft, R. (ed.), *Bestendig Handboek Verbintenissenrecht*, Mechelen: Kluwer, VI.4–6.

422 Van Eecke, P. (2009) "De elektronische handtekening in het recht", *T.B.H.*, 349; De Groote, B. (2001) "Het bewijs in de elektronische handel – Enkele bedenkingen", *A.J.T.*, 899; Mougenot, D. (2002) *Droit des obligations: la preuve*, Brussel: Larcier, 311.

423 See section 3.4.2.

424 Minjauw, H., Vandendriessche, J. (2008) "Titel VI. Het bewijsrecht in burgerlijke zaken", in: Roodhooft, R. (ed.), *Bestendig Handboek Verbintenissenrecht*, Mechelen: Kluwer, VI.3–10–11. In practice, the matter of identification or appropriation will only be raised if the party against whom the writing is invoked disputes that he authored or appropriated that writing.

127. Similar conclusions can be drawn for other types of communication through electronic information, such as Short Message Service (SMS) messages, instant messaging, blogs and social media communications such as status updates and tweets.[425] While these types of electronic information could be considered as writing[426], they are generally not signed and thus their qualification as a private instrument will fail. As a result, they will at most constitute beginning of evidence in writing, if their authorship can be established – through identification of the author or appropriation by the person against whom they are invoked – and if they make the alleged fact probable.[427] Sould this qualification fail, they will constitute presumptions at most.

3.5.2. Logs

128. Logs are records generated by computer systems that document the activities and transactions to which they were part, thereby providing an audit trail.[428] They could be considered to be an important element during an e-commerce transaction, where they can document what occurred between the

---

Absence of such dispute could be considered as appropriation. Samyn, B. (2013) "Sms is maar begin van bewijs", *De Juristenkrant*, nr. 276, 2. In general, it can be held that the threshold for acceptance of writing as beginning of evidence in writing has been put lower than that for instruments. De Page, H. (1967) *Traité élémentaire de droit civil Belge, Tome Troisième (Les Obligations)*, Brussel: Bruylant, 910–911.

425 Minjauw, H., Vandendriessche, J. (2008) "Titel VI. Het bewijsrecht in burgerlijke zaken", in: Roodhooft, R. (ed.), *Bestendig Handboek Verbintenissenrecht*, Mechelen: Kluwer, VI.4–6; De Groote, B. (2001) "Het bewijs in de elektronische handel – Enkele bedenkingen", *A.J.T.*, 899; Mougenot, D. (2002) *Droit des obligations: la preuve*, Brussel: Larcier, 311.

426 Some authors still dispute whether such information – for instance SMS messages – can indeed be considered as writing. Wagner, K. (2008) "Recente ontwikkelingen met betrekking tot het bewijs in burgerlijke zaken", in: Serrus, D. (ed.), *Actualia Gerechtelijk Recht*, Gent: Larcier, 187.

427 The Ghent Appeals Court, for instance, ruled that – in the absence of a public or private instrument – SMS messages could constitute beginning of evidence in writing. Here, it was found that the fact that the phone number from which the SMS message was sent is known to belong to the party against whom the SMS message was invoked constituted sufficient proof of appropriation, even though tampering with these matters is relatively easy from a technical viewpoint. In this case, the authorship of the SMS message was not disputed, thus confirming the appropriation. While accepting the qualification of the SMS message as beginning of evidence in writing, the Court rejected that this message and the presumptions delivered as supplementary evidence constituted sufficient proof of the alleged agreement, thus emphasizing the importance of such supplementary evidence. Samyn, B. (2013) "Sms is maar begin van bewijs", *De Juristenkrant*, nr. 276, 2. This case also serves to illustrate that the threshold for acceptance of identification of authorship or appropriation under beginning of evidence in writing is lower than under instruments, as noted under footnote 424.

428 Different types of logging exist, which can provide a wide range of information. Some logs can be aimed at providing documentation of a particular transaction, while others aim to fulfill broader data mining purposes. Regarding the use of different types of logs in e-commerce, see: Kohavi, R. (2001) "Mining e-commerce data: the good, the bad, and the ugly", in: X., *KDD '01 Proceedings of the seventh ACM SIGKDD international conference on Knowledge discovery and data mining*, New York: ACM, 8–13; Suneetha, K.R., Krishnamoorthi, R. (2009)

seller – being the company or person maintaining that e-commerce platform – and the buyer – being the consumer making a purchase transaction on that e-commerce platform. For instance, when the user registers an account on an e-commerce platform and clicks on icons and buttons to make and confirm his purchase, these activities will leave traces in the logs of that platform.[429] From a probative point of view, it could then be expected that – should a dispute arise – the parties would want to use those logs to provide proof of what occurred between them.[430]

129. Following a broad interpretation of the notion of writing, a log could principally be considered to constitute writing, as it concerns an expression of a language, using understandable signs, with relative durability.[431]

130. Logs are not typically signed.[432] As a result, they cannot qualify as a private instrument. They could be found to constitute beginning of evidence in writing, insofar as they are considered to be a writing that makes the alleged fact probable and that is appropriated by the person against whom it is invoked. However, this last element may prove difficult to apply to logs. For instance, if during an e-commerce transaction a log-file is generated by the server on which the e-commerce platform runs, then it cannot be invoked against the consumer if it is found that he has not authored the log, or if he has not appropriated it. Moreover, if the seller is considered to be the author of the log, he principally cannot invoke it in his own favor as the log is unilaterally created.[433] The

---

"Identifying User Behavior by Analyzing Web Server Access Log File", *International Journal of Computer Science and Network Security*, 327–332.

429 Cornelis, L., Goethals, P. (2000) "Contractuele aspecten van e-commerce", in: X, *De elektronische handel*, Antwerpen: Kluwer, 1–49.

430 This makes that logs are not so much an *ex ante* overview of what parties agreed and what following such agreement should occur between them – as contracts typically are – but an *ex post* account of what in reality occurred between them, regardless of what was agreed to occur.

431 Van Eecke, P. (2009) "De elektronische handtekening in het recht", *T.B.H.*, 333; Storme, M.E. (2001) "De invoering van de elektronische handtekening in ons bewijsrecht", *RW*, 1514–1515; Minjauw, H., Vandendriessche, J. (2008) "Titel VI. Het bewijsrecht in burgerlijke zaken", in: Roodhooft, R. (ed.), *Bestendig Handboek Verbintenissenrecht*, Mechelen: Kluwer, VI.4–7; Steennot, R. (1999) "Juridische problemen in het kader van de elektronische handel", *T.B.H.*, 671.

432 While in some cases logs could be secured or encrypted, this will generally not constitute a valid electronic signature in the sense of article 1322 Belgian Civil Code. Minjauw, H., Vandendriessche, J. (2008) "Titel VI. Het bewijsrecht in burgerlijke zaken", in: Roodhooft, R. (ed.), *Bestendig Handboek Verbintenissenrecht*, Mechelen: Kluwer, VI.4–7–8; Mougenot, D. (2002) *Droit des obligations: la preuve*, Brussel: Larcier, 301.

433 As is the case for, for instance, account books, domestic papers and registers, see section 1.4.4. This follows the adage "*nul ne peut se créer un titre à soi-même*", meaning that nobody can create a title in his own favor. This also means that even if a log would be validly signed, its qualification as a private instrument would be dubious as it still constitutes a title created

question of authorship is therefore critical to the qualification of the log.[434] When it cannot be sufficiently certainly be proven that the log has been authored or appropriated by the consumer, it is more likely to be considered as a factual presumption at most.[435] As presumptions, logs can be considered as the known fact from which an unknown fact is deducted. For this qualification to stand, logs must display clearly established facts, from which a plausible and justifiable conclusion is drawn, where the judge takes into account only weighty, certain and concordant presumptions.[436]

131. When logs are qualified as presumptions, their probative value is limited. They will not be considered as complete evidence and, therefore, are subject to the judge's appreciation, in the cases for which the use of presumptions as evidence is even allowed.[437] Moreover, if the accuracy or integrity of a log is disputed, the fact of the log from which the presumption is drawn will not be considered to have been sufficiently established.[438] Therefore, logs are more likely to take up a supplementary role, providing facts in support of other legal facts that can be proven by all means.[439]

3.5.3. Payment transactions

132. Another aspect of the rise of e-commerce is that also payment transactions are increasingly conducted over the Internet, with most banks offering online account and payment services referred to as e-banking. The question is then how these transactions are to be proven. Traditionally, banks relied on the use of logs to record transactions – such as money withdrawal or wire transfers – made by their customers at electronic terminals.[440] As discussed in the previous section, logs are most likely to be considered as presumptions at most, thus being

---

unilaterally by one party. See also: Montero, E. (2009), "À propos de la valeur probante des e-mails", note to Ghent Appeals Court 10 March 2008, *D.A.-O.R.*, 317.

434 Mougenot finds that some authors argue that the log is controlled by the operator of the server that generates the log, whereas other authors argue it to be the user who generates the log by his interaction with that server, or even that it could be argued to be a joint effort. However, as the user principally cannot verify or correct the logs, it seems difficult to argue that he really has appropriated their content. Mougenot, D. (1997) "Droit de la preuve et technologies nouvelles, synthese et perspectives", in: Mougenot, R., *La preuve*, Liège: CUP, 83–84.

435 Cornelis, L., Goethals, P. (2000) "Contractuele aspecten van e-commerce", in: X, *De elektronische handel*, Antwerpen: Kluwer, 1–49; Mougenot, D. (2002) *Droit des obligations: la preuve*, Brussel: Larcier, 302.

436 See section 1.5.2.

437 Where the limitations of article 1341 Belgian Civil Code do not apply, or where one of the exceptions thereto apply.

438 Minjauw, H., Vandendriessche, J. (2008) "Titel VI. Het bewijsrecht in burgerlijke zaken", in: Roodhooft, R. (ed.), *Bestendig Handboek Verbintenissenrecht*, Mechelen: Kluwer, VI.3–55.

439 As the limitation of article 1341 Belgian Civil Code only applies to legal acts.

440 Minjauw, H., Vandendriessche, J. (2008) "Titel VI. Het bewijsrecht in burgerlijke zaken", in: Roodhooft, R. (ed.), *Bestendig Handboek Verbintenissenrecht*, Mechelen: Kluwer, VI.4–7.

subjected to the judge's full appreciation.[441] Even the use of a PIN code in such transactions is unlikely to provide a higher probative value, as this method is not necessarily considered to constitute a valid electronic signature.[442]

133. While technically different from conducting transactions on a terminal at the bank's premises, e-banking is not that much different from a probative point of view. Here, logs will also be used to record the user's transactions.[443] Where a valid electronic signature is used, the transaction could be recorded as part of a private instrument.[444]

134. One important element found in jurisprudence is that account statements can be presumed to be correct if the account holder has not protested them within reasonable time.[445] As a result, such account statements could play a role in providing evidence of financial transactions, for instance through beginning of evidence in writing.[446] Payments on their own can be considered as legal acts, thus making the proof thereof subject to the rules of article 1341 Belgian Civil Code.[447]

3.5.4. Audiovisual electronic information

135. One of the basic characteristics of electronic information is that it is not limited to a single form. This means that electronic information does not consist solely of legible text, but can also be applied to spoken words and sounds, photographic content or videography. Digital music distribution platforms – such as iTunes – photo-sharing platforms – such as Instagram – and video-sharing platforms – such as YouTube – are growing in popularity and as a result make up an important part of the electronic information created and shared around the world. As the traditional rules of Belgian civil evidence law are primarily aimed at governing the probative value of paper documents, their application to these different types of electronic information may be problematic.

441 See section 3.5.2. While it could be argued that the log records the actions of the user here, the degree of control exercised by the controller of the log server and other logging equipment over these logs will also determine whether or not a log could be used as evidence against the user. Even when admissible, it will still have to be determined whether the log can be considered to be appropriated by the user in order for it to be qualified as a beginning of evidence in writing. If these two points fail, only a qualification of the log as presumption will remain.

442 Minjauw, H., Vandendriessche, J. (2008) "Titel VI. Het bewijsrecht in burgerlijke zaken", in: Roodhooft, R. (ed.), *Bestendig Handboek Verbintenissenrecht*, Mechelen: Kluwer, VI.4–7; Mougenot, D. (2002) *Droit des obligations: la preuve*, Brussel: Larcier, 301.

443 Minjauw, H., Vandendriessche, J. (2008) "Titel VI. Het bewijsrecht in burgerlijke zaken", in: Roodhooft, R. (ed.), *Bestendig Handboek Verbintenissenrecht*, Mechelen: Kluwer, VI.4–8.

444 *Id.*

445 Stevens, O. (2010), note to Brussels 14 March 2008, *T.B.H.*, 109–116.

446 Mougenot, D. (2007), "Paiement et commencement de preuve par écrit", *P&B*, 289–290.

447 *Ibid.*, 289.

136. The first question that needs to be answered is whether or not electronic information in the form of sound, pictures or video can constitute a writing. Traditionally, audio and video could be refused probative value on the grounds that it required additional equipment to be accessed.[448] With the acceptance of text in the form of electronic information – which by nature always requires equipment to interpret the computer language – this position seems less sustainable.[449] This is because, according to the principle of functional equivalence, the requirement for a document in writing can be satisfied by means of a series of interpretable signs accessible for later consultation, regardless of their medium and the modalities of transmission thereof.[450] It has been accepted that these signs may be expressed in a computer language, which requires computer equipment to process the series of signs in order for it to become understandable for humans.[451] While audio and video in the form of electronic information could be argued to also fulfill that requirement, it may still prove difficult to argue that audio and video in electronic form can really fulfill the functional requirements of a document in writing.[452] Where the qualification of audio and video in electronic form as writing would succeed, a qualification as private instrument – if that information has been validly signed – or as beginning of evidence in writing – if it makes the alleged fact probable and is appropriated by against whom it is invoked – would become possible. Where such would not be the case, a qualification as presumption would be the sole remaining option.[453] Conversations conducted by technological means – such as cell phones – are principally not recorded and can thus not be used as

---

448 De Corte, R. (2001) "Elektronische handtekening en identificatie in de virtuele wereld", *P&B*, 217.

449 For instance, in criminal law, it has been accepted that electronic information includes text, audio and video. Proposal for an act regarding informatics crime, *Parl. St. Kamer* 1999–2000, 0213/1, 12; Van Eecke, P. (2004) *Naar een juridische status voor de elektronische handtekening: Een rol voor de handtekening in de informatiemaatschappij?*, PhD thesis KU Leuven – Faculty of Law, 695.

450 Article 16 §2 Act of 11 March 2003, current article XII.15 §2 Code of Economic Law.

451 Van Eecke, P. (2009) "De elektronische handtekening in het recht", *T.B.H.*, 333.

452 Vandendriessche, for instance, references that while some authors believe that a broad interpretation of the notion of writing should also include audio and video in electronic form, it does seem that courts are still reluctant to accept it as such. Minjauw, H., Vandendriessche, J. (2008) "Titel VI. Het bewijsrecht in burgerlijke zaken", in: Roodhooft, R. (ed.), *Bestendig Handboek Verbintenissenrecht*, Mechelen: Kluwer, VI.4–5.

453 Minjauw, H., Vandendriessche, J. (2008) "Titel VI. Het bewijsrecht in burgerlijke zaken", in: Roodhooft, R. (ed.), *Bestendig Handboek Verbintenissenrecht*, Mechelen: Kluwer, VI.4–5; Mougenot, D. (2002) *Droit des obligations: la preuve*, Brussel: Larcier, 293. Van Gerven argues that even the qualification of picture and film as presumption may not hold, given the possibility of falsification and the difficulty to prove authenticity and integrity. Van Gerven, W., Covemaker, S. (2006) *Verbintenissenrecht*, Leuven: Acco, 698. However, Belgian case law does demonstrate clear examples where sound recordings were accepted as presumptions. Cass. 24 November 1961, *Pas.* 1962, I, 367; Aps, F. (2000) "Het "recht op nieuwsgierigheid tussen echtgenoten" en de toelaatbaarheid van geluidsmateriaal in het kader van een echtscheidingsprocedure op grond van bepaalde feiten", *Echtscheidingsjournaal*, 31–32.

evidence, unless a party to a conversation would testify as a witness.[454] When recorded, a conversation could serve as presumption, where permitted.[455]

137. Another concern regarding the use of these types of electronic information is whether or not they have been lawfully obtained.[456] Pictures and video could be taken without the party involved knowing it. Likewise, conversations could be recorded without the consent of all parties involved. In such cases, the production of these types of electronic information may constitute a breach of law, for instance by potentially infringing the general right to privacy and data protection legislation, as well as legislation protecting electronic communications.[457] As a result, the judge may deny their admissibility.

4. DIGITALIZATION AND THE ORIGINALITY REQUIREMENT

138. The previous sections provided an overview of the changes to the rules on evidence in Belgian civil law brought about by the process of digitalization. First, conclusions will be drawn from this overview with regard to the influence of digitalization on the classic evidence rules. Second, what exactly the position of the originality requirement is in this context will be assessed.

4.1. INFLUENCE OF DIGITALIZATION IN THE BELGIAN CIVIL CODE

139. Rather than formulating a new legal framework aimed specifically at regulating the probative value of electronic information, the Belgian legislator has clearly decided to maintain the existing legal framework regarding evidence under civil law and to allow for the application of these rules to electronic

---

Regarding the authenticity of such recordings, Aps refers to the possibility of the judge to appoint an expert to verify this.

454 Minjauw, H., Vandendriessche, J. (2008) "Titel VI. Het bewijsrecht in burgerlijke zaken", in: Roodhooft, R. (ed.), *Bestendig Handboek Verbintenissenrecht*, Mechelen: Kluwer, VI.4–6.

455 Mourlon Beernaert, F., Gaudy, A. (2006) "Partie VI. Le droit de la preuve – La preuve par présomption", in: X, *Obligations. Traité théorique et pratique*, Brussel: Kluwer, VI.4.4 – 5.

456 Allemeersch, B., Schollen, P. (2002) "Behoorlijk bewijs in burgerlijke zaken over de geoorloofdheidsvereiste in het burgerlijk bewijsrecht", *RW*, 43–45; Aps, F. (2000) "Het "recht op nieuwsgierigheid tussen echtgenoten" en de toelaatbaarheid van geluidsmateriaal in het kader van een echtscheidingsprocedure op grond van bepaalde feiten", *Echtscheidingsjournaal*, 31–34; Mougenot, D. (2002) *Droit des obligations: la preuve*, Brussel: Larcier, 293.

457 In Belgium: article 22 Belgian Constitution; Act of 8 December 1992 protecting the personal sphere against the processing of personal data, *Belgian State Gazette* 18 March 1993; articles 259*bis* and 314*bis* Belgian Criminal Code; article 124 Act of 13 June 2005 concerning electronic communication, *Belgian State Gazette* 20 June 2005.

information. To facilitate this, it was also decided to limit the number of amendments to the existing rules of evidence under civil law, and to introduce the application of those rules to electronic information by means of the principle of functional equivalence and the introduction of an electronic signature, laid down in separate acts. As a result, the position of electronic information under Belgian civil evidence law is more a continuation of existing and established practices, rather than moving into a new direction.

140. One element that was already developing in jurisprudence and legal doctrine is the acceptance of electronic information as writing. Moreover, this notion was later laid down into law by the principle of functional equivalence.[458] Given the preference of the Belgian rules of civil evidence for evidence in writing, this acceptance was necessary for electronic information to be accorded significant probative value. Prior to this evolution, electronic information could at most be considered to be a factual presumption, thus enjoying a low admissibility and probative value. However, it could be questioned whether this acceptance on its own is sufficient to fully integrate electronic information into the rules of Belgian civil evidence law. After all, the core element that constitutes an original under the rules of the Civil Code is the signature.[459]

141. A second important element for the acceptance of electronic information as evidence under civil law is therefore the introduction of electronic signatures. Given the high value of signatures – an absolute requirement for the qualification of evidence as an original instrument – the impossibility to affix a handwritten signature to electronic information had severely restricted the probative value of that electronic information. Now, if electronic information is signed with a valid electronic signature, then it can be accorded the high probative value of an original private instrument. The introduction of electronic signatures into Belgian civil evidence law has been twofold. First, the signature requirement of article 1322 Belgian Civil Code was broadened to allow a signature to be created by electronic means. Subsequently, in transposing an EU Directive, the legislator introduced three types of electronic signatures, with varying degrees of reliability and trustworthiness. While the electronic signature is principally technology-neutral, it is clear that some preference is given to the use of a qualified electronic signature – relying on a PKI infrastructure and qualified certificates – due to its automatic equivalence to a handwritten signature. Other types – the common and advanced electronic signature – cannot be denied legal

458 Original article 16 of the Act of 11 March 2003, current article XII.15 of the Code of Economic Law.

459 Gobert, D., Montero, E. (2000) "La signature dans les contrats et les paiements électroniques: l'approche fonctionelle", in: Montero, E. (ed.) *Commerce électronique: le temps des certitudes*, Brussels: Bruylant, 67.

value solely due to their nature, but are still subjected to the judge's appreciation of their value regarding identification, non-repudiation and integrity.

142. The underlying principle in the evolution of electronic information to qualify as writing and the introduction of electronic signatures is that of functional equivalence. This principle states, once and for all, that contracts can be concluded by electronic means, as long as those means satisfy the functional requirements to the conclusion of such contracts. Clarifying this principle, the legislator references the acceptance of electronic information as writing and the acceptance of electronic signatures as equal to handwritten signatures, if all requirements thereto are met. However, as it is not explained how electronic information could fulfill such functional requirements, this principle could be argued to result in some legal uncertainty.

143. The acceptance of electronic information as writing and the potential equivalence between electronic and handwritten signatures has significant consequences. It allows for the qualification of electronic information as a private instrument or – where a valid signature is lacking – beginning of evidence in writing – thereby raising the probative value of that information. However, the nature of electronic information – intrinsically susceptible to manipulation – may still prove to limit its probative value. Therefore, it is important to clearly demonstrate that the author of electronic information is identified and authenticated, that his authorship cannot be repudiated and that the integrity of the information is attested to. Where electronic information would qualify as beginning of evidence in writing, appropriation will be the main matter to prove.

144. Despite these significant evolutions, a number of gaps in the legal framework remain. For instance, electronic public instruments are currently still not possible, even though several legal amendments thereto have been foreseen during the past two decades. Similarly, while the rising importance of trust services has led to an important role for Trusted Third Parties, this figure has – until the adoption of Regulation 910/2014 – not been given a legal framework yet, even though such framework was effectively adopted in Belgium, but never entered into force before being abolished again.[460] Moreover, while the electronic

[460] This legal framework was established by the Act of 15 May 2007, holding the establishment of a legal framework for certain providers of trust services, *Belgian State Gazette* 17 July 2007. However, the executive measures required for this legal framework to become operational were never adopted, meaning that while this act did exist, it bore no practical use. Minjauw, H., Vandendriessche, J. (2008) "Titel VI. Het bewijsrecht in burgerlijke zaken", in: Roodhooft, R. (ed.), *Bestendig Handboek Verbintenissenrecht*, Mechelen: Kluwer, VI.4–10; Dumortier, J., Somers, G. (2007) "De wet van 15 mei 2007 tot vaststelling van een juridisch kader voor sommige verleners van vertrouwensdiensten: een eerste verkenning", *T.B.H.*, 649–659. The act was eventually repealed by article 33 of the Act of 21 July 2016 executing and

signature has indisputable theoretical value, its use in practice has proven to be limited.[461]

4.2. WHERETO WITH ORIGINALITY?

145. Two questions that inevitably rise are: can the originality requirement still be fulfilled in the context of electronic information, and is there still a need for this requirement in the current society?

146. The first question has already been answered positively in the previous sections. Thanks to the acceptance of electronic information as writing and the introduction of electronic signatures, it is perfectly possible to establish an electronic original.[462] There is, however, some variation in terms of how this requirement is fulfilled.

147. Under the rules on evidence regarding paper instruments, the formalities regarding the originality requirement essentially prescribed a documentary exchange. In such exchange, each party with a discernible interest would receive an original, signed by all other parties, with discernible interests.[463] This exchange has been somewhat altered when transferring electronic information. If electronic information is duly signed electronically and subsequently transmitted, each party will receive a version of that electronic information with a valid electronic signature. In other words, while the information transmitted is essentially duplicated, the duplicated signature retains its validity, thereby establishing the duplicate as an original instrument and not just a copy.[464] The

supplementing Regulation 910/2014 of the European Parliament and of the Council of 23 July 2014 concerning electronic identification and trust services for electronic transactions in the internal market and repealing Directive 1999/93/EC, inserting title 2 in book XII "Law of the electronic economy" in the Code of Economic Law and inserting the definitions for title 2 of book XII and of the enforcement rules of title 2 of book XII in the books I, XV and XVII in the Code of Economic Law, *Belgian State Gazette* 28 September 2016.

461 This much was acknowledged by the European Commission in proposing its overhaul of the legal framework on electronic signatures. Commission staff working document of 7 June 2012 impact assessment accompanying the document proposal for a regulation of the European Parliament and of the Council on electronic identification and trust services for electronic transactions in the internal market, *SWD(2012) 135 final*, 9–12; Graux, H. (2011) "Rethinking the e-signatures directive: on laws, trust services and the digital single market", *Digital Evidence & Electronic Signature Law Review*, Vol. 8, 9–24.

462 Demoulin, M., Soyez, S. (2012) "L'authenticité, de l'original papier à la copie numérique – Les enjeux juridiques et archivistiques de la numérisation", in: Duranti, L., Schaeffer, E. (eds) *The Memory of the World in the Digital Age: Digitization and Preservation*, Conference proceedings of UNESCO: Vancouver, 26–28 September 2013, 748.

463 Under the rule of article 1325 Belgian Civil Code.

464 Gobert, D., Montero, E. (2000) "La signature dans les contrats et les paiements électroniques: l'approche fonctionelle", in: Montero, E. (ed.) *Commerce électronique: le temps des certitudes*, Brussels: Bruylant, 68.

main difference is that the transmitting party does not lose his version of the original, as used to be the case in paper documentary exchanges. The electronic documentary exchange, therefore, allows for the creation of an unlimited number of originals, which was impossible under the paper documentary exchange – as each reproduction would require the manual placement of a signature to make that reproduction an original. While it is certain that this constitutes a change from the practice for paper documents, it can be held to not significantly deviate from the legislator's intention for the originality requirement.[465]

148. An important point to raise here, is that the nature of an original should be viewed separately from the information carrier. While in paper documents, the information and the signature are inextricably linked to their carrier – thus also resulting in the fact that duplication of this information to another non-signed carrier constitutes a copy – this is not the case for electronic information. Duly signed electronic information can – together with its signature – be moved freely between information carriers, *e.g.* hard drives, USB-drives, discs or others. In order for an instrument to remain an original, it is therefore not required that the information remains on its first carrier. Only the presence of the signature is required for the status of original to be preserved. As with paper instruments, the original would *de facto* always remain linked to its first carrier, there are authors that erroneously assume that this 'original carrier' is a part of the originality requirement.[466]

149. There is, however, some concern regarding the long-term validity of electronic signatures. While a handwritten signature will remain valid *in perpetuum*, the qualified electronic signature is bound to the validity of its certificates. If such certificate expires or is revoked, the electronic signature can no longer be validated. The result is that it is possible that validly signed electronic information could lose its status of original – if that signature cannot be validated – and can become a copy.[467] This problem could be mitigated by adopting a preservation strategy.

150. The conclusion to the questions asked here can then be that electronic information can indeed fulfill the originality requirement, and that – barring

465 *Id.*

466 As observed by: Demoulin, M., Soyez, S. (2012) "L'authenticité, de l'original papier à la copie numérique – Les enjeux juridiques et archivistiques de la numérisation", in: Duranti, L., Schaeffer, E. (eds) *The Memory of the World in the Digital Age: Digitization and Preservation*, Conference proceedings of UNESCO: Vancouver, 26–28 September 2013, 749.

467 Gobert, D., Montero, E. (2000) "La signature dans les contrats et les paiements électroniques: l'approche fonctionelle", in: Montero, E. (ed.) *Commerce électronique: le temps des certitudes*, Brussels: Bruylant, 68.

a few *caveats* addressed here – the originality requirement can still fulfill its legislative purposes.[468]

151. In recent years, the original-copy dichotomy has taken on a new dimension. Within archival practice, there is a growing demand to replace paper archives with electronic reproductions. Such electronic archives take up less space and can be made more broadly accessible. This has posed certain legal hindrances: an electronic reproduction of a paper original is not electronically signed – unless the parties to that instrument were to expressly electronically sign it, which may not always be feasible from a practical viewpoint – and therefore constitutes a copy.[469] From a probative point of view, it could therefore be unwise to replace paper originals with electronic copies. This problem, in archival science addressed as substitution[470], has found no widespread legal answer to date.[471]

152. The Belgian legislator has expressed a clear intention to address this matter. In recent years, a number of legislative acts on economic matters have been bundled into the Belgian Code of Economic Law.[472] As noted previously, the Act of 11 March 2003 has already been inserted into Book XII of this Code. While it was the intention of the legislator to also insert the Act of 9 July 2001 into the same Book, this did not happen immediately.[473] Under the 53rd Parliamentary session, a proposal was introduced to this end.[474] That proposal

468 During the preparatory discussions on the UNCITRAL Model Law on Electronic Commerce (1996) there was also uncertainty regarding whether the notion of originality still makes sense in an electronic environment. An article was inserted (article 8) eventually that deals specifically with this matter. Demoulin, M. (2014) *Droit du commerce électronique et équivalents fonctionnels*, Brussels: Larcier, 193–194. While the UNCITRAL Model Law was a clear source of inspiration for the EU's Directive on Electronic Commerce, this directive does not include a reference to the originality principle.

469 As noted above, this loss of originality is solely due to the reproduction not being signed automatically, and not due to the information being duplicated to another carrier.

470 Note that substitution includes the destruction of paper originals after their electronic representatives have been produced, which is precisely where the problem lies. No probative problem is posed if the original paper instrument remains available together with an electronic copy, as the original could then still be procured when so demanded.

471 At this point, certain sector-specific rules have been introduced to allow for substitution in particular cases. This fragmented approach, however, can be argued to result in legal uncertainty. While this problem certainly merits more research, it is beyond the scope of this work to delve into this matter further.

472 Information on this codification project – in Dutch – can be found at: *economie.fgov.be/nl/fod/codificatie_economische_wetgeving*.

473 This could be derived from the text itself: Article XII.15 §2 of the Code of Economic Law – formerly article 16 §2 of the Act of 11 March 2003 – originally referred to the electronic signature of article XII.25 §4 of the same Code. This article XII.25 did, however, at that time not yet exist. In the Act of 11 March 2003, this was a reference to article 4 §4 of the Act of 9 July 2001. The legislator later corrected the erroneous reference.

474 Proposal to amend the legislation introducing the law of electronic commerce, *Parl. St. Kamer* 2012–2013, 2745/1.

also included an article that would add a new paragraph to article 1334 of the Belgian Civil Code, holding that when the original instrument no longer exists, a digital copy thereof has the same probative value as the private instrument of which it – barring proof to the contrary – is presumed to be a reliable and durable copy if produced by means of a qualified electronic archival service.[475] This proposal, however, was not enacted at the time.[476] However, in implementing the EU eIDAS Regulation, the Belgian legislator revisited this matter. In 2016, the Belgian legislator inserted the provisions of the Act of 9 July 2001 into book XII of the Code of Economic Law, and thereby repealing the original Act of 9 July 2001.[477] Additionally, this act also added the aforementioned new paragraph to article 1334 of the Belgian Civil Code, giving digital copies the same probative value as private instruments, if they were created using a qualified electronic archival service and where the original instrument no longer exists.[478]

5. CONCLUSION

153. The main conclusion to be drawn, after analyzing the basic tenets of Belgian civil evidence law, is that the rules found in the Belgian Civil Code display a clear preference for evidence in writing. This is explicated in, for instance, the rule of article 1341 Belgian Civil Code that prohibits the use of witnesses and presumptions to provide evidence of legal acts in cases where the sum exceeds EUR 375, as well as against written instruments. This means that such types of non-written evidence can only be used when small amounts are at

---

475 Article 8 proposal to amend the legislation introducing the law of electronic commerce, *Parl. St. Kamer* 2012–2013, 2745/1, 47.

476 In part, this was due to the proposal's coincidence with the European proposal for a regulation replacing Directive 1999/93/EC. It was remarked that it would be unwise to introduce new Belgian legislation that could end up contradicting European legislation at that point. Proposal to amend the legislation introducing the law of electronic commerce - Committee report, *Parl. St. Kamer* 2012–2013, 2745/7, 12. In the end, the proposal was scrapped as a result of the dissolution of Parliament before the 2014 federal election.

477 Articles 2 – 31 Act of 21 July 2016 executing and supplementing Regulation 910/2014 of the European Parliament and of the Council of 23 July 2014 concerning electronic identification and trust services for electronic transactions in the internal market and repealing Directive 1999/93/EC, inserting title 2 in book XII "Law of the electronic economy" in the Code of Economic Law and inserting the definitions for title 2 of book XII and of the enforcement rules of title 2 of book XII in the books I, XV and XVII in the Code of Economic Law, *Belgian State Gazette* 28 September 2016.

478 Article 34 Act of 21 July 2016 executing and supplementing Regulation 910/2014 of the European Parliament and of the Council of 23 July 2014 concerning electronic identification and trust services for electronic transactions in the internal market and repealing Directive 1999/93/EC, inserting title 2 in book XII "Law of the electronic economy" in the Code of Economic Law and inserting the definitions for title 2 of book XII and of the enforcement rules of title 2 of book XII in the books I, XV and XVII in the Code of Economic Law, *Belgian State Gazette* 28 September 2016.

play, when legal facts need to be proven or when one of the exceptions to this rule apply – either beginning of evidence in writing or the impossibility to produce written evidence. The preference for written evidence is further evidenced in the hierarchy of probative value, reserving full value for written instruments.

154. The high probative value of written instruments reveals a second element, the signature. The highest probative value can be accorded only when a valid signature is present, an absolute requirement for the qualification of evidence as an original private or public instrument. The absence of a signature automatically leads to a lower qualification, beginning of evidence in writing at best. This type of evidence is not only accorded a lower probative value, it must also be supplemented by additional evidence. Similarly, presumptions – which may also lack a valid signature and are not necessarily presented in writing – are accorded an even lower value, and thus serve mostly as such supplementary evidence, in cases where their use is even admitted.

155. It is in this setting, historically aimed to solely apply to paper documents and handwritten signatures, that electronic information must seek its probative value. The application of the traditional rules of Belgian civil evidence law has been facilitated with a minimum of legislative amendments. Alongside the more low-key acceptance of electronic information as a potential writing and the introduction of the principle of functional equivalence, the most notable legislative intervention has been the introduction of electronic signatures. While principally being technology-neutral – thereby requiring the judge to weigh the value of every electronic signature presented to him – there is a clear preference for the qualified electronic signature, demonstrated through its automated equivalence to handwritten signatures.

156. The historical reason for this preference for written evidence can be explained in many ways, as a matter of economy of procedure for instance. As paper documents are more difficult to falsify than, for instance, oral statements, they are considered to be more trustworthy. Moreover, paper documents can be easily verified, meaning that for the establishment of the legal truth it will be sufficient if such document corresponds to a number of predefined requirements. The establishment of the legal truth during civil proceedings can, therefore, be found to rely on reasoned assumptions of veracity to certain extent.

157. These assumptions rely on three principles, which must be found present for paper documents, electronic information and signatures in any form. First, the author of the information or signature must be identified. While the term identification is commonly used here, it has become clear that this does not only include the pointing out of a person as the author, but also the verification of whether or not that person is who he purports to be, being authentication.

Second, it must be ensured that the author cannot deny his authorship, which means that the non-repudiation must be proven. Third, the integrity of the information must be proven, meaning that it must be assured that the information has not been tampered with since a certain point in time – typically the moment of signing.

158. While the electronic signature must correspond to these principles as well, as found in the requirements of article 1322 Belgian Civil Code and in the requirements for an advanced and qualified electronic signature under the Act of 9 July 2001, it is also found to provide certain proof of the trustworthiness of the electronic information to which is affixed, very much like a handwritten signature was accepted to provide proof of integrity of the document to which it was affixed. While the notion of writing has been liberalized over the years – first allowing various techniques of printing documents instead of handwriting them and later accepting electronic information as a writing – the signature could be argued to have become more strictly regulated over the years.[479] However, the electronic signature has been found to be barely used in practice even though it is such an important element of Belgian civil evidence law. The theoretical discussion on which electronic signature to use, therefore, seems not to have resulted in significant practical difficulties thus far.

159. It is against this background that the principle of originality must be evaluated. From a historical viewpoint, the specific formalities currently found in the Belgian Civil Code were only introduced relatively recently. Despite these stricter formalities – followed by a number of formalization waves in jurisprudence and doctrine in the 19th and 20th century – case law does demonstrate certain leniency in probative matters. If parties accept the validity of a copy in their dispute, that copy will have full probative force between them.

160. With regard to the originality requirement, the signature is also the main constitutive element. Only duly signed documents can be regarded as originals. This is an important finding with regard to the digitalization process: with the introduction of electronic signatures, also electronic information can satisfy the originality requirement. While some authors have linked originality to the information carrier – holding that only the first carrier can be regarded as original – this theory must be rejected as false. The main problem with originality in a digital context relates to the documentary transfer. While with a paper documentary transfer one party would lose possession of that information, this

479 The quality assurances expected from an electronic signature can be argued to be more onerous than those of a handwritten signature. Moreover, where the legislator requires the use of a particular technique for producing electronic signatures – such as the use of the e-ID in labor contracts – the legislator seems to demonstrate a lack of trust in this evolution. Van Eecke, P. (2009) "De elektronische handtekening in het recht", *T.B.H.*, 347–348.

is not the case with electronic information transfers. Here, the party transferring duly signed electronic information will remain in possession of that information. The receiving party will also enter into possession of this information, together with the valid signature. In other words, while the information is essentially duplicated, the transferred information constitutes not a mere copy, but also an original. Until now, the main problem was lay with the Belgian Civil Code's dichotomy between originals and copies, which accorded a lower probative value to (electronic) documents that were not validly signed. This proved to be a problem for the substitution of paper documents by electronic copies. New rules adopted in implementing the EU eIDAS Regulation have provided a partial solution in solving this problem by imposing a non-discrimination principle for electronic documents and by allowing for substitution – albeit under certain restrictions.

CHAPTER IV
ORIGINALITY IN ADMINISTRATIVE LAW

1. ORIGINALITY IN ADMINISTRATIVE LAW

1.1. ADMINISTRATIVE LAW AND PRESERVATION OF INFORMATION

161. Administrative law aims to regulate the conduct and actions of governmental entities.[480] Unlike Napoleonic civil law, which builds upon a rich history of laws and customs, administrative law is a relatively recent branch of law.[481] The development of administrative law can be considered a direct consequence of the expanding role of the state throughout the late 19th and 20th centuries. After all, as the state started to provide more and more services, the potentiality of conflicts between government and citizens rose accordingly.[482] In this regard, administrative law aims to limit the chances for conflict to arise, and to provide effective protection to the citizen should a conflict still arise.

162. Administrative law is by nature a diverse field.[483] Different branches and levels of governmental actors generally operate under their own set of rules. This leads to a plethora of specific rules of administrative law – each applying only to a particular administrative entity – accompanied by general principles of administrative law, common to all administrative entities. Within the Belgian legal order, the foremost principles of administrative law are the so-called general principles of good governance.[484] Amongst others, these principles require that

---

480 Dujardin, J., Van Damme, M., Vande Lanotte, J., Mast, A. (2009) *Overzicht van het Belgisch Administratief Recht*, Mechelen: Kluwer, 3.

481 In Belgium, for instance, the highest administrative court – the Council of State – was only founded in 1946, though a similar court has existed in France since 1799. An even more recent development is the Dutch general administrative law (Algemene wet bestuursrecht), adopted in 1992.

482 Dujardin, J., Van Damme, M., Vande Lanotte, J., Mast, A. (2009) *Overzicht van het Belgisch Administratief Recht*, Mechelen: Kluwer, 717.

483 There are only few states that, like the Netherlands, have adopted a general act or code of administrative law.

484 Dutch: *Algemene beginselen van behoorlijk bestuur.*

governmental actors display sufficient diligence and reason in their actions, that their actions are thoroughly motivated and that their actions are within the reasonable expectations of their subjects.[485] Another general principle under the rule of law regulating, to some extent, the conduct of administrative entities is that of freedom of information. In Belgium, this principle – referred to as the right to publicity of governance – is enshrined in article 32 of the Constitution, as well as several federal and state laws.[486]

163. From these principles, it can already be understood that administrative entities will be required to preserve certain information in order to prove their compliance with the general principles of good governance and to fulfill freedom of information requests.

1.2. PRESERVATION AND ORIGINALITY

164. When considering the duty to preserve certain information imposed on administrative entities, the question arises as to whether or not that information must be preserved in its original form. Here, the Belgian Archival Act does not provide much clarity. The act only refers to 'archival documents', without specifying the scope of this term. The Royal Decree of 18 August 2010 implementing articles 5 and 6 of the act determines that the archival documents must be durably preserved and maintain their authenticity, integrity, order, accessibility and readability (article 3). Regarding originality, the act and its executing decrees only determine that search instruments with which records can be retrieved – such as index cards or databases – should be transferred to the archival authorities in original or in copy.[487]

165. The Flemish Archival Decree also uses the term 'archival documents', and defines it as "*all documents that regardless of their date, form, stage of development, or type of carrier, are by their intrinsic nature destined to remain into the custody of a caretaker who has received, acquired, or created them in consequence of his activities or tasks, or for the purpose of asserting his rights*" (article 3, 2°). The decree also holds that all due professional care must be exercised in the maintenance of the archival documents (article 5, §2). The

---

485 Dujardin, J., Van Damme, M., Vande Lanotte, J., Mast, A. (2009) *Overzicht van het Belgisch Administratief Recht*, Mechelen: Kluwer, 46–73.

486 See for instance: article 32 Belgian Constitution; Act of 11 April 1994 concerning the publicity of governance, *Belgian State Gazette* 30 June 1994; Decree of 26 March 2004 concerning the publicity of governance, *Belgian State Gazette* 1 July 2004; Ordonnance of 30 March 1995 concerning the publicity of governance, *Belgian State Gazette* 23 June 1995.

487 Article 18 Royal Decree of 18 August 2010 executing articles 1, 5 and 6*bis* of the Archival Act of 24 June 1955, *Belgian State Gazette* 23 September 2010.

Decree of 21 March 2014 regulating archival management specifies that this means that archival documents and their metadata must maintain their authenticity, trustworthiness, integrity and usability (article 2). The Wallonian Archival Decree and the Brussels Archival Ordonnance contain language similar to their Flemish counterpart.

166. Similar language is also used concerning the publicity of governance. Here, an administrative document can be defined as each carrier, in any form, of information at the disposal of an administrative entity.[488] The reference to the information carrier means that this term is not limited to paper records, but also spans any form of electronic information.[489] Moreover, the reference to administrative *documents* rather than administrative *acts* must be understood as broadening the scope to also include, for instance, preparatory documents.[490] However, here the manner in which the information to which citizens can request access must be preserved is not determined.

167. Since law does not appear to provide a clear answer on the question of originality, reference will have to be made to archival science. Here, an archival document or record can be considered as a "*document made or received in the course of a practical activity as an instrument or a by-product of such activity, and set aside for action or reference*".[491] Preservation is defined as "*the whole of the principles, policies, rules and strategies aimed at prolonging the existence of an object by maintaining it in a condition suitable for use, either in its original format or in a more persistent format, while leaving intact the object's intellectual form*" (emphasis added).[492] The legislative acts discussed here also make reference to the notion of authenticity, which is defined within archival science as "*the trustworthiness of a record as a record; i.e., the quality of a record that is what it purports to be and that is free from tampering or corruption*".[493]

168. In the regular use of the word, an original can be defined as the first form or source of something, that from which other work is derived or copied.[494] Here, it is clear that in principle there can only be a single original, even though in the legal sense there can be more originals.[495] The reason for this is that in the scope of Belgian civil law an original is a document which demonstrates the intention of the parties as primarily evidenced by their signatures, of which there can

488 See, for instance, article 3, 4° Decree of 26 March 2004 concerning the publicity of governance, *Belgian State Gazette* 1 July 2004.
489 *Gedr. St. Kamer* 1992–93, nr.839/1, explanatory note, 5.
490 *Parl. St. Senaat* B.Z. 1991–92, nr. 100–49/20, 8–10.
491 InterPARES 2 (2008) "The InterPARES 2 Project Glossary", *interpares.org*, 38.
492 *Ibid.*, 36.
493 *Ibid.*, 8.
494 See the discussion in chapter III.
495 As, for instance, provided by article 1325 of the Belgian Civil Code.

indeed be more than one.[496] From an archival point of view, an original record can be defined as "*the first copy or archetype of a record; that from which another instrument is transcribed, copied, or initiated*", which more closely relates to the dictionary definition of originality.[497] Under these definitions, an original record can be considered to be authentic, in the sense that the first archetype of a record – as created by its originator – is in principle what it purports to be and has not been tampered with.[498] The reverse, however, is not necessarily true: an authenticated copy is authentic, but remains a copy.[499] However, from the definition of preservation, it can be gathered that there is a preference to preserve the original form of a record, unless a more persistent format would be better suited for archival purposes. The Belgian State Archives also state that, in principle, only original archival documents must be transferred to the central archival authorities.[500] This suggests that archival records should indeed, or at least ideally, be original in the meaning of the word as it is used in archival science.

169. The link between originality and preservation becomes especially apparent in the field of diplomatics, where an original is the "*first complete and effective document, that is, an original must present the qualities of primitiveness, completeness and effectiveness*".[501] Diplomatics is the study of "*the genesis, forms and transmission of archival documents, and their relationship with the facts represented in them and with their creator, in order to identify, evaluate, and communicate their true nature*".[502] This relates to the earlier overview of the origins of archives. At first, records derived their authenticity from being stored in a designated place, which as noted was mostly maintained by public authorities.[503] Of course, this system could not prevent the deposition of forgeries in these proto-archives, which is why law – mainly starting with the *Codex Iuris Civilis* – laid down rules of formalities.[504] The study of diplomatics later emerged as the critical study of archival documents, in order to ascertain whether records are authentic or forgeries.[505] Within this field, from which

---

496 See also: Van den Eynde, S. (2002) "DAVID: Authenticiteit, integriteit en originaliteit van elektronische archiefstukken", *ICRI research report*, 14.

497 InterPARES 2 (2008) "The InterPARES 2 Project Glossary", *interpares.org*, 33.

498 If the record would be tampered with, it would lose its sense of originality.

499 Van den Eynde, S. (2002) "DAVID: Authenticiteit, integriteit en originaliteit van elektronische archiefstukken", *ICRI research report*, 17.

500 Devolder, K., Verachten, L. (2013) *Overbrenging van digitale archieven*, Brussels: Belgian State Archives, 6.

501 Duranti, L. (1998) *Diplomatics: New Uses for an Old Science*, Lanham: Scarecrow Press, 165; Pearce-Moses, R. (2005) *A Glossary of Archival and Records Terminology*, Chicago: The Society of American Archivists, 280.

502 InterPARES 2 (2008) "The InterPARES 2 Project Glossary", *interpares.org*, 17.

503 Duranti, L. (1998) *Diplomatics: New Uses for an Old Science*, Lanham: Scarecrow Press, 36.

504 *Id.*

505 Ross, S. (2007) "Digital Preservation, Archival Science and Methodological Foundations for Digital Libraries", Keynote Address at the 11th European Conference on Digital Libraries

archival science developed, originality is then one of the core criteria on which the trustworthiness of records is assessed.[506] The historical origins of archives show that archival science has always had a preference for originals.[507]

2. DIGITALIZATION IN ADMINISTRATIVE LAW

2.1. DIGITALIZATION AND ARCHIVES

170. During the last two decades, society has seen a significant growth in digitalization procedures. More and more information processes are being conducted electronically, which has two main implications.[508] First, there is a growing body of so-called *digital born* information, meaning information that was first created electronically.[509] Second, there is the process of digitalizing non-electronic information. In this last process, information that was first created on a non-electronic information carrier, generally paper, is being transferred to electronic information carriers.[510] These processes of digitalization impact the archival requirement found in administrative law in several ways, each of which will be further explored under this section.[511] Archival scientists have gone as far as referring to a paradigm shift, meaning that the advent of electronic information in archives has led to new observations "*that cannot be explained in the terms of the old framework*" and thus "*begin to put into question its validity*" in order to find a new way of thinking about existing concepts.[512]

(ECDL), Budapest (17 September 2007), 8; Cook, T. (1997) "What is past is prologue", *Archivaria*, Vol. 43, 45.

506 Bushey, J. E. (2005) *Born digital images as reliable and authentic records,* Unpublished thesis University of British Columbia, Vancouver, 10.

507 Even though it has been posited that originality as used in diplomatics and archival science differs from the concept of originality in earlier ages. Bedos-Rezak, B. M. (2011) *When Ego Was Imago: Signs of Identity in the Middle Ages,* Leiden: Brill, 38.

508 Boudrez, F., Dekeyser, H., Dumortier, J. (2005) *Digital Archiving: The New Challenge?*, Mont Saint Guilbert: IRIS, 15–16.

509 Important to note here is that this electronic information can take many forms. While some forms – e.g. word processor files – may resemble traditional paper records, there are also forms of electronic information that have no non-electronic counterpart. Examples include information posted on social media networks, and the use of audiovisual media such as vlogs and videostreams.

510 A notable example is the digitalization conducted by many libraries, sometimes also involving private companies such as Google Books' Library Project.

511 On the impact on archival science in general: Duranti, L. (2001) "The impact of digital technology on archival science", *Archival Science*, Vol. 1, 39.

512 Duranti, L. (2001) "The impact of digital technology on archival science", *Archival Science*, Vol. 1, 41; Taylor, H. A. (1987) "Transformation in the Archives: Technological Adjustment or paradigm Shift?", *Archivaria*, Vol. 25, 12–28; Macneil, H. (1994) "Archival Theory and Practice: Between Two Paradigms", *Archivaria*, Vol. 37, 6–20.

171. First, there is the question of whether information can be created electronically. Several laws prescribe formalities with which information must comply, such as the use of paper or that information must be signed.[513] Here, the question arises as to what extent electronically created information can comply with such requirements and, hence, whether or not electronic information processes can be used to replace traditional non-digital processes.[514] In the first place, this means that in any case the extent to which the procurement of a paper document is an existential condition for the validity of the administrative action must be assessed. In second order, this question also refers to the matter of probative value of electronic information, and in so doing it is of the utmost importance to archives as well, since the task of archives to preserve information also extends to the preservation of the probative value thereof.[515]

172. Second, once electronic information is created, it must also be maintained. While this does not pose significant problems for paper records – documents created centuries ago can still be accessible and understandable today – it does pose a significant problem for electronic information.[516] As electronic information at its basic bit-level cannot be readily understood by humans; there is an inherent reliance on computer hardware and software to interpret this information in a human-readable way. And given the fast evolution in the fields of computer hardware and software, it is by no means unthinkable that certain hardware or software platforms can be rendered obsolete, which exposes the information created using those platforms to the risk of becoming inaccessible.[517] This problem can be referred to as digital obsolescence.[518] For archives, this means that measures must be taken to ensure the durable

---

513 In Belgian law, there are even instances where the use of carbon paper is regulated (article 2, §5 Royal Decree of 17 June 2004 concerning the declaration upon admission to a hospital). Other laws prescribe the use of paper forms (article 161 Electoral Code).

514 As discussed in chapter III, Belgian civil law has to this end seen the dual introduction of the principle of functional equivalence and the electronic signature.

515 Diplomatics could, for instance, be considered as providing the tools for "*assessing the trustworthiness of records as evidence after the fact of their creation*". Meehan, J. (2003) *Towards an archival concept of evidence*, unpublished University of British Columbia thesis, 14.

516 A good example is the Domesday Book, a tax census record completed in 1086. This volume, nearly a millennium old, can still be accessed and understood to this day. However, a 1986 digitalization of the volume was nearly lost due to the technology used in the digitalization process becoming obsolete. *bbc.co.uk/history/domesday.*

517 Rothenberg, for instance, points out a number of other cases in which important information – including US census data and Vietnam war reports – were almost lost due to the nearing obsolescence of the media on which the information was stored: Rothenberg, J. (1995) "Ensuring the longevity of digital documents", *Scientific American*, Vol. 272, 42–43.

518 InterPARES 2 (2008) "The InterPARES 2 Project Glossary", *interpares.org*, 32. Additionally, electronic storage media are susceptible to deterioration. Magnetic storage devices may experience decay in their magnetic orientation, while CD-based storage may experience chemical deterioration.

accessibility and readability of electronic information.[519] While in practice some strategies to this end have already been developed, how some of those strategies – and in particular migration – may conflict with legal requirements will be explained below.[520]

173. Third, the second digitalization process, in which electronic equivalents are created from non-electronic information, poses a particular problem for archives. As electronic archives can be easier to maintain and require less storage facilities, there is a clear interest to conduct digitalization efforts. After such digitalization, the archive could continue the maintenance of its electronic archives and subsequently discontinue their non-electronic archives. Where under the first point made here the question was whether it is – from a legal point of view – possible to create original electronic archival information, the question now becomes whether it is possible to substitute original non-electronic information with their electronic equivalents, whereby this substitution includes the subsequent destruction of the non-electronic information.

2.2. ORIGINAL ELECTRONIC INFORMATION

174. Prior to examining this issue further, one additional matter that must be addressed here is that of competence. It is clear that a public sector entity can only take the administrative decisions to which it has competence. In the absence of this competence, or the delegation of that competence from the competent civil servant – such as a minister or an alderman – to the entity in question, a valid decision can in principle not be taken, regardless of whether a paper-based or electronic procedure is followed. The following paragraphs, therefore, depart from the assumption that the entity in question is competent to conduct a particular administrative process, and only questions whether or not that process can be operated electronically.

175. The first question that must be analyzed here inquires about whether the documentary processes that later become subject to public sector archival requirements can be conducted by electronic means. This means that from the viewpoint of the administrative decision process, it must be assessed whether or not a paper document is a constitutive requirement for valid decision-making. Moreover, while the information that is created in these processes only becomes subject to archival requirements after its creation, it is from an archival point

---

519 As opposed to paper-based information "*preservation as applied to electronic records no longer refers to the protection of the medium of the records, but to that of their meaning and trustworthiness as records*". Duranti, L. (2001) "The impact of digital technology on archival science", *Archival Science*, Vol. 1, 46.

520 See also: Boudrez, F., Dekeyser, H., Dumortier, J. (2005) *Digital Archiving: the new challenge?*, Brussels: I.R.I.S. Group, 81–89.

of view important to know whether electronic information can satisfy the requirements of authenticity, integrity and originality in order for the archival records to maintain their probative force.

176. Regarding probative value, it is clear that the judge presiding over the case will first refer to specific laws, where available, in administrative disputes. A police report, for instance, will generally be subjected to the rules of evidence under criminal procedure law. For private law instruments, reference will be made to the rules on evidence found in Belgian civil law. From a procedural point of view, administrative law courts generally operate under their own set of rules, different from the civil law procedural rules.[521] However, when the procedural rules of an administrative court do not regulate a particular element, reference must be made to Belgian civil procedural rules as suppletive law, if the application of such rules would be reconcilable with the specific nature of procedures before that administrative court.[522]

177. Moreover, "*principles common to all branches of law and that are at the foundation of the Judicial Code, can also be applied to administrative courts*".[523] One of these principles is the signature. This, together with the requirement of writing, forms the basis of the rules on evidence under Belgian civil law, and forms a constitutive element of a valid administrative decision as well. This becomes clear from case law at the Council of State, where the validity of a signature was judged according to the same standards set by case law and literature regarding the signature in Belgian civil law, and where the absence of a valid signature invalidated the administrative act in question.[524] In terms of the signature, the notion utilized in Belgian civil law can therefore be understood to also apply to administrative law, unless a more specific law would determine otherwise.[525] Therefore, in order to understand whether public sector information processes can be conducted electronically, how digitalization is operationalized under Belgian civil law must also be assessed.

178. As noted in chapter III, the general principle of Belgian civil rules on evidence is a preference for evidence in writing, either by a private instrument between parties or by an instrument by a public notary – a deed.[526] Private

---

521 The Council of State, for instance, has made it clear that the Belgian Judicial Code is not applicable to administrative courts as such. It also does not form the common procedural law for administrative courts, barring a specific provision to this end. Council of State 22 December 2010, nr. 210.056, *RW* 2011–2012, case note Dirk de Bruyn, 615.

522 *Id.*

523 Council of State 22 December 2010, nr. 210.056, *RW* 2011–2012, 614 (own translation).

524 Council of State 8 May 2009, nr. 193.106, 6–7.

525 *Pandectes Belges*, v° Signature, nr. 1; Wagner, K. (2008) "Recente ontwikkelingen met betrekking tot het bewijs in burgerlijke zaken", in: Serrus, D. (ed.), *Actualia Gerechtelijk Recht*, Gent: Larcier, 141–142.

526 Article 1341 Belgian Civil Code.

instruments can be considered as documents drafted between a creditor and debtor, without intervention by a public official such as a notary, signed by both parties and in which they acknowledge certain obligations or legal facts, thereby constituting a legal act.[527] Such document must describe the full extent of the legal acts its documents, it must be appropriated by the person against whom it is invoked, and it must be signed by the party against whom it is invoked.[528] When the document describes mutual obligations, there must be as many originals as there are parties with a discernible interest.[529] Proof against this instrument can only be provided by another instrument, oath, or confession.[530] Similar, yet stricter, rules apply for public instruments, mainly with regard to the involvement of the public notary in the creation of this instrument.[531] The result is a higher degree of proof, due to the nature of his profession, statements by a public official are considered as irrefutable by counterproof, unless they are challenged on the grounds of fraud or forgery.[532] When there is a writing, yet one of the formalities for private or public instruments – generally the signature – is not fulfilled, that writing can at most be considered as beginning of evidence in writing, which is accorded a much lower probative value.[533]

179. At the level of the European Union, electronic signatures have been regulated since 1999.[534] This was followed by the so-called E-Commerce Directive in 2000, which holds that contracts can be concluded electronically.[535] The principles proclaimed by these directives were transposed to Belgian

527 Van Gerven, W., Covemaker, S. (2006) *Verbintenissenrecht*, Leuven: Acco, 675; Minjauw, H., Vandendriessche, J. (2008) "Titel VI. Het bewijsrecht in burgerlijke zaken", in: Roodhooft, R. (ed.), *Bestendig Handboek Verbintenissenrecht*, Mechelen: Kluwer, VI.3–21; Dumortier, J. (2010) *ICT-Recht*, Leuven: Acco, 128.

528 De Page, H. (1967) *Traité élémentaire de droit civil Belge, Tome Troisième (Les Obligations)*, Brussel: Bruylant, 788–790; Van Eecke, P. (2004) *Naar een juridische status voor de elektronische handtekening: Een rol voor de handtekening in de informatiemaatschappij?*, PhD thesis KU Leuven – Faculty of Law, 324; Cornelis, L. (2000) *Algemene theorie van de verbintenis*, Antwerpen: Intersentia, 221.

529 Article 1325 Belgian Civil Code.

530 Minjauw, H., Vandendriessche, J. (2008) "Titel VI. Het bewijsrecht in burgerlijke zaken", in: Roodhooft, R. (ed.), *Bestendig Handboek Verbintenissenrecht*, Mechelen: Kluwer, VI.3–35.

531 Articles 1317–1318 Belgian Civil Code.

532 Article 1319 Belgian Civil Code.

533 Minjauw, H., Vandendriessche, J. (2008) "Titel VI. Het bewijsrecht in burgerlijke zaken", in: Roodhooft, R. (ed.), *Bestendig Handboek Verbintenissenrecht*, Mechelen: Kluwer, VI.3–11; Cornelis, L. (2000) *Algemene theorie van de verbintenis*, Antwerpen: Intersentia, 223.

534 Directive 1999/93/EC of the European Parliament and of the Council of 13 December 1999 on a Community framework for electronic signatures, *OJ* L 13 of 19 January 2000, 12–20. This directive has been replaced by: Regulation (EU) No 910/2014 of the European Parliament and of the Council of 23 July 2014 on electronic identification and trust services for electronic transactions in the internal market and repealing Directive 1999/93/EC, *OJ* L 257 of 28 August 2014, 73–114.

535 Article 9 Directive 2000/31/EC of the European Parliament and of the Council of 8 June 2000 on certain legal aspects of information society services, in particular electronic commerce, in the Internal Market ('Directive on electronic commerce'), *OJ* L 178 of 17 July 2000, 1–16.

law.[536] As a result, Belgian law fully recognizes that a signature can be created electronically, if it can be attributed to a particular person and if it can demonstrate the integrity of the information to which it is affixed.[537] Furthermore, three distinct types of electronic signatures have been introduced – in advancing degree of probative value: the common electronic signature, the advanced electronic signature and the qualified electronic signature – some of which using cryptographic techniques and certificates, and of which one type – the qualified electronic signature – is assimilated with the handwritten signature.[538] Moreover, it is now also fully recognized by law that electronic information can satisfy the requirement of writing, as long as this electronic information is functionally equivalent thereto.[539]

180. From this, it follows that it is indeed possible to conduct certain information processes in an electronic manner, and that the resulting electronic information can be accorded the same probative value as paper-based records, at least if the requirements of a writing and the signature are satisfactorily fulfilled by the electronic means used. The question is then whether the law also allows public sector entities to conduct their information processes electronically.

181. At present, there are only fairly few legal provisions that explicitly refer to the possibility to conduct those processes electronically.[540] However, given that the legislator has adopted the principle of functional equivalence, such explicit reference may not even be necessary. If it can be established that electronic procedures can equivalently fulfill the formalities imposed on the prescribed (paper-based) procedure, then the conclusion is that such electronic procedure is allowed, unless expressly prohibited.[541] Formalities are mostly imposed

---

536 For the signature: Act of 20 October 2000 introducing the use of means of telecommunication and of the electronic signature in judicial and extrajudicial proceedings, *Belgian State Gazette* 22 December 2000; Act of 9 July 2001 concerning the determination of certain rules regarding the legal framework for electronic signatures, electronic certified mail and certification services, *Belgian State Gazette* 29 September 2001. For e-commerce: Act of 11 March 2003 concerning certain legal aspects of the services of the information society, *Belgian State Gazette* 17 March 2003.

537 Article 1322 Belgian Civil Code.

538 As defined under the Act of 9 July 2001.

539 Article 16 Act of 11 March 2003, current article XII.15 Code of Economic Law.

540 One example is article 4/1 Act of 24 February 2003 concerning the modernization of the management of social security and concerning the electronic communication between enterprises and the federal government, which holds that communications between social security entities can be conducted and signed electronically. Article 100/2 of the Social Penal Code allows police reports to be drafted and signed electronically. Article 158, §4 of the Act of 30 December 2009 holding diverse provisions states that communications between the state and the Public Centers for Social Welfare can be conducted and signed electronically. Article I.14, 11° Code of Economic Law allows online patent applications to be signed electronically.

541 Boudrez, F., Dekeyser, H. (2004) "Digitaal archiefbeheer in de praktijk", Antwerpen: Stadsarchief, 20.

for three distinct purposes: (1) to identify parties, (2) to preserve the integrity of the information and (3) to protect the parties.[542] For each formality, which purpose it serves, and whether an electronic information process could fulfill that purpose in an equivalent manner, must then be assessed.[543] Where such is the case, an electronic process can replace the non-electronic process. For some formalities, however, the conclusion will be that an electronic process cannot fulfill the purposes of the formalities imposed, and thus cannot replace the non-electronic process.

182. However, this approach can only provide little legal certainty. After all, the assessment of whether an electronic information process, including the electronic signature, can provide a functional equivalent to the formalities and their purposes found in non-electronic procedures is often more an exercise of opinion than of fact. Only the judge presiding over a case in which electronic evidence is presented can decide whether this evidence is functionally equivalent to its non-electronic counterparts.[544] Moreover, whether the procurement of paper documents is not an existential condition for valid administrative decision-making must also be assessed. Where such is the case, an electronic process could not result in a validly taken decision, even if the electronic process could be argued to be functionally equivalent to the paper-based procedure.

183. As a result, public sector actors should take due care in deciding whether or not to allow electronic information processes when the law prescribes a non-electronic process, at least in the absence of clear instructions regarding the admission of electronic processes.[545] In many cases, digitalization of

542 *Id.*

543 Important here is that attention must be paid to both the formality and to its purpose. For instance, an electronic document can fulfill the formality of consecutively numbered pages. However, the goal of this formality is to protect the integrity of the information, given that it will be difficult to tamper with such documents with paper documents. Here, it must be held that electronic information fails that purpose, as inserting new or different information in an electronic consecutively numbered document is easier than it is for paper documents. Thus, while the formality *in se* can be fulfilled, the purpose requires a different approach at the electronic realm.

544 Van Eecke, P. (2009) "De elektronische handtekening in het recht", *T.B.H.*, 339–340; Dumortier, J., Dekeyser, H. (2003) "Hoofdstuk V. Ruimen van juridische obstakels bij contracten langs elektronische weg", in: Van Eecke, P., J. Dumortier (ed.) *Elektronische Handel – Commentaar bij de wetten van 11 maart 2003*, Brugge: die Keure, 167–168.

545 An example of a general framework that principally allows electronic information processes within public sector entities, is the Brussels Capital Region Ordonnance of 13 February 2014 concerning communication using electronic means in the framework of interactions with the governments of the Brussels Capital Region, *Belgian State Gazette* 5 March 2014. The goal of this general framework is to provide common ground for the digitalization of government communications, in order to not have to change each legal provision that would refer to a non-electronic procedure. This would allow administrations to determine the most practical means in which such electronic communication must be conducted, before

administrative information processes will only begin after legislation has been adopted to facilitate this digitalization. While an earlier start is possible, such would require a certain measure of risk assessment and management.[546]

2.3. PRESERVATION OF ELECTRONIC INFORMATION

184. The first issue discussed in the previous section concerned whether or not trustworthy electronic information could be established in the context of archival requirements. The question then becomes how this trustworthiness can be durably maintained. This matter, therefore, concerns not the creation of electronic information, but what happens with that information throughout its preservation.

185. As noted previously, electronic information relies on hardware and software platforms in order to be interpretable by humans. However, given the speed at which those platforms evolve, there is a clear risk that the precise combination of hardware and software on which a particular piece of electronic information relies might become unavailable. If certain hardware becomes unavailable[547], or if older software is not compatible with newer hardware[548], electronic information created using that combination of hard- and software can no longer be accessed. Measures must, therefore, be taken to ensure the durable accessibility of electronic information. As opposed to paper-based information "*preservation as applied to electronic records no longer refers to the protection of the medium of the records, but to that of their meaning and trustworthiness as records*".[549]

---

in a second stage including those procedures in existing legal provisions. Brussels Capital Region Parliament 2012–2013, *A-444/1*, 2. This ordinance is based on the provisions on electronic communications found in section 2.3 of the Dutch Act of 4 June 1992 on general administrative law, *Stb.* 1992, 315.

546 Dumortier, J. (2015) "Goede praktijken digitaal-vriendelijke regelgeving voor de Vlaamse overheid", presented at workshop digital-friendly regulation, Brussels, 26 January, 5.

547 For instance, it is becoming increasingly difficult to still find a functioning floppy disk drive. Even the more recent CD-ROM drive is becoming a rarity in modern computers. When a technology is phased out, and production of new hardware ceases, archives must rely on the availability of spare parts to access the electronic information created using that technology.

548 Given the changes in computer architectures, software written for older architectures may not run on newer platforms. An example is software for Mac OS X written for the IBM PowerPC architecture used by Apple before 2006, which is incompatible with the Intel x86 architecture used thereafter. Additionally, newer software versions may not be compatible with information created using older software versions. For instance, current Microsoft Word versions do not natively support Word documents created using pre-1997 versions of the same word processing software package.

549 Duranti, L. (2001) "The impact of digital technology on archival science", *Archival Science*, Vol. 1, 46.

186. While the preservation of a hard-copy could be suggested for purely text-based information[550] – thereby requiring the electronic information to be printed onto a paper carrier – it is clear that such would not be a feasible solution for all types of electronic information and it would only increase the burden of physical archives and forego the advantages of electronic archiving. The two most feasible strategies for the durable preservation of electronic information are emulation and migration.

187. The aim of emulation is to preserve the electronic information as 'purely' as possible. As electronic information is not intrinsically linked to a particular medium, it is possible to regularly move this information from one medium to another. In so doing, the devastating effects of the natural degradation of the medium – such as CD-ROMs – can be avoided and the information can always be accessible from the latest platforms and storage media, thus providing at least a partial solution to the potential hardware issues of digital obsolescence. The remaining problem here is then mostly software-related. As noted previously, software platforms may at a certain moment become outdated and will then no longer receive the updates required to keep the software running on newer platforms; this is a point in time when this software becomes legacy software. As it is practically unfeasible to preserve and to maintain legacy software and the hardware systems they require –because of the eventual lack of spare parts to maintain such systems for instance – emulation focuses on developing solutions to create an environment on new software platforms in which legacy software can run as if it were natively.[551] In essence, emulation is a good preservation strategy as it allows all electronic information to be preserved 'untouched'.[552] However, the development of emulation software is a difficult and expensive undertaking. In many cases, developers will need to reverse engineer the platform they are trying to emulate, adding to the overall difficulty of this solution.[553] Moreover, emulators may also become obsolete when the hardware platform for which they were developed is phased out. In such a scenario, a new emulator would have to be developed, further increasing the cost of the emulation strategy.

188. While emulation focuses on not changing the underlying file structure of the electronic information it preserves, migration focuses on doing just that. When migrating electronic information, the information is transferred to

---

550 Boudrez, F., Dekeyser, H., Dumortier, J. (2005) *Digital Archiving: the new challenge?*, Brussels: I.R.I.S. Group, 81–82.

551 InterPARES 2 (2008) "The InterPARES 2 Project Glossary", *interpares.org*, 20.

552 Some authors consider emulation to be the most desirable preservation strategy as it allows information to be looked at in the exact way it was intended to be seen. Rothenberg, J. (2000) *An experiment in Using Emulation to Preserve Digital Publications*, Amsterdam: Koninklijke Bibliotheek, 74p.

553 Boudrez, F., Dekeyser, H., Dumortier, J. (2005) *Digital Archiving: the new challenge?*, Brussels: I.R.I.S. Group, 83–84.

another file type that is considered more well-suited for durable preservation.[554] By focusing on the file format, migration assumes durable support for a format or standard and not for a particular software or hardware platform. As such, its feasibility can be considered higher than emulation, at a lower cost. However, there are also clear disadvantages to this strategy.[555] First, migration assumes the availability of a standard as well as the long-term maintenance of that standard. As the development of standards takes time, migration may thus become difficult to execute at short notice. It should also be noted that standards can also become obsolete when they are replaced by new standards. In such an event, re-migration will become inevitable. A second and more important disadvantage is that migration affects the bit structure of electronic information. While electronic information is not bound to a physical medium – and can thus be freely moved to a new storage medium in order to avoid the information becoming inaccessible due to the deterioration of the first medium – there are certain characteristics of electronic information that can be bound to a particular file type. For instance, electronic information created in particular word processor software may lose its layout – or parts thereof – when migrated to another format. Another matter of import here is the electronic signature, as will be explored in the following paragraphs.

189. Article 1322 of the Belgian Civil Code requires that an electronic signature attests to the identity of the person signing the information, and to the integrity of that information. While there are several ways in which this can be achieved from a technical viewpoint, it is clear that in practice most parties will rely on the digital signature technique, as required for the production of a qualified electronic signature. This technique allows for the detection of even the smallest bit-level change to the signed electronic information, as such a change would prevent the successful validation of the electronic signature.[556] Since migration introduces exactly such changes to the signed electronic information, the electronic signature is then at risk of becoming invalid. The resulting migrated electronic information would then, given the absence of a valid signature, lose its status as original under the Belgian general principles on evidence.[557]

---

[554] Ideally, this file type would be standardized and non-proprietary, in order to increase the chance of it being durably supported. An example is the PDF/A standard (ISO 19005), which is aimed at durable preservation.

[555] Rothenberg, for instance, is highly critical of reliance on standards and migration in general: Rothenberg, J. (1999) *Avoiding Technological Quicksand: Finding a Viable Technical Foundation for Digital Preservation*, Washington D.C.: Council on Library and Information Resources, 35p.

[556] Dekeyser, H., Dumortier, J. (2004) "Juridische obstakels voor de elektronische handel op het vlak van archivering en datering", *FPS Economy, SME, Self-employed and Energy*, 23–24.

[557] More on the originality issue can be found in the following section, 3.4.

190. Efforts have been made at ensuring the durable preservation of electronic signatures. One proposition is to preserve the validation chain.[558] This would include validating the electronic signature soon after signing, and subsequently preserving the electronic information – with electronic signature – as well as the certificate and the validation information. While preservation of the validation chain would allow an electronic signature to be validated long after signing, this still requires the electronic signature itself to remain valid. In other words, this solution does not solve the problem of migration, where changes in the file format would invalidate the electronic signature. While it has been proposed to re-sign the migrated information, this solution is unsatisfactory as it essentially entails creating newly signed electronic information since law does not provide for the re-signing of previously signed information.[559]

191. The only solution, at least for the time being, appears to preserve validly signed electronic information as is, together with the electronic signature's validation chain, in order to ensure the durable validity of the electronic signature. Here, a trusted third party, more precisely a trusted archival service, could be employed to ensure this durable preservation.[560] Although such trusted archival service has not been regulated at the European level – *e.g.* in the eIDAS Regulation – the Belgian federal legislator did adopt a limited framework for this in book XII of the Code of Economic Law.[561]

192. As is clear from the previous overview, no preservation strategy is perfect. In all cases, different advantages and disadvantages will need to be weighed against each other. While emulation offers the possibility to access electronic information as it was originally created, the development of suitable emulators – and their upkeep – is both costly and time-consuming. The focus of migration on the file format with which the electronic information is associated allows for a cheaper solution, although its reliance on standards and the unavoidable changes it makes to the bit structure of electronic information may diminish the feasibility or desirability of this strategy. One possible solution is to establish a middle ground strategy[562] in which the best elements of both options are used.

---

558 ETSI (2012) "Electronic Signatures and Infrastructures (ESI); CMS Advanced Electronic Signatures (CAdES)", *ETSI TS 101 733 V2.1.1*; Dekeyser, H., Dumortier, J. (2004) "Juridische obstakels voor de elektronische handel op het vlak van archivering en datering", *FPS Economy, SME, Self-employed and Energy*, 25; Boudrez, F. (2005) "Digitale handtekeningen en archiefdocumenten", *edavid.be*, 8–9.

559 Moreover, in the context of public administrations it must be borne in mind that the parties that originally signed the information may have already left the public service, thereby making them no longer competent to sign this information. Dekeyser, H., Dumortier, J. (2004) "Juridische obstakels voor de elektronische handel op het vlak van archivering en datering", *FPS Economy, SME, Self-employed and Energy*, 26.

560 *Ibid.*, 27.

561 Articles XII.27 – XII.29 Code of Economic Law.

562 Boudrez, F., Dekeyser, H., Dumortier, J. (2005) *Digital Archiving: the new challenge?*, Brussels: I.R.I.S. Group, 87–89.

When maintaining the electronic information as it was created alongside a migrated version, the durable preservation could be ensured through migration while at the same time keeping open other options – such as emulation – for which the untouched information is needed.[563] While from a probative point of view this would not lead to the most desirable result – which would of course be full and irrefutable proof – it must be remarked that at the present moment no perfect solution appears to exist to ensure the long-term preservation of signed electronic information. Moreover, when a judge must assess the value of evidence put forward, all elements regarding the creation of the information, its managements and its preservation can be taken into account in assessing its authenticity, integrity and overall trustworthiness.[564] In doing so, a well-considered archival strategy – while not irrefutable proof in itself – could still support the trustworthiness of electronic information.

2.4. SUBSTITUTION OF NON-ELECTRONIC INFORMATION

193. While the issues discussed in the previous sections are of concern to archivists too, it is especially this last matter that strikes at the core of archival science. If substitution were to be allowed – *i.e.* if the archivist could destroy a paper record after producing an electronic equivalent thereof – this could be understood as limiting the role of archivists to solely preserving the contents of the archival records under their custody, thereby not requiring the preservation of the physical attributes of the record, such as its age, material and wear and tear.[565] Important factors here are the originality and authenticity of the record.[566] If an electronic equivalent cannot display the same traits of originality and authenticity as its non-electronic counterpart, the latter can principally not be destroyed and substituted by the former.

194. Perhaps one of the most important traits of the archivist – for the purposes of this research – is that this person can be regarded as a trusted custodian, being a "*neutral third party who must demonstrate that it has no reason to alter or to allow others to alter the records in its care, and that it has the knowledge required for attesting to, and ensuring the continuing authenticity*

563 *Id*; Duranti, L. (2001) "The impact of digital technology on archival science", *Archival Science*, Vol. 1, 46.
564 Demoulin, M. (2012) "L'archivage électronique et le droit", in: Demoulin, M. (Ed.) *L'archivage électronique et le droit*, Brussels: Larcier, 33–34.
565 This is contrary to the belief that it is the duty of the archivist to preserve the record in its entirety, including the format in which it was presented to him. Thomassen, T. (2011) "A first introduction to archival science", *Archival Science*, Vol. 1, 373–385.
566 Boudrez, F., Drossens, P. (2010) "Substitutie: Magda?", *edavid.be*, 1–2.

of, the records".[567] With regard to electronic information, it should be remarked that the custodianship of the archivist has "*always been linked inextricably to the protection and safeguarding of evidence*" and that while electronic information may change the way in which archivists exercise physical ownership over their records, this is just a change in means by which the archivist exercises custodial responsibility and not a change in the substance of that task.[568] By ensuring the authenticity of the records under archival care, the archivist is of utmost importance in ensuring the enduring trustworthiness of archival records.

195. Apart from the concerns this topic may raise for archival scientists, the legal aspects of substitution have not proven to be an easy matter either. As can be gathered from the current state of the art in the general rules on evidence under Belgian law, electronic equivalents of a non-electronic record are still often viewed as being 'copies' – as opposed to 'originals' – and are thus accorded a lesser legal value. Therefore, a non-electronic record cannot always be substituted by an electronic surrogate, unless specific rules would allow such procedure. Under the general rules on evidence, article 1334 of the Belgian Civil Code initially held that when the original still exists, parties can always demand that this original be procured, rather than just its copies. When the original no longer exists – as would be the case if under substitution the original is destroyed and only copies remain – these copies will only have limited probative value, should a dispute arise.[569, 570] A deviation was only recently included to provide probative value to a digital copy, but only under certain conditions.[571]

196. The legal concerns on this matter originate from the same idea as the archival concerns mentioned earlier in this section, namely that the information carrier and the actual information have become so intertwined that they are often regarded as synonymous, and that the first information carrier is regarded as an essential component of an original.[572] However, as noted in section 3.2, it is clear

567 Duranti, L. (2009) "From Digital Diplomatics to Digital Records Forensics", *Archivaria*, Vol. 68, 41; Duranti, L. (ed.) (2002) "The Long-term Preservation of Authentic Electronic Records: Findings of the InterPARES Project – Authenticity Task Force Report", *interpares.org*, 21.

568 Macneil, H. (1994) "Archival Theory and Practice: Between Two Paradigms", *Archivaria*, Vol. 37, 16.

569 Of course, when a copy is presented as evidence and there is no dispute between parties on its correctness, it will simply be accepted as proof. However, it remains that parties can with any means of law dispute this copy. Demoulin, M., Soyez, S. (2013) "L'authenticité, de l'original papier à la copie numérique", in: Duranti, L., Schaffer, E. (Eds.) *The Memory of the World in the Digital Age: Digitization and Preservation*, Vancouver: UNESCO, 755–756.

570 Article 1335 Belgian Civil Code holds that regular copies can only be considered as beginning of evidence in writing. However, copies produced by notaries or at court's order can be accorded a higher probative value, even up to having the same probative value as their originals.

571 Article 1334, second paragraph Belgian Civil Code.

572 Gobert, D., Montero, E. (2001) "L'ouverture de la preuve littérale aux écrits sous forme électronique", *J.T.*, 127.

that the general principles on evidence in Belgian law determine that it is the signature that makes an original, and not necessarily the first carrier.[573] Therefore, duly signed electronic information can maintain its originality even as it moves freely between different information carriers.[574] As a result, substitution should be possible if preservation of only the information itself is required, if the signature can be validly carried over and if specific rules do not stipulate otherwise. However, there are also cases where the preservation of the information carrier can be required, for instance when law prescribes the use of a particular form.[575] In such cases, the paper-based process can be considered as a constitutive element of valid administrative decision-making, and must therefore be respected.

197. It becomes clear that the signature itself presents a particular issue to substitution. If non-electronic information is signed, then the contents of that information could fairly easily and reliably be transposed to electronic information. However, case law is clear that the digitalization of the signature itself no longer satisfies the requirements of a handwritten signature, nor does it satisfy the requirements of the electronic signature as found in article 1322 of the Belgian Civil Code.[576] This could pose a problem in the context of administrative procedures, where certain actions require the valid signature of the competent civil servant. If this signature cannot be validly digitalized, then the resulting information cannot be considered to have been duly signed. The result would be a copy of limited probative value, and substitution would then not be recommendable.

198. What can be gathered from this is that the original-copy dichotomy in the general rules on evidence in Belgian law pose a threat to substitution. It must, therefore, be ensured that the digitalized versions of information can be considered as originals, if the probative value of that information is to be preserved. Moreover, requirements regarding the information carrier could provide a further barrier to substitution. These preliminary findings lead to three cases:

(1) The information carrier is relevant. This is the case where law prescribes the use of a particular information carrier.[577] Here, what the purpose of

---

573 Demoulin, M., Soyez, S. (2013) "L'authenticité, de l'original papier à la copie numérique", in: Duranti, L., Schaffer, E. (Eds.) *The Memory of the World in the Digital Age: Digitization and Preservation*, Vancouver: UNESCO, 749.

574 *Ibid.*, 747–748.

575 Dumortier, J. (2015) "Naar een Vlaams beleid inzake substitutie?", *vlaanderen.be*, 2.

576 Council of State, nr. 193.106, 8 May 2009. In this case, the Council of State found that a scan of a handwritten signature does not correspond to either a handwritten or an electronic signature, and therefore did not constitute a valid signature.

577 Important to note is that in this sense, the information carrier can be considered to be an essential part of the original. There are even instances of documents in law designated as original, but which are not necessarily signed. Demoulin, M., Soyez, S. (2013) "L'authenticité,

this carrier is, and whether this purpose could be transposed to electronic processes, must be assessed.[578] For instance, sometimes the carrier is meant to provide certain guarantees regarding the authenticity and integrity of electronic information. While simple transposition of only the information to electronic information would result in the loss of those guarantees, electronic information processes can also provide alternative guarantees on authenticity and integrity. In other cases, however, the paper-based process is integral to valid administrative decision-making and cannot be replaced by an electronic process.

(2) The information carrier is irrelevant, and the information is not signed. In this case, information can be transposed to an electronic information carrier. Here, substitution should in principle be possible, unless there are indications to the contrary.

(3) The information carrier is irrelevant, and the information is signed. As noted above, simple transposition of the signature to electronic information does not result in a valid signature or electronic signature. Thus, additional measures must be taken to ensure that the electronic information is validly signed and can thus constitute an original. Only in the exception provided by article 1334, second paragraph of the Belgian Civil Code would substitution be possible.

199. Given the numerous variables in these scenarios that could result in legal uncertainty, it is not possible to provide a definitive answer on the legality of substitution, at least not in the absence of a more elaborate legal framework. While under the current state of the art no such general legal framework on substitution exists, the legislator has decided to specifically allow substitution in a number of cases. In these cases, it is specified that the transposed electronic information can have the same probative value as their non-electronic counterparts.[579] Sometimes specific requirements are included with which the digitalized information must comply.[580] These provisions are, however, very limited in their scope of application, which is mostly confined to use within a particular administrative entity or process.[581] The more broad provision of article 1334, second paragraph of the Belgian Civil Code has an important

de l'original papier à la copie numérique", in: Duranti, L., Schaffer, E. (Eds.) *The Memory of the World in the Digital Age: Digitization and Preservation*, Vancouver: UNESCO, 749.

578 Boudrez, F., Drossens, P. (2010) "Substitutie: Magda?", *edavid.be*, 3.

579 Examples include the Act of 2 May 1956 concerning the postal cheque, *Belgian State Gazette* 13 June 1956; the Act of 4 December 1990 concerning financial transactions and financial markets, *Belgian State Gazette* 22 December 1990; the Act of 21 August 2008 concerning the foundation and organization of the eHealth platform and other provisions, *Belgian State Gazette* 13 October 2008.

580 As is the case for article 36/1 of the Act of 21 August 2008.

581 However, it has been argued that if the intention of the legislator was to truly solve the preservation problem of these administrations, the probative value of the digitalized

limitation, in that it requires the use of a qualified archival service. With regard to the digitalization of invoices, the Belgian federal tax administration has drafted a circular letter detailing how substitution can be performed in this field.[582] In short, invoices can either be preserved on paper, or electronically. When a paper invoice is digitalized, it must either be scanned and signed using an advanced electronic signature, or scanned and sealed by algorithm. Additionally, electronically created invoices can be preserved by writing them to WORM-media. This circular letter, however, cannot be considered as instituting a general method of substitution.

200. For the administrative entities falling under the scope of Belgian federal archival law, attention must also be paid to the fact that this legal framework does not foresee substitution. As a result, the destruction of non-electronic archival information following the transposition of this information to electronic information processes is subject to the agreement of the state archivist or those mandated thereto.[583] It may then be questioned whether the provisions instituting probative value for electronic equivalents of information in particular cases, as discussed in the previous paragraph, can be considered as derogating from the general principles of archival law.[584] If such would not be the case, then those provisions must be interpreted as only allowing the creation of electronic equivalents with probative value alongside their non-electronic counterparts, and not as allowing the subsequent destruction of those non-electronic originals. The Belgian State Archives make a distinction between archival information marked for permanent preservation and information marked for destruction after its preservation term has lapsed. Only the latter information can become the subject of substitution, under permission of the state archivist.[585] A very different approach can be found in the Netherlands, where the administrations creating the information themselves can decide on the substitution thereof.[586] Guidelines are provided to assist administrations in this process.[587]

201. In conclusion, it can be held that substitution remains a thorny issue from the perspectives of both archival science and law. While the Belgian legislator

---

information should extend beyond its administration of origin. Dumortier, J. (2015) "Naar een Vlaams beleid inzake substitutie?", *vlaanderen.be*, 5.

582 Circular letter of 13 May 2008, nr. AOIF 16/2008 (E.T.112.081).

583 Article 5 Belgian Archival Act.

584 Demoulin, M., Soyez, S. (2012) "L'archivage électronique dans le secteur public", in: Demoulin, M. (Ed.) *L'archivage électronique et le droit*, Brussels: Larcier, 46–47.

585 Depoortere, R. (2010) "Substitutie in België, magda?", presented at VVBAD studiedag Substitutie: Magda?, Brussels, 1 April, 5.

586 Article 7 Dutch Archival Act of 28 April 1995, *Stb.* 1995, 276.

587 Article 26b Archival Regulation of 15 December 2009, *Stcrt.* 2010, 70; Archief 2020 (2014) "Handreiking vervanging archiefbescheiden", *archief2020.nl;* Dumortier, J. (2015) "Naar een Vlaams beleid inzake substitutie?", *vlaanderen.be*, 15–17.

has intervened to allow substitution in a number of particular cases, there is no general legal framework on substitution as yet – barring the broader provision of article 1334, second paragraph Belgian Civil Code. The result is that substitution remains an exercise of risk management for the administrative entities that wish to engage in this form of digitalization. First, it must be assessed whether paper-based information does not constitute an existential condition for valid administrative decision-making. Second, where such is not the case, the old original-copy dichotomy of the general rules on evidence remains in place, which means that validly signed non-electronic information must be transposed into validly signed electronic information. Where such is not possible and no specific provision on substitution is foreseen, the resulting electronic information will be regarded as a copy, and thus be accorded lower probative value. While in practice this does not appear to have resulted in major issues to date, the risk that it will one day, of course, remains. It is therefore up to Belgian legislators – at federal and state level – to provide a clear legal framework on this matter.

3. CONCLUSION

202. From what has been described here, it follows that there is a clear link between the activities of governmental entities and administrations on the one hand and those of archives on the other. Public sector actors are bound to preserve information within the exercise of their functions, mainly for the purposes of government accountability and transparency. The result is the inclusion of information preservation requirements under archival law, which can be considered to be part of administrative law. Although administrative law itself is a fairly recent branch of law, the link between archives and public sector entities goes back to Antiquity, and even lies at the origins of archives.

203. Within these archives, there is a clear preference to preserve original information. Originality is here to be understood as referring to the first form of information, from which other versions – copies – are derived. While this notion of originality does not directly correspond to the originality requirement found in Belgian civil law – where there can be more than one original and where the signature is the hallmark of originality – both originality requirements do at least serve the same purpose to some extent. Civil law's preference for written and signed information stems from the desire to ensure the reliability of evidence, and to provide all parties with the same probative means.[588] Similarly, it was found here that the reliance of diplomatics and archival science on original information is meant to ensure that information's integrity and authenticity,

[588] Aubry, C., Rau, C.F., Bartin, E. (1922) *Cours de droit civil français*, Tome XII, Paris: Marchal et Billard, 188–189.

which in turn serves to support the trustworthiness of that information as evidence. The purpose of the formalities that define the originality notion in Belgian civil law is, therefore, the same under the rules on evidence as it is to archival law: they protect information against fraud and forgeries, in order to ensure the reliability of that information for later (probative) use.

204. The digitalization of society and information processes has of course also had an impact on the functioning of archives. For the purposes of this research, three distinct issues were identified where this impact is most notable: (1) whether information processes designed for non-electronic information can be replaced with electronic information processes; (2) whether such electronically created information can durably be preserved; and (3) whether electronic information can substitute non-electronic information, whereby the non-electronic information is destroyed after the creation of its electronic equivalent.

205. In principle, information processes could be conducted electronically, given that law since long recognizes electronic signatures and that electronic information can satisfy the requirement of a writing. Duly signed electronic information can, thus, be accorded the same probative value as a signed written act. However, there are quite a few cases in law where specific formalities are imposed, which means that the issues of whether and how electronic information processes can satisfy the purposes of those formalities must be assessed on a case-by-case basis. In the absence of any clear provisions on the admissibility of electronic information processes in a particular case, this is mainly a risk management exercise.

206. Once electronic information has been validly created, its preservation poses the next issue. As electronic information relies on a particular combination of computer hard- and software in order to be understandable, measures must be taken to ensure that this information does not become inaccessible due to digital obsolescence. The two most well-known initiatives undertaken by archives both have their particular drawbacks. Emulation preserves the electronic information as is, but relies on software that is both costly and time-consuming to develop. Migration is a more manageable strategy, but its inherent changes at the bit-level of the electronic information and risks invalidating the electronic signature. If the electronic signature becomes invalid, the probative value of that electronic information will be lowered significantly. However, even without changes at the bit-level, the certificates used in creating the electronic signature may expire, thus again impeding later validation of the electronic signature. Preserving the complete validation chain, as part of a comprehensive preservation strategy, can be proposed.

207. While the first issue concerned so-called *digital born* electronic information, the last issue focuses on substitution, being the replacement of non-electronic information by their electronic counterparts. Here, reference must be made to the originality requirement under Belgian civil law, as electronic equivalents risk being considered as copies of lesser probative value if they cannot be regarded as originals. Substitution of signed information is, therefore, only recommendable if a valid electronic signature can be produced, or where the legislator has foreseen specific provisions regulating the probative value of electronic equivalents. Additionally, specific formalities regarding the information carrier may prevent substitution. Moreover, public sector entities are subjected to the Belgian Archival Act, which holds that the state archivist must agree with the destruction of information, thus requiring the involvement of this person in the substitution process. As under the previous issues, the decision on whether to implement substitution is, in the absence of a clear legal framework on this matter, largely a risk management exercise.

208. From this, it becomes clear that the digitalization process has impacted the originality requirement under Belgian administrative law in two main ways. First, there is the introduction of *digital born* electronic information processes, which requires the acceptance of electronic originals. As the rules on evidence of Belgian civil law can also apply here, the groundwork for such acceptance has already been laid. However, specific formalities may still prevent the creation of an electronic original. Moreover, the durable preservation of electronic signatures remains a difficult matter, and still encompasses the risk of the duly signed electronic information losing its originality should the electronic signature lose its validity over time. Second, there is the substitution of non-electronic information by its electronic counterparts. Here, the original – copy dichotomy is still very much present, resulting in a risk for the electronic substitutes to be accorded the lower probative value of a copy.

209. Despite these challenges to the originality notion posed by digitalization processes, the legislator has only infrequently intervened, mainly by adopting provisions allowing the use of electronic information processes and – somewhat rarer – by providing for probative value for electronic substitutes. While the theoretical risk concerning lack or loss of originality of electronic information is clear, it must be said that no major practical issues have risen thus far. The question is then whether it is wise to rely on such an outcome where probative matters are at stake. It is clear that the legislator, in strictly regulating the civil law rules on evidence and in imposing formalities, has wanted to ensure that all parties to an agreement can obtain trustworthy evidence of high probative value. However, in regulating some aspects of the digitalization process – namely by accepting the electronic signature and electronic information as writing, while foregoing comprehensively regulating other aspects of this same process – such as durable preservation and substitution – it is also clear that these parties are now at risk of being confronted with evidence of a possibly lower probative value. And as becomes clear from the research conducted here, this is not just a matter for civil parties but has consequences for the preservation requirements imposed on public sector entities as well.

CHAPTER V
ORIGINALITY IN FISCAL LAW

1. ORIGINALITY IN FISCAL LAW

1.1. THE INVOICE

210. In this chapter, we focus on one of the most important documents within commercial transactions, namely the invoice.[589] Even though many legislative texts refer to the figure of the invoice, the notion is not clearly defined by law.[590] Nevertheless, literature and case law uncover two important functions of the invoice. On the one hand, the invoice serves as a confirmation of delivery, listing the nature, amount and price of what has been delivered.[591] On the other hand, the invoice confirms a claim of debt: after goods or services have been delivered, they need to be paid for.[592] However, while these two functions can be distinguished from one another, they are of course intrinsically connected.[593]

211. While the invoice is in the first place a commercial document - with particular rules surrounding its use by merchants - it can be issued by any legal or natural person.[594] It is an integral part of a firm's accounting, serving as proof of a transaction.[595] It provides information to the recipient with regard

---

589 Gobert, D. (2003) "La Directive du 20 Décembre 2001: Vers une discrimination de traitement entre la facture papier et la facture électronique?", in: Montero, E., Demoulin, M., Gobert, D. (Eds.) *Commerce électronique: de la théorie à la pratique, Cahiers du CRID, n° 23*, Brussels: Bruylant, 7.

590 Ballon, G. (2008) "Inleiding", in: Ballon, G., Samoy, I., Byl, T., Deschoolmeester, F., Dumortier, J., Goethals, T., Govers, M., Swaenepoel, E. (Eds) *De factuur en verwante documenten*, Brugge: Vanden Broele, 9; Gobert, D. (2001) "Vers une discrimination de traitement entre la facture papier et la facture électronique?", *Cahier du Juriste*, nr. 4–5/2001, 45.

591 *Ibid.*, 9–10.

592 *Ibid.*, 10–11.

593 Cloquet, A. (1954) *Factuur*, Brussels: Larcier; Ballon, G. (2008) "Inleiding", in: Ballon, G., Samoy, I., Byl, T., Deschoolmeester, F., Dumortier, J., Goethals, T., Govers, M., Swaenepoel, E. (Eds) *De factuur en verwante documenten*, Brugge: Vanden Broele, 11.

594 Ballon, G. (2008) "Inleiding", in: Ballon, G., Samoy, I., Byl, T., Deschoolmeester, F., Dumortier, J., Goethals, T., Govers, M., Swaenepoel, E. (Eds) *De factuur en verwante documenten*, Brugge: Vanden Broele, 12.

595 Amand, C. (2008) "De gemiste besparingen van de elektronische facturatie in Europa", *Tijdschrift voor Fiscaal Recht*, nr. 343, 573.

to the underlying debt claim. This is particularly important in transactions in which the buyer is a consumer, as consumer law imposes specific information requirements. It also provides important fiscal information, more particularly with regard to the value added tax (VAT). Because of this, the use of invoices has been made mandatory under fiscal law at both the national and European level.[596]

212. While the invoice is, for instance, also an important document in direct taxes, the originality question there is more related to the originality of signatures, within the framework of procedural matters for instance. One example of this concerns the petition against tax assessments, which must be submitted with an original signature.[597] If this petition is submitted by e-mail, without an original signature, then it cannot be accepted as valid, unless the originally signed document is submitted as well.[598]

213. The position of the invoice as a document providing information to the recipient and providing proof of the transaction for the issuer means that at least two copies of the invoice are needed.[599] The invoice must be issued at the latest on the 15th day of the month following that in which the taxable event took place.[600] A late invoice could have certain fiscal consequences, but will generally still be accepted as valid – and thus as payable – at least within a reasonable term.[601]

214. Invoices do not need to be signed in order to be valid. The issuer's signature on the invoice will generally be considered – barring proof to the contrary – as a presumption that payment has been fulfilled.[602] The recipient's signature on the invoice will likewise be considered as a presumption of acceptance of the invoice.[603]

---

596 E.g. for Belgian law, see Article 53 Belgian Act introducing the VAT Code, *Belgian State Gazette* 17 July 1969 (hereinafter: Belgian VAT Code). For European law, see articles 220–225 Council Directive 2006/112/EC of 28 November 2006 on the common system of value added tax, *OJ* L 347 of 11 December 2006, 1–118 (hereinafter: VAT Directive).

597 Article 371 Belgian Code of Income Tax 1992, *Belgian State Gazette* 30 July 1992.

598 Rb. Antwerpen, 5 June 2015, nr. 14/1851/A.

599 Ballon, G. (2008) "Inleiding", in: Ballon, G., Samoy, I., Byl, T., Deschoolmeester, F., Dumortier, J., Goethals, T., Govers, M., Swaenepoel, E. (Eds) *De factuur en verwante documenten*, Brugge: Vanden Broele, 17–18.

600 Article 4 Royal Decree nr. 1 of 29 December 1992 regarding the regulation for the fulfillment of the value added tax, *Belgian State Gazette* 31 December 1992.

601 Ballon, G. (2008) "Inleiding", in: Ballon, G., Samoy, I., Byl, T., Deschoolmeester, F., Dumortier, J., Goethals, T., Govers, M., Swaenepoel, E. (Eds) *De factuur en verwante documenten*, Brugge: Vanden Broele, 18–19.

602 *Ibid.*, 20.

603 *Id.*

215. Invoices can be subjected to a number of formal requirements. For instance, in Belgian VAT law it is – amongst others – required for an invoice to state the date of creation; its sequential number; the name, address and VAT identification number of the issuer; the date on which the taxable event took place; the information necessary to determine the taxable event and the applicable tariff; the price per unit; the amount delivered; the total amount of the payment due; etc.[604] While it is not mandatory, generally speaking, for an invoice to explicitly state its nature as an invoice, it is common practice to do so.[605]

1.2. PROBATIVE VALUE OF THE INVOICE

216. The invoice is in the first place a confirmation of the underlying agreement, and particularly of the debt claim following from that agreement. It therefore cannot be considered as establishing an agreement on its own.[606] When an invoice is accepted, it can at most provide proof of the underlying agreement.[607]

217. Against the issuer of the invoice, this document can provide proof of the obligations of that party following from the agreement – insofar as they can be derived from the invoice.[608] In that sense, the invoice can be considered as a written extrajudicial confession by the issuer.[609] As noted previously, an invoice does not need to be signed. The issuer's signature on the invoice will – barring proof to the contrary – be considered as an indication that the underlying debt claim has been fulfilled, as will other notes on the invoice such as "paid" or "fulfilled". The recipient can use the probative rules of commercial law against the merchant-issuer of the invoice, even if he is not a merchant himself.

218. Against the recipient of the invoice, the underlying agreement can be proven by the invoice if the recipient is a merchant.[610] Here, it is presumed that

604 Article 5 Royal Decree nr. 1 of 29 December 1992 regarding the regulation for the fulfillment of the value added tax, *Belgian State Gazette* 31 December 1992.

605 Ballon, G. (2008) "Inleiding", in: Ballon, G., Samoy, I., Byl, T., Deschoolmeester, F., Dumortier, J., Goethals, T., Govers, M., Swaenepoel, E. (Eds) *De factuur en verwante documenten*, Brugge: Vanden Broele, 23–24.

606 Deschoolmeester, F. (2008) "De factuur in het bewijsrecht", in: Ballon, G., Samoy, I., Byl, T., Deschoolmeester, F., Dumortier, J., Goethals, T., Govers, M., Swaenepoel, E. (Eds) *De factuur en verwante documenten*, Brugge: Vanden Broele, 45.

607 *Id.*

608 Deschoolmeester, F. (2008) "De factuur in het bewijsrecht", in: Ballon, G., Samoy, I., Byl, T., Deschoolmeester, F., Dumortier, J., Goethals, T., Govers, M., Swaenepoel, E. (Eds) *De factuur en verwante documenten*, Brugge: Vanden Broele, 48.

609 *Id.*

610 Article 25, 2° Belgian Code of Commercial Law.

the invoice provides a trustworthy record of that agreement, barring proof to the contrary.[611] Together with accounting books, the invoice therefore forms non-absolute proof in commercial transactions.[612] The merchant-recipient can still protest the invoice, given that – as noted in chapter III – presumptions only have a fairly limited probative value in civil law. When the recipient is not a merchant, protesting the invoice is not necessary in principle. The more unregulated means of evidence of commercial law are not applicable against a non-merchant.[613] This means that the rules of evidence of civil law come into play in this instance. As noted in chapter III, this will – amongst others – require written evidence for transactions exceeding EUR 375.[614] Presumptions, as created by the invoice, can only be used to prove transactions of lower amounts. Accounting books cannot be used as evidence against a non-merchant.[615]

1.3. PRESERVATION OF INVOICES

219. All invoices or copies thereof must be preserved.[616] A taxable person must preserve copies of the invoices issued by himself and everyone must preserve incoming invoices.[617] The duration of preservation can be determined by the Member States.[618] In Belgium, this is currently seven years – starting 1 January of the year following their issuance – down from ten years before 2006.[619] However, for non-VAT obliged persons – such as regular consumers – it is accepted that they should only preserve the invoices they receive for five years.[620]

220. When preserving invoices, it is important that the legibility of the invoices, the authenticity of their origin, and the integrity of their content is

611 Deschoolmeester, F. (2008) "De factuur in het bewijsrecht", in: Ballon, G., Samoy, I., Byl, T., Deschoolmeester, F., Dumortier, J., Goethals, T., Govers, M., Swaenepoel, E. (Eds) *De factuur en verwante documenten*, Brugge: Vanden Broele, 50.

612 For accounting books, see article 20 Belgian Code of Commercial Law.

613 Deschoolmeester, F. (2008) "De factuur in het bewijsrecht", in: Ballon, G., Samoy, I., Byl, T., Deschoolmeester, F., Dumortier, J., Goethals, T., Govers, M., Swaenepoel, E. (Eds) *De factuur en verwante documenten*, Brugge: Vanden Broele, 53.

614 See article 1341 Belgian Civil Code.

615 Article 1329 Belgian Civil Code.

616 Article 244 VAT Directive.

617 Article 60, §1 Belgian VAT Code.

618 Article 247 VAT Directive.

619 Article 60, §3 Belgian VAT Code; Govers, M. (2008) "De factuur en verwante documenten in het fiscaal recht", in: Ballon, G., Samoy, I., Byl, T., Deschoolmeester, F., Dumortier, J., Goethals, T., Govers, M., Swaenepoel, E. (Eds) *De factuur en verwante documenten*, Brugge: Vanden Broele, 311.

620 Govers, M. (2008) "De factuur en verwante documenten in het fiscaal recht", in: Ballon, G., Samoy, I., Byl, T., Deschoolmeester, F., Dumortier, J., Goethals, T., Govers, M., Swaenepoel, E. (Eds) *De factuur en verwante documenten*, Brugge: Vanden Broele, 312.

guaranteed throughout the preservation period.[621] Accounting books, original invoices, and copies thereof must be made available to tax administrations when needed.[622]

221. From this, it appears that there is no direct obligation to preserve only the original invoice. However, the Court of Justice of the European Union stated in this regard that EU VAT law allows "*the Member States to regard as an invoice not only the original but also any other document serving as an invoice that fulfils the criteria determined by the Member States themselves, and confer on them the power to require production of the original invoice in order to establish the right to deduct input tax, as well as the power, where a taxable person no longer holds the original, to admit other evidence that the transaction in respect of which the deduction is claimed actually took place*".[623] Furthermore, the Court found that Member States can allow taxable persons to prove their entitlement to a tax refund "*by submitting a duplicate invoice or import document where the original has been lost for reasons beyond his control, provided that the transaction which led to the application for a refund occurred and there is no risk of further applications for a refund*".[624] This would indicate that – as in civil law – there is a clear preference for the original, which can be demanded at all times. Copies then only have probative value where the original is no longer available.

2. DIGITALIZATION IN FISCAL LAW

2.1. ELECTRONIC INVOICES

222. A direct result of the informatization of society is that invoices are only very rarely still drafted by hand. Most invoices will be created electronically, on a computer and will subsequently be printed. From a legal point of view, it makes little difference whether an invoice is drafted by hand or electronically if the transmission is conducted by paper. A more important matter is the electronic transmission and preservation of invoices.[625] In such case, an invoice is created electronically, transmitted to the recipient electronically and preserved electronically for accounting and fiscal purposes. Such fully electronic invoicing process could eliminate most of the manual procedures that are involved in

621 Article 246 VAT Directive; article 60, §5 Belgian VAT Code.
622 Article 61 Belgian VAT Code.
623 CJEU, John Reisdorf *v.* Finanzamt Köln-West, C-85/95, paragraph 31.
624 CJEU, Société générale des grandes sources d'eaux minérales françaises *v.* Bundesamt für Finanzen, C-361/96, paragraph 31.
625 Dumortier, J. (2008) "Elektronische facturen", in: Ballon, G., Samoy, I., Byl, T., Deschoolmeester, F., Dumortier, J., Goethals, T., Govers, M., Swaenepoel, E. (Eds) *De factuur en verwante documenten*, Brugge: Vanden Broele, 411.

issuing, sending and preserving paper-based invoices, and can be considered as both a substantially cost-reducing and an environmentally friendly effort.[626]

223. Such electronically created and preserved invoices have two important consequences.[627] First, electronic data can easily be manipulated, unless it is preserved in an unalterable file format. Second, electronic data requires computer hard- and software in order to be legible. Moreover, as electronic data is not tied to a particular carrier – in the way information on a paper document is – the distinction between originals and copies becomes irrelevant.[628] Given these issues, it is important to assess whether an invoice can indeed be created and transmitted electronically, and whether it can be preserved electronically.

2.2. LEGAL FRAMEWORK ON ELECTRONIC INVOICES

224. At the European level, the legislator already adopted a directive that allowed for electronic invoicing in 2001.[629] Concretely, this directive added to the EU's VAT framework that invoices can be issued by electronic means under two conditions: (1) the recipient must accept to do so; and (2) "*provided that the authenticity of the origin and integrity of the contents are guaranteed*".[630] The directive recognized two means to do so: (1) the use of an advanced electronic signature – although Member States may require the use of a qualified electronic signature – and (2) the use of Electronic Data Interchange (EDI).[631] Oddly, these are two very different technologies. While the advanced electronic signature clearly serves a security purpose in this context – as opposed to its natural function of creating legally valid signatures – EDI is only a technology for

626 Gobert, D. (2001) " Vers une discrimination de traitement entre la facture papier et la facture électronique?", *Cahier du Juriste*, nr. 4–5/2001, 45; De Bruyn, J., Van Eecke, P. (2011) "Afdeling 3 – Elektronische facturatie", in: Van Eecke, P. (Ed.) *Recht en elektronische handel*, Gent: Larcier, 227–228; Amand, C. (2008) "De gemiste besparingen van de elektronische facturatie in Europa", *Tijdschrift voor Fiscaal Recht*, nr. 343, 573; PricewaterhouseCoopers (2005) "e-Invoicing and e-Archiving taking the next step", *pwc.com*, 12–14.

627 Dumortier, J. (2008) "Elektronische facturen", in: Ballon, G., Samoy, I., Byl, T., Deschoolmeester, F., Dumortier, J., Goethals, T., Govers, M., Swaenepoel, E. (Eds) *De factuur en verwante documenten*, Brugge: Vanden Broele, 412.

628 *Ibid.*, 413.

629 Council Directive 2001/115/EC of 20 December 2001 amending Directive 77/388/EEC with a view to simplifying, modernising and harmonising the conditions laid down for invoicing in respect of value added tax, *OJ* L 15 of 17 January 2002, 24–28.

630 Article 2 Directive 2001/115/EC; Nordén, A. (2006) "Electronic Invoicing in the Light of European Community Directive 2001/115/EC", in: Schulz, A. (Ed.) *Legal Aspects of an E-Commerce Transaction*, Munich: Sellier, 211.

631 EDI is a means for machine-to-machine communication. In the context of invoices, it allows one company's accounting software to send the data for an electronic invoice directly to the accounting software of another company, without human interference. EDI itself, however, is an umbrella term for this process, and not a standard on its own. In fact, several EDI standards have been adopted throughout the years.

electronic business-to-business communication and does not provide inherent security guarantees.[632] With regard to preservation, the directive held that the "*authenticity of the origin and integrity of the content of the invoices, as well as their readability, must be guaranteed throughout the storage period*".[633] To ensure this, Member States "*may require that invoices be stored in the original form in which they were sent, whether paper or electronic*". Data guaranteeing the authenticity of the origin and integrity of the content could also be required to be stored. The directive was to be transposed by the Member States by 2004, thus officially inaugurating the electronic invoice in the EU.[634] In Belgium this was achieved on 28 January 2004.[635]

225. It should, however, be noted that before the directive there was already some evolution toward electronic invoicing within the Member States, albeit in very divergent ways.[636] Most Member States – except for Greece –already accepted the notion of electronic invoicing.[637] Germany, however, required a paper document to be transmitted alongside the electronic data. In several other Member States, such as Belgium, prior permission from the tax authorities was required in order to issue and to receive electronic invoices.[638] This was to be made possible in 1993 by the then article 53*octies*, §1 of the Belgian VAT Code. However, that article required a Royal Decree, which was never adopted, thereby meaning that this provision never entered into practice. The Belgian VAT administration then instated a system of temporary licenses to issue electronic invoices.[639] These licenses were either individual – for individual issuers of electronic invoices – or general – to providers of electronic invoicing services.[640]

---

632 Nordén, A. (2006) "Electronic Invoicing in the Light of European Community Directive 2001/115/EC", in: Schulz, A. (Ed.) *Legal Aspects of an E-Commerce Transaction*, Munich: Sellier, 214–215.

633 Article 2 Directive 2001/115/EC.

634 Article 5 Directive 2001/115/EC.

635 Act of 28 January 2004 amending the VAT Code, *Belgian State Gazette* 10 February 2004. Together with the Royal Decree of 16 February 2004 amending Royal Decree nr. 1 of 29 December 1992 regarding the regulation for the fulfillment of the value added tax, *Belgian State Gazette* 27 February 2004.

636 PriceWaterhouseCoopers (1999) "Study on the requirements imposed by the Member States, for the purpose of charging taxes, for invoices produced by electronic or other means – final report 23 August 1999", *ec.europa.eu*, 61–65.

637 Gobert, D. (2001) " Vers une discrimination de traitement entre la facture papier et la facture électronique?", *Cahier du Juriste*, nr. 4–5/2001, 46; Nordén, A. (2006) "Electronic Invoicing in the Light of European Community Directive 2001/115/EC", in: Schulz, A. (Ed.) *Legal Aspects of an E-Commerce Transaction*, Munich: Sellier, 211.

638 Massin, I., Vanderstichelen, B. (2002) "Nieuwe algemene vergunning inzake elektronische facturatie", *Fiscoloog*, nr. 848, 3–5.

639 Amand, C. (2008) "De gemiste besparingen van de elektronische facturatie in Europa", *Tijdschrift voor Fiscaal Recht*, nr. 343, 574.

640 Dumortier, J. (2008) "Elektronische facturen", in: Ballon, G., Samoy, I., Byl, T., Deschoolmeester, F., Dumortier, J., Goethals, T., Govers, M., Swaenepoel, E. (Eds) *De factuur en verwante documenten*, Brugge: Vanden Broele, 419–420.

The 2001 directive can therefore be considered as a necessary step to harmonize the European practice on electronic invoicing, in order to make cross-border electronic invoicing within the EU a possibility.

226. In 2006, the previous EU VAT framework – to which the 2001 directive made amendments – was repealed and replaced by a new VAT Directive.[641] This directive maintains the provisions on the electronic invoice, holding that "*Member States shall accept documents or messages on paper or in electronic form as invoices if they meet the conditions laid down*" therein.[642] It maintains that invoices can be transmitted electronically, if the recipient agrees thereto.[643] The authenticity of the origin of the electronic invoice and the integrity of its content can also still be guaranteed through an advanced electronic signature – unless a Member State requires the use of a qualified electronic signature – or through EDI.[644] Furthermore, "*Member States may not impose on taxable persons supplying goods or services in their territory any other obligations or formalities relating to the sending or making available of invoices by electronic means*".[645] Still, the "*authenticity of the origin and the integrity of the content of the invoices stored, as well as their legibility, must be guaranteed throughout the storage period*"[646], for which Member States "*may require that invoices be stored in the original form in which they were sent or made available, whether paper or electronic*", including "*the data guaranteeing the authenticity of the origin of the invoices and the integrity of their content*".[647] Another interesting element is that for batches of several invoices, "*the details common to the individual invoices may be mentioned only once if, for each invoice, all the information is accessible*".[648] In an ongoing business relationship, this would allow certain information, such as general terms, to be sent once – for instance at the beginning of that relation. Later electronic invoices would then only need to convey information directly related to that particular invoice, and no longer provide other information.[649]

227. As it concerns a directive, these provisions were to be implemented by the Member States in their national legal frameworks.[650] Later on, in 2009, the

---

641 Article 411 VAT Directive.
642 Article 218 VAT Directive.
643 Article 232 VAT Directive.
644 Article 233 VAT Directive.
645 Article 234 VAT Directive.
646 Article 246 VAT Directive.
647 Article 247 VAT Directive.
648 Article 236 VAT Directive.
649 Dumortier, J. (2008) "Elektronische facturen", in: Ballon, G., Samoy, I., Byl, T., Deschoolmeester, F., Dumortier, J., Goethals, T., Govers, M., Swaenepoel, E. (Eds) *De factuur en verwante documenten*, Brugge: Vanden Broele, 432.
650 For Belgium, this was in the Belgian VAT Code and Royal Decree nr. 1 of 29 December 1992 regarding the regulation for the fulfillment of the value added tax, *Belgian State Gazette* 31 December 1992.

Belgian legislator removed the explicit reference to the electronic signature and EDI for electronic invoice transmission in an attempt to simplify electronic invoicing.[651] The provisions regarding the preservation of electronic invoices, however, remained in place.[652] The European legislator followed a similar path in 2010 by adopting a new directive that relaxed the rules regarding the electronic invoice.[653] While this new directive, for instance, still refers to the electronic signature and EDI, these are now just considered as "*examples of technologies that ensure the authenticity of the origin and the integrity of the content of an electronic invoice*", instead of the only available options.[654] Acceptance of the electronic invoice by the recipient is still a prerequisite. This directive necessitated another change in the Belgian legislation, adopted in 2012.[655] Two circular letters were issued by the Belgian tax administration in order to clarify these provisions.[656]

2.3. THE ELECTRONIC INVOICE IN PRACTICE

2.3.1. Issuing and preserving electronic invoices

228. It is perfectly possible to transmit invoices electronically between parties, insofar as the recipient have accepted to do so. Such acceptance could be tacit, much like payment of the invoice can be considered as a tacit acceptance of that invoice's contents.[657] While it is not determined explicitly what to do in the event that the recipient does not accept to receive electronic invoices, it would seem logical that in such case a paper invoice will have to be delivered.[658] Even in the cases where the use of an invoice is required by law, reference could be made to the principle of functional equivalence – introduced by the e-commerce

651 Royal Decree of 15 December 2009 amending Royal Decree nr. 1 of 29 December 1992 regarding the regulation for the fulfillment of the value added tax, *Belgian State Gazette* 21 December 2009.

652 Article 60 Belgian VAT Code.

653 Council Directive 2010/45/EU of 13 July 2010 amending Directive 2006/112/EC on the common system of value added tax as regards the rules on invoicing, *OJ* L 189 of 22 July 2010, 1–8.

654 Article 1(22) Directive 2010/45/EU.

655 Act of 17 December 2012 amending the VAT Code, *Belgian State Gazette* 21 December 2012. Together with the Royal Decree of 19 December 2012 amending Royal Decree nr. 1 of 29 December 1992 regarding the regulation for the fulfillment of the value added tax, *Belgian State Gazette* 21 December 2012.

656 Circular AFZ nr. 02/2013 (*AFZ/2011-0272*) of 23 January 2013; Circular AAFisc Nr. 14/2014 (*nr. E.T. 120.000*) of 4 April 2014.

657 Dumortier, J. (2008) "Elektronische facturen", in: Ballon, G., Samoy, I., Byl, T., Deschoolmeester, F., Dumortier, J., Goethals, T., Govers, M., Swaenepoel, E. (Eds) *De factuur en verwante documenten*, Brugge: Vanden Broele, 415–422.

658 Massin, I. (2014) "'Bedrijfscontrole': zelfcontrole en (externe) audit 'aanbevolen'", *Fiscoloog*, nr. 1383.

directive.[659] This means that if the formal requirements imposed on invoices can be fulfilled by an electronic process, invoices can principally be issued electronically. However, it must be borne in mind that the principle of functional equivalence only applies to electronic contracts, and cannot be applied to just any domain. It is up to the issuer of the electronic invoice to ensure that the invoice is received and usable.[660] This means that he needs to ensure that the invoice is sent to the correct (electronic) address, and that the invoice can be opened and read.

229. If such electronically transmitted invoice is later to serve as evidence, it must be assessed whether the authenticity of the invoice has been guaranteed. This means that it must be assured that the invoice really emanated from whom it purports to be. Oddly, while the same risk of falsification exists for paper invoices – see for instance the recent wave of invoice fraud – such authentication requirement has not traditionally been imposed on paper invoices.[661] Here, the use of the digital signature technique and the preservation of the electronic invoice on a non-erasable storage medium – such as a WORM[662] disc – can provide such guarantees.[663] It should also be borne in mind that the use of a digital signature in this context only serves as security element, and not as an acknowledgment that the invoice has been paid.[664] The obligation of using this technique as a means to secure the electronic invoice is therefore not contrary to article 229 of the VAT Directive, which states that Member States cannot require invoices to be signed, as that article refers to the use of the signature on paper invoices.[665]

2.3.2. Substituting paper invoices

230. Since 2006 it has been possible to preserve paper invoices in either their original format or electronically in Belgium.[666] Since then, article 60 of the VAT Code held that paper invoices could be preserved electronically, if the authenticity of the origin and the integrity of the content could be guaranteed.

---

659 Dumortier, J. (2008) "Elektronische facturen", in: Ballon, G., Samoy, I., Byl, T., Deschoolmeester, F., Dumortier, J., Goethals, T., Govers, M., Swaenepoel, E. (Eds) *De factuur en verwante documenten*, Brugge: Vanden Broele, 415–416.

660 *Ibid.*, 422.

661 *Ibid.*, 423–424.

662 Write Once, Read Many: this is a storage medium to which information can be written. Once the information is written, it cannot be erased or altered anymore, it can only be read.

663 Dumortier, J. (2008) "Elektronische facturen", in: Ballon, G., Samoy, I., Byl, T., Deschoolmeester, F., Dumortier, J., Goethals, T., Govers, M., Swaenepoel, E. (Eds) *De factuur en verwante documenten*, Brugge: Vanden Broele, 416.

664 *Id.*

665 *Ibid.*, 421.

666 Act of 27 December 2005 holding diverse provisions, *Belgian State Gazette* 30 December 2005.

This provision therefore effectively allowed paper invoices to be substituted by electronic reproductions thereof. In 2008, the Belgian tax authorities adopted a circular letter that detailed the procedure hereto, which will be discussed in the following paragraphs.[667]

231. It is important to note that the 2008 circular letter only concerns invoices originally issued on paper, and not those originally issued electronically. The latter will be discussed in the next subsection. Generally, four scenarios for outgoing invoices can be distinguished under the circular letter. Everyone obliged to preserve such invoices will therefore have to choose one of these scenarios. Mixing the different preservation strategies listed here is not allowed for outgoing invoices.

232. First, there is the paper preservation. In this scenario, a paper invoice is issued to the recipient. The issuer will produce a second paper copy of that invoice, and preserve that paper copy during the legally determined preservation period of seven years. Since the invoice was created by electronic means[668] – for instance using word processing software or accounting software – the electronic version of that invoice will have to be preserved as well, for a duration of five years.[669]

233. Second, there is the digital preservation on WORM-media. In this scenario, one paper copy of the invoice is produced to issue to the recipient. The issuer will then make a daily electronic archive of that day's invoices – respecting their numbering order – to a WORM storage medium.[670] The information must be written in a readily accessible and readable format – for the purposes of facilitating audits by the tax administration – and be preserved within Belgium.[671]

234. Third, there is the digital preservation using an advanced electronic signature. In this scenario, one paper copy will again be issued to the recipient. The issuer will then immediately secure the electronic data of the invoice with an advanced electronic signature and preserve that secured data.[672]

---

667 Circular letter nr. AOIF 16/2008 (E.T.112.081) of 13 May 2008 (hereinafter: Circular AOIF 2008).

668 The circular letter describes a different procedure for invoices created purely manually. However, given the increasing rarity of this scenario, this procedure will not be further discussed here.

669 Paragraph 73 Circular AOIF 2008.

670 Paragraph 74 Circular AOIF 2008.

671 Paragraph 75 Circular AOIF 2008.

672 Paragraph 79 Circular AOIF 2008.

235. Fourth, there is the digital preservation using sealing algorithms. In this scenario, a seal will be affixed to both the paper version issued to the recipient and the electronic data.[673] The seal is generated through a mathematic calculation, the precise method for which is explained in the circular letter.[674] After the paper version and the electronic data have been sealed, their contents can no longer be altered.

236. In each of these four scenarios, the issuer's client received a paper invoice. This recipient – in the case he is a VAT subject – can preserve the incoming invoices in any way he wants. It is, for instance, possible for the recipient to decide to digitalize the invoice and preserve it electronically – unless the paper invoice has been signed, in which case the originally signed paper invoice must be preserved.[675] The paper invoices will then only need to be preserved for one month following their electronic preservation. While there is in principle no particular technology that must be used here, the tax administration's circular letter specifically describes a procedure to scan the original paper invoice.[676] Here, it is also important that whatever procedure is chosen can guarantee the authenticity and integrity of the invoice. Adding an advanced electronic signature to the scanned invoice, or using a sealing algorithm, could provide such guarantees.

2.3.3. Preserving electronic invoices

237. In 2014, the Belgian tax administration issued another circular letter, this time specifically describing the electronic invoice.[677] The circular letter confirms that an electronic invoice must be issued and received electronically.[678] Merely drafting the invoice electronically and subsequently printing it out before sending it to the recipient therefore does not qualify as an electronic invoice. Conversely, however, when a paper invoice is digitalized, it does become an electronic invoice.

238. The circular letter confirms the need for acceptance by the recipient – as foreseen in the European VAT framework. One explanation for this need for acceptance is that the recipient will need the right hardware, software and a network connection in order to receive and read the electronic invoice, thus

---

673 Paragraph 80 Circular AOIF 2008.

674 Paragraphs 81–82 Circular AOIF 2008.

675 Paragraphs 37 and 43 Circular AOIF 2008; Dumortier, J. (2008) "Elektronische facturen", in: Ballon, G., Samoy, I., Byl, T., Deschoolmeester, F., Dumortier, J., Goethals, T., Govers, M., Swaenepoel, E. (Eds) *De factuur en verwante documenten*, Brugge: Vanden Broele, 437–438.

676 Paragraphs 45–46 Circular AOIF 2008.

677 Circular AAFisc Nr. 14/2014 (*nr. E.T. 120.000*) of 4 April 2014 (hereinafter: Circular AAFisc 2014).

678 Paragraph 17 Circular AAFisc 2014.

necessitating an agreement on those points.[679] Such acceptance can be made explicit through the adoption of a specific agreement hereto, or tacit through the subsequent payment of the electronic invoice.[680]

239. In terms of preserving the electronic invoice, the circular letter confirms that the authenticity of the origin must be ensured, meaning that the identity of the issuer of the invoice must be guaranteed.[681] By this time, use of the advanced electronic signature and EDI are still recommended techniques to do so, but they are no longer the only ones allowed. Similarly, the integrity of the contents of the electronic invoice must be ensured, meaning that it must be guaranteed that the invoice has not been changed since the moment of issuing for the entirety of the preservation period.[682] Here the advanced electronic signature and EDI can also be used, but other techniques are allowed as well. Last, the readability of the electronic invoice must be ensured.[683]

240. The freedom to choose the technique with which to ensure the authenticity, integrity and readability of the electronic invoice implies that those required to preserve electronic invoices must document their choice in order to prove their compliance with these requirements to the competent VAT administrations.[684] Moreover, when new techniques are implemented during the preservation period of electronic invoices, it must be proven that these new techniques do not diminish the authenticity, integrity and readability of electronic invoices originally preserved using a different technique.[685] If, for instance, an electronically signed invoice would be migrated to a different format, then the electronic signature will principally be broken due to the resulting changes in the bitstream. In this case, the migration process must be thoroughly documented – proving that the electronic invoice was validly signed before the migration – or an originally signed electronic invoice must be preserved alongside a migrated invoice.

241. The circular letter also points out the use of a qualified electronic signature – for instance using the Belgian e-ID – as a means to ensure the authenticity, integrity and readability of the electronic invoice.[686] Another possibility is to use business controls to create an audit trail documenting all transactions of the company and the associated documents.[687] In order to be

---

679 Paragraph 21 Circular AAFisc 2014.
680 Paragraph 22 Circular AAFisc 2014.
681 Paragraph 26 Circular AAFisc 2014.
682 Paragraph 29 Circular AAFisc 2014.
683 Paragraph 32 Circular AAFisc 2014.
684 Paragraph 34 Circular AAFisc 2014.
685 *Id.*
686 Paragraph 36 Circular AAFisc 2014.
687 Paragraphs 40–42 Circular AAFisc 2014.

reliable, such audit trail must allow probative documents and existing links between actions and those documents to establish whether the electronic invoice really reflects a corresponding action – *e.g.* a delivery of goods or services. One possibility of such an audit trail is to match the order with the invoice.[688] The circular letter further details how certain processes and logs can contribute to audit trails establishing the required authenticity, integrity and readability of the electronic invoice.[689]

2.3.4. Digitalization and originality

242. As noted previously, one general principle of invoices is that an invoice must be issued to the recipient, whereas the issuer maintains a copy.[690] This need for two copies of the invoice demonstrates the dual nature of the invoice as being on the one hand a document that must be issued to the recipient of goods and services subjected to VAT, and as a document for the internal accounting and control purposes of the issuer on the other. However, the former reference to two copies whereby only one is the original did, of course, stem from a pre-digital era, in which delivering a paper invoice to a recipient meant that the issuer lost possession of that same paper invoice. This is no longer relevant in a digital era, where the issuer can endlessly transfer – and in so doing duplicates – electronic information without himself losing possession over that information. As was also the case in the civil law discussion of chapter III, the original-copy dichotomy therefore holds little relevance in workflows that are increasingly digitalized.

243. Nevertheless, while the original-copy distinction was still present in VAT law in some form and for a while, the previous sections discussed the introduction of an advanced recognition of substitution. An invoice received on paper – the 'original' according to traditional VAT law – may be substituted by an electronic reproduction and may subsequently – after one month – be destroyed. Of course, this is true insofar as that electronic reproduction can guarantee the authenticity, integrity and readability of the invoice. While such electronic reproduction must in the strict sense of the original-copy dichotomy be considered as a copy, it can gain the recognition and value of an original, if the requirements thereof are fulfilled.

244. By now, and to further underline that guaranteeing the authenticity and the integrity of the invoice is now the main goal in preserving invoices, the references to the 'original format' have been removed from the Belgian VAT

---

688 Paragraph 43 Circular AAFisc 2014.
689 Circular AAFisc 2014.
690 For Belgium, see article 53 VAT Code.

Code. One remaining *caveat* is that there can, in principle, only be one invoice per taxable event. If, for instance, a customer loses an invoice issued to him and requests a new one, the new version will have to explicitly state that it is a duplicate of the original invoice.

3. CONCLUSION

245. The originality requirement in VAT law mainly stems from the dual nature of the invoice as being both a document for the recipient and a document for the issuer's own accounting purposes. It is in that duality that an original-copy dichotomy was created, with the recipient receiving the original invoice and the issuer maintaining a copy. Similar to what was found in the previous chapters on civil law and administrative law, it can be held that the purpose of such formality is to protect information against fraud and forgeries, in order to ensure the reliability of that information for later (probative) use.

246. However, as seen previously in the discussion on civil law, such original-copy dichotomy makes little sense in the context of digitialized business processes. VAT law is no stranger to such digitalization, where the use of electronic invoices is said to be an environmentally friendly and cost-saving measure.

247. The EU first adopted rules regarding electronic invoices in VAT law 17 years ago, and has regularly updated this legal framework. As a result, invoices can now be created, transmitted and preserved fully electronically, provided that the recipient agrees thereto. The Belgian legislator has duly implemented these rules in its national corpus, and has removed the original-copy dichotomy. Now, the main requirement for invoices – electronic or otherwise – is that they guarantee their authenticity and integrity, and that they are readable. While at first only the techniques of the advanced electronic signature and EDI could guarantee such authenticity and integrity, the legislator now leaves it up to parties to determine how they wish to comply with this requirement. Of course, when in doubt, the techniques of the advanced electronic signature and EDI can still be used, and will undoubtedly be accepted by both courts and tax administrations.

248. Moreover, tax administrations have provided guidance on the preservation of invoices through circular letters. Important here is that these circular letters also detail the procedure for substitution of paper invoices by electronic representations thereof. As a result, paper invoices can be destroyed after their digitalization, provided that the digital reproduction can attest to the authenticity and integrity of the invoice.

249. The previous findings lead to a very different result than what was the case for civil law and administrative law. Regarding civil law, it was found that the original-copy dichotomy is still very much present, and that only a recent legislative amendment provides a partial solution by imposing a non-discrimination principle for electronic documents and by allowing for substitution under certain restrictions. However, substitution under those new rules requires the use of a qualified archival service, whereas fiscal law leaves the method for substitution up to the parties. Moreover, an original under civil law requires a signature, which is not the case for the invoice under fiscal law. Under administrative law, it was found that substitution still remains a thorny matter, with clear rules or guidance as found in fiscal law being largely absent. Fiscal law is therefore unique in its abolishment of the original-copy dichotomy and its full acceptance of substitution.

CHAPTER VI
BLOCKCHAIN

1. DEVELOPMENT AND TECHNICAL BACKGROUND OF BLOCKCHAIN

250. Blockchain technology originated with the creation of bitcoin. In the following paragraphs, we will briefly explain the background and workings of blockchain using bitcoin as its core example.[691] While a number of operational elements will of course differ, depending on the precise use case, bitcoin provides a good example to illustrate the basic tenets of blockchain. Next, we will highlight some of the further developments in wider blockchain use cases.

1.1. BACKGROUND

251. Crypto-anarchists have been developing virtual alternative currencies using cryptography since the early 1990s,, by using public-key encryption to allow for the use of pseudonymous identifiers for instance.[692] Examples include loyalty programs and prepaid cards – such as InternetCash, Flooz and Beenz – digital gold currencies – such as e-gold and e-bullion – and centralized transfer systems – such as Liberty Reserve. David Chaum first developed a system allowing for anonymous money transfers, called DigiCash.[693] Wei Dai expanded on that idea with b-money, which included a proof of work function.[694] Further contributions in this field were made by Nick Szabo's 'bit gold' – which included a distributed proof of work string as ownership title – and Hal Finney's Reusable Proofs of Work. The next step in this development would be Satoshi Nakamoto's bitcoin in 2008.[695]

---

691 This section was first developed, more elaborately, at: Vandezande, N. (2018) *Virtual Currencies: A Legal Framework*, Cambridge: Intersentia, 50–69.

692 Pseudonymity and anonymity being the core elements of May's crypto-anarchism: May, T.C. (1994) "Cyphernomicon", *spinnaker.com/crypt/cyphernomicon/CP-FAQ*.

693 Based on the idea of blind signatures: Chaum, D. (1983) "Blind signatures for untraceable payments", *Advances in Cryptology Proceedings of Crypto*, Vol. 82, 199–203.

694 Dai, W. (1998) "B-money", *weidai.com/bmoney.txt*.

695 Nakamoto, S. (2008) "Bitcoin: A Peer-to-Peer Electronic Cash System", *bitcoin.org/bitcoin.pdf*.

252. Bitcoin can best be viewed in light of its historical context, right within the global financial crisis that was unfolding back in 2008. Traditional payments were still fairly slow and expensive, and relied on a whole range of financial intermediaries. Electronic payments were slow to catch on, and mobile and other contactless payment technologies were still in development or in early infancy at best. It is not that hard to imagine the appeal of a fully electronic, fast and cheap means of payment within that context, one relying on cryptographic proof rather than on trust in financial intermediaries.

253. The Bitcoin network became operational in early 2009, with its basic tenets being that users maintain the decentralized network through their computer's calculating power, being rewarded new units of bitcoin for 'mining' a new block, with those rewards halving every four years and no new units of bitcoin being generated once 21 million units have been mined.[696] Initially, the value of bitcoin was close to zero as no entities accepted it as means of payment. In 2010, the first bitcoin exchanges were founded, allowing users to exchange legal tender and similar instruments for bitcoin.[697] In 2011, the value started going up and achieved parity with the US dollar.[698] In 2013, some online and brick-and-mortar retailers started to accept bitcoin, and a first price bubble briefly made the value rise above USD 1,000.[699] An important factor for this growth was the development of intermediaries that accept payments in bitcoin on behalf of retailers and convert those bitcoins into legal tender or similar instruments and thus limit the retailer's exposure to bitcoin's value fluctuations.[700] From 2014 on, the value of bitcoin declined somewhat, hovering around the USD 500 mark. In 2016 and more so in 2017, the value rose dramatically again, even breaching the USD 20,000 mark in late 2017. However, since early 2018, the value appears to be in a downward trajectory again.[701]

254. The success of bitcoin has, of course, spawned numerous copies aiming to reproduce some of that success. Some of these cryptocurrencies use the same algorithm as bitcoin, but there are also examples – such as Litecoin and Dogecoin – that use different algorithms. There are also cryptocurrencies that have split off from the Bitcoin blockchain in a so-called hard fork. Examples

---

696 *Mail-archive.com/cryptography@metzdowd.com/msg10142.html.*

697 The first exchange was Mt. Gox, which handled over 70% of all bitcoin trades before collapsing in late 2013. McMillan, R. Metz, C. (2013) "The rise and fall of the world's largest bitcoin exchange", *Wired*, 6 November 2013. Mt. Gox was soon followed by other exchanges such as OKCoin, BitInstant, Bitstamp, BTC China, and Coinbase.

698 Wallace, B. (2011) "The rise and fall of bitcoin", *Wired*, 23 November 2011.

699 For instance, bitcoin has at some point been accepted by Overstock, Dell, Expedia, Newegg, Time and Microsoft.

700 The two major bitcoin payment processors, BitPay and Coinbase, collectively serve over 90,000 businesses. *Bitpay.com, coinbase.com.*

701 *Coinmarketcap.com/currencies/bitcoin/#charts.*

of these include Bitcoin Cash, Bitcoin Gold and Bitcoin Private. Such forks are the result of disagreements within the bitcoin community, with some wanting to keep the main source code as original as possible and others wanting to implement the necessary changes to make the system more performant.

1.2. TECHNICAL ASPECTS

255. The following paragraphs will provide a step-by-step analysis of how the Bitcoin system functions.[702]

256. Cryptocurrencies such as bitcoin are managed through wallets. These wallets – accessible through web browsers or applications – connect to the peer-to-peer network underlying the cryptocurrency. In essence, a wallet stores addresses, each of which represents a balance of units of cryptocurrency.[703] In public-key cryptography, corresponding key pairs – one key being private and the other key being public – are issued, which allows the recipient of a signed message to use the public key to determine that this message was signed by the holder of the corresponding private key.[704] The addresses in cryptocurrency wallets are public keys, and the wallet user holds the corresponding private keys. Any outgoing transaction from a cryptocurrency address must therefore be confirmed with the corresponding private key.[705] Of course, this also means that if a private key is lost or stolen, the units of cryptocurrency in the corresponding address can no longer be used.

257. In order to execute a transaction, the recipient of the units of cryptocurrency must provide his or her address – the public key – to the sender. The sender will then set up the transaction and sign using the private key corresponding to the public key of his or her own address.[706] Alternatively, a cryptocurrency user can engage in mining activities, whereby new units of cryptocurrency are issued upon successfully mining a new block.

258. Cryptocurrency transactions must be confirmed in order to prevent double-spending. This is one of the main issues in electronic transactions.

---

[702] Based on: Peck, M. (2012) "The cryptoanarchists' answer to cash", *IEEE Spectrum*, June 2012, 51–56.

[703] Peck, M. (2012) "The cryptoanarchists' answer to cash", *IEEE Spectrum*, June 2012, 54.

[704] Bollen, R. (2013) "The Legal Status of Online Currencies: Are Bitcoins the Future?", *Journal of Banking and Finance Law and Practice*, vol. 24, nr. 4, 272–293.

[705] Stokes, R. (2012) "Virtual money laundering: the case of Bitcoin and the Linden dollar", *Information & Communications Technology Law*, vol. 21, nr. 3, 224.

[706] Peck, M. (2012) "The cryptoanarchists' answer to cash", *IEEE Spectrum*, June 2012, 54; Brito, J., Castillo, A. (2013) *Bitcoin: A Primer for Policymakers*, Arlington: George Mason University Mercatus Center, 7.

Whereas in physical exchanges there is a clear handover of possession from one party to the other, in electronic exchanges information is essentially duplicated. As noted previously, in the chapter on civil law, this can cause confusion on the originality of such duplicated electronic information, but it is an even more pressing problem for electronic transactions: if the funds do not actually leave the wallet of the sender, then they can be spent more than once. This double-spending problem is addressed in bitcoin by recording only the earliest transaction and ignoring subsequent contradicting transactions.[707] To determine the earliest transaction, each transaction is timestamped and recorded in a public ledger, called the blockchain.[708] As the term indicates, this is a chain of cryptographically linked blocks in which transactions are recorded. Once recorded in the blockchain, a transaction is considered to have been confirmed.[709] In the case of Bitcoin, new blocks are added approximately every 10 minutes, but other cryptocurrencies can have faster confirmation times – such as Litecoin's 2.5 minutes or Dogecoin's 1 minute. In principle, there is no direct attestation that a certain cryptocurrency address belongs to a particular person.[710] While this is what has given cryptocurrencies an air of anonymity, it should be clarified that in many cases it is possible to derive a person's identity from its publicly recorded transaction history or through its appropriation of an address.[711]

259. The blockchain is stored decentralized, meaning that all participants in the network will store a copy of the entire ledger. This is to ensure that the blockchain cannot be controlled by a single entity.[712] By submitting every transaction to the entire network, the blockchain relies on computational trust, rather than on trust in a single entity.[713] However, it has already been shown that public blockchains – such as Bitcoin or Ethereum – still gravitate towards *de facto* centralization, as often only a very small group controls the majority of the network's computing power.[714] Moreover, many companies interested

---

707 Turpin, J. (2014) "Bitcoin: the economic case for a global virtual currency operating in an unexplored legal framework", *Indiana Journal of Global Legal Studies*, Vol. 21, 340.

708 Kien-Meng Ly, M. (2014) "Coining Bitcoin's 'legal-bits': examining the regulatory framework for Bitcoin and virtual currencies", *Harvard Journal of Law & Technology*, vol. 27, nr. 2, 590.

709 Dion, D. (2013) "I'll gladly trade you two bits on Tuesday for a byte today: Bitcoin, regulating fraud in the e-conomy of hacker-cash", *Journal of Law, Technology & Policy*, 168.

710 Dion, D. (2013) "I'll gladly trade you two bits on Tuesday for a byte today: Bitcoin, regulating fraud in the e-conomy of hacker-cash", *Journal of Law, Technology & Policy*, 168.

711 De Filippi, P. (2014) "Bitcoin: a regulatory nightmare to a libertarian dream", *Internet Policy Review*, vol. 3, nr. 2, 1–2.

712 Kaplanov, N. (2012) "Nerdy Money: Bitcoin, the Private Digital Currency, and the Case Against its Regulation", *Loyola Consumer Law Review*, Vol. 25, 117.

713 Bayern, S. (2014) "Of Bitcoins, independently wealthy software, and the zero-member LLC", *Northwestern University law Review Online*, Vol. 108, 1487.

714 Gencer, A. E., Basu, S., Eyal, I., van Renesse, R., Gün Sirer, E. (2018) "Decentralization in Bitcoin and Ethereum Networks", *arxiv.org/pdf/1801.03998.pdf*.

in developing blockchain-based solutions wish to keep the system under their own centralized control, thereby creating so-called private or permissioned blockchains that take away most of the intended decentralization.[715]

260. As already hinted at previously, the process of mining takes transactions, bundles them into blocks and adds those blocks to the blockchain. Because these blocks are cryptographically linked to one another, altering or withdrawing a transaction would require the re-computation of the corresponding block and of all subsequent blocks. Given that this is considered unfeasible, transactions are considered irrevocable when added to the blockchain.[716] Concretely, a block consists of transactions, the hash value of the previous block – thus providing that cryptographic link between blocks – and a nonce. In cryptocurrencies, the resulting hash value of a block must correspond to certain characteristics. In the case of Bitcoin, for instance, the hash value must begin with a predefined number of zeroes.[717] Because of this, miners add a random number – the nonce – to the block. Essentially, they will thus try out different numbers until they have found one that makes the block's hash value comply with the required format, which is what is considered their proof-of-work. The required format determines the difficulty of mining, which can be adjusted depending on the network's available computing power in order to maintain a steady rate of adding new blocks.[718]

261. As has becomes clear from the previous paragraph, mining is the backbone of a successful blockchain. Nevertheless, this process requires an ever-increasing amount of computing power. In the case of more popular cryptocurrencies, such as bitcoin, this even requires specialized hardware, as well as a lot of energy to power and cool that hardware. Because of the costs associated with this, many mining operations have already moved to countries where such costs are more bearable, such as China or Iceland. The main incentive for people to direct their computing power to mining is that the successful miner of a new block will automatically be awarded with new units of cryptocurrency. The amount of that reward is predefined in the underlying code, and is thus not subject to a policy decision by a central entity. In many cases, the mining reward may decrease over time – as is the case in bitcoin, where the reward is halved every four years. Moreover, some cryptocurrencies, such as bitcoin, have

---

715 Finck, M. (2017) "Blockchain Regulation", *Max Planck Institute for Innovation and Competition Research Paper No. 17-13*, 6.

716 Pflaum, I., Hateley, E. (2014) "A bit of a problem: National and extraterritorial regulation of virtual currency in the age of financial disintermediation", *Georgetown Journal of International Law*, Vol. 45, 1175.

717 Twomey, P. (2013) "Halting a shift in the paradigm: the need for Bitcoin regulation", *Trinity College Law Review*, Vol. 16, 69.

718 Pflaum, I., Hateley, E. (2014) "A bit of a problem: National and extraterritorial regulation of virtual currency in the age of financial disintermediation", *Georgetown Journal of International Law*, Vol. 45, 1178.

a built-in cap after which no new units are created. In such an event, miners will have to find another way to make their activity profitable, by levying transaction fees for instance.

1.3. USE CASE DEVELOPMENTS

262. As noted previously, the cryptocurrency bitcoin was the very first use case of the blockchain technology. By now, myriads of other use cases are being developed.

263. One example is using blockchain as a platform to issue and trade private corporate bonds.[719] This would develop an alternative security market competing with traditional exchanges such as NASDAQ and NYSE. These traditional exchanges have also explored such blockchain-powered private trading platforms.[720]

264. The idea of transactions recorded on a blockchain as being irreversible and immutable has generated interest in using this technology for record-keeping purposes. A blockchain transaction could, for instance, also include encrypted records.[721]

265. Perhaps the most debated use case for blockchain technology is that of self-executing smart contracts. Here, we can look at the Ethereum blockchain, which implemented a scripting language to allow for the development of applications running on that blockchain. The idea here is that a contract could be coded, and thus be deployed as an application. Once all particulars of the contract are included in that application, it could run by itself without the need for further human intervention – thus attempting to counter the risk of the counterparty not being obliging to the contract. Examples include using the blockchain technology to register contracts, to enact voting systems, etc.[722] Nevertheless, the coding of smart contracts has proven to be a work in progress, as even a small error in the code could result in unwanted outcomes. A clear example of this is the DAO, which served as a self-executing venture capital

---

[719] Santos, M. (2018) "CEO of Overstock.com buys world's first Bitcoin bond for $500,000", *99bitcoins.com*, 2 January.

[720] Metz, C. (2015) "Bitcoin May Never Make It to Wall Street, But Its Tech Will", *Wired,* 12 May 2015; Hern, A. (2015) "Nasdaq bets on bitcoin's blockchain as the future of finance", *The Guardian,* 13 May 2015; Intercontinental Exchange (2015) "NYSE to Launch NYSE Bitcoin Index, NYXBT", *Business Wire,* 19 May 2015.

[721] Pflaum, I., Hateley, E. (2014) "A bit of a problem: National and extraterritorial regulation of virtual currency in the age of financial disintermediation", *Georgetown Journal of International Law,* Vol. 45, 1181.

[722] *Github.com/ethereum/wiki/wiki/White-Paper.*

fund. Through an error in the code, about USD 50 million worth of investments was siphoned away by a malicious party.[723]

266. Even though cryptocurrencies have received a bad reputation due to their perceived anonymity, blockchain can actually also be used for the reverse: to serve as an identity register. Estonia, for instance, runs a pilot project allowing citizens to verify records on governmental databases, and is working on a blockchain-based identity program within its e-residency project.[724] Private initiatives, such as ShoCard, are also being developed to this effect.

267. While many of the developments in blockchain use cases remain within the financial sphere, it should be made clear that the technology is being investigated for much broader use cases as well. For instance, the technology can be used for supply chain tracking[725]; university degrees could be recorded on blockchain[726]; applications are being developed to manage IP rights on blockchains[727]; blockchain could support firms in complying with maritime insurance requirements[728], etc. It could then be argued that blockchain may become a foundational technology that has the potential to create new paradigms in existing fields.[729] It should, however, be cautioned that there are also clear cases in which blockchain may not be the most suitable technology.[730] The coming years will therefore be pivotal in separating the use cases where blockchain makes sense from the use cases where blockchain provides little to no added value.

2. BLOCKCHAIN AND ELECTRONIC SIGNATURES

268. In the chapter on civil law, we discussed the figure of the electronic signature as established by European law and as implemented within the Belgian legal order. While the European eIDAS regulation is in principle technology-

---

723 Siegel, D. (2016) "Understanding The DAO Attack", *CoinDesk*, 27 June.

724 *E-estonia.com/solutions/security-and-safety/ksi-blockchain*; *medium.com/e-residency-blog/welcome-to-the-blockchain-nation-5d9b46c06fd4*.

725 Higgins, S. (2017) "Air France Tests Blockchain for Supply Chain Tracking", *CoinDesk*, 5 October.

726 Haig, S. (2017) "MIT to Issue Diplomas Using Bitcoin Blockchain", *Bitcoin.com*, 22 October.

727 Del Castillo, M. (2017) "Fight for Your Right: Universal Music Veteran Launches Ethereum IP Platform", *CoinDesk*, 5 October; see also *Mycelia*.

728 O'Leary, R. R. (2017) "Shipping Giant Maersk to Deploy Blockchain Maritime Insurance Solution", *CoinDesk*, 6 September.

729 Iansiti, M., Lakhani, K. R. (2017) "The Truth About Blockchain", *Harvard Business Review*, January-February, 118–127.

730 Wüst, K., Gervais, A. (2017) "Do you need a Blockchain?", *IACR Cryptology ePrint Archive 2017*, 375.

neutral[731], it was already established that the European and national legislators mainly look at the technique of the digital signature in order to provide an advanced or a qualified electronic signature. The digital signature incorporates the cryptographic techniques of a PKI and hashing, both of which are used in the blockchain technology as well.

269. To recapitulate, the digital signature allows a user to calculate the hash value of the information that is to be protected. This hash value is encrypted using that user's private key. The recipient of the resulting digital signature can decrypt the hash value using the corresponding public key and can calculate the hash value of the information he has received. If both hash values are the same, the information has been proven to be unaltered since the moment of signing.

270. As noted previously, blockchain uses the same cryptographic techniques, but in a somewhat different way. A transaction to be recorded on the blockchain is signed using the private key corresponding to the public key associated with the address from which the transaction originates. Transactions are recorded in blocks, which are cryptographically linked by including the previous block's hash value in the next block.

271. The European legislator has identified three levels of electronic signatures. The most basic electronic signature is defined as "*data in electronic form which is attached to or logically associated with other data in electronic form and which is used by the signatory to sign*".[732] This is a very broad definition that could span many different forms of signing. It could then be argued here that the private key – being electronic data used to sign a blockchain transaction and associated with the public key/address – could indeed constitute such basic electronic signature.

272. For an advanced electronic signature, it is additionally required that "(a) it is uniquely linked to the signatory; (b) it is capable of identifying the signatory; (c) it is created using electronic signature creation data that the signatory can, with a high level of confidence, use under his sole control; and (d) it is linked to the data signed therewith in such a way that any subsequent change in the data is detectable".[733] In this paragraph, we will examine each of those elements.

A PKI ensures a link between both keys of a key pair, but does not link those keys to a specific signatory on its own. It is of course possible to ensure such a link, by making the use of a key pair subject to additional authentication requirements for instance – such as a password, PIN code or even biometrics – that do guarantee a link with a specific signatory. In this sense, it must then be

731 See recital 27 eIDAS Regulation.
732 Article 3(10) eIDAS Regulation.
733 Article 3(11) eIDAS Regulation, referring to article 26 of the same text.

acknowledged that there is not – at least not at this point in time – one specific blockchain standard. Additional authentication requirements as described here are certainly not part of some of the original blockchain implementations – such as bitcoin – but could be implemented in future blockchain use cases. Nevertheless, the lack of a standard in this regard means that a case-by-case analysis is still needed, as not every blockchain implementation will thus be able to ensure a unique link between the key pair and the signatory.

A similar conclusion can be drawn with regard to the identification of the signatory. Initial blockchain implementations, such as bitcoin, ensure a form of pseudonymity by only identifying addresses and not the users behind those addresses. Regardless, it is clear that in many cases identification of a particular user is still possible – either by that user's appropriation of an address or by analyzing an address's transactional history. In such event, it could be argued that even in the supposedly 'anonymous' blockchains, identification will often be possible, albeit not necessarily intentional. Moreover, in permissioned blockchains it is certainly possible – even necessary – to identify users. While this is also a case-by-case analysis is still required given the wide range of operational factors involved, the general conclusion is that identification of the signatory can be made possible.

A private key could, in principle, be argued to be under the sole control of the signatory. This is, at least, the intention with which such key is used within a PKI. It is then up to the holder of the key to ensure that the private key remains under his sole control. For instance, additional measures could be taken to protect this key, such as storing it on a secure device and protecting it through encryption.

Last, the signature must be linked with the signed data in such a way that subsequent changes in that data become detectable. In blockchain this is achieved by recording transactions in blocks that are cryptographically linked. Once recorded, a transaction can therefore – in theory – not be altered. However, this is a separate process from the signing of a transaction using the private key. While blockchain therefore does allow for subsequent changes in data to be detectable, this feature is not a direct result of the signing itself. It is therefore arguable whether or not this satisfies this last requirement of the advanced electronic signature.

273. For the qualified electronic signature, it is additionally required that the signature is created "*by a qualified electronic signature creation device, and which is based on a qualified certificate for electronic signatures*".[734] Here, is it clear that most implementations of blockchain technology will not comply with these requirements. As noted previously, the pseudonymity of certain blockchain implementations – such as bitcoin – can even be argued to run counter to the idea of certification. Nevertheless, it is possible to implement blockchain in such

---

[734] Article 3(12) eIDAS Regulation.

a way –through a permissioned blockchain for instance – that these requirements could be fulfilled. Here, a case-by-case analysis therefore also remains necessary.

3. BLOCKCHAIN FOR AUTHENTICITY AND INTEGRITY

274. A signature can fulfill several functions. In the chapter on civil law, two of the most important functions identified were authenticity and integrity. A signature must be able to identify the signatory, and thus attest to the origin of the signed content. At the same time, the signed content must remain unaltered since the moment of signing. In this section, whether blockchain can provide for such authenticity and integrity will be analyzed.

275. As noted in the previous section, a public and private key of a PKI key pair are cryptographically linked to each other. However, keys are not directly linked to a particular signatory, unless they are accompanied by a trustworthy certificate that specifies which key pair has been issued to a particular signatory. Blockchain technology in itself does not provide for such assurance, and certain instances of blockchain – such as bitcoin – may even be resistant to the idea of identifying the users behind key pairs. But, as already explained in the previous section, it is certainly possible to add this functionality to a particular case of blockchain implementation. This will, for instance, likely be the case for permissioned blockchains, where a particular company or consortium will want to control who has access to its blockchain. In this case, assurances on the identity of signatories – thus providing for authenticity – will be needed. Several projects are even underway to use blockchain as a means to provide for secure digital identities.[735] If such blockchain identities can be considered trustworthy and can be linked to key pairs used to sign blockchain transactions, then they could provide for the necessary authenticity.

276. Second, a signature must display integrity, meaning that the signed content has not been altered since the moment of signing. As noted in the previous section, blockchain achieves this by recording all transactions in blocks that are cryptographically linked. Once a transaction has been recorded, it can therefore in principle no longer be altered. This approach has several benefits.[736] First, once recorded on a blockchain, a transaction can be considered

---

[735] See, for instance: *cloudblogs.microsoft.com/enterprisemobility/2018/02/12/decentralized-digital-identities-and-blockchain-the-future-as-we-see-it; ibm.com/blockchain/solutions/identity; civic.com/products/secure-identity-platform.*

[736] See also: Saelemans, S. (2017) "An analysis of the legal effect of an electronic signature used to sign an agreement in a blockchain application, under Dutch law", *Master thesis Vrije Universiteit Amsterdam,* 38–39.

as validated and remaining valid. Such validation will therefore not have to be stored elsewhere, something that is the case for electronic signatures whose certificates may expire. Second, the decentralized nature of blockchain makes that transactions should remain accessible, unlike the case where signed content is stored by a single entity. Given the principal immutability of transactions recorded on a blockchain, a signed transaction should therefore be able to assure its integrity once recorded on that blockchain.[737]

277. However, an important *caveat* of using blockchain to ensure authenticity and integrity of records is that the records may be preserved separately from the blockchain itself. The reason for this is that the blockchain principally stores hashes, from which it is not possible to derive the underlying data. In order to verify the integrity of the data, a hash of that data will have to be calculated and compared with the hash stored on the blockchain – much like in the digital signature technique.[738] Steps will therefore still have to be taken to preserve the data for which authenticity and integrity is to be ensured. In such a case, blockchain can provide a tool to verify the integrity of data, but does not assure it in itself. While there are projects underway that would allow records to be stored on the blockchain itself, it may prove unfeasible to use blockchain as a fully-fledged data repository due to elements such as block-size, transaction confirmation time, etc. In most cases, data will therefore remain outside of the blockchain, with only a referral to that data stored on the blockchain. As a result of these shortcomings, blockchain will need more development before being considered a suitable record management tool under archival science.[739]

4. CONCLUSION

278. This chapter's goal has been to assess whether the currently popular blockchain technology could be used as a means to satisfy the originality requirement as analyzed under this research. The focus of this analysis has been put on the use of blockchain to provide electronic signatures on the one hand, and the use of blockchain as a means to assure authenticity and integrity on the other.

---

737 Nevertheless, attention should be paid to some of the remaining weaknesses of the technology – or rather to: particular implementations of this technology – that could cast doubt over the immutability of transactions.

738 Lemieux, V. (2016) "Trusting records: is Blockchain technology the answer?", *Records Management Journal*, Vol. 26, 130–131.

739 Lemieux, V. (2017) "Blockchain Technology for Recordkeeping", *SSHRC Knowledge Synthesis Grant Competition on "How can emerging technologies be leveraged to benefit Canadians?"*, Volume 1 – Report.

279. For electronic signatures, it is clear that blockchain technology does not use the digital signature technique as it is traditionally used in electronic signatures. Since the European legal framework on electronic signatures is in principle technology-neutral, this is not necessarily a problem as long as the requirements for the different levels of electronic signatures are fulfilled. Here, it can be argued that a signed blockchain transaction could in any case be considered as a basic electronic signature. For the advanced electronic signature, the outcome will depend on a range of operational factors that may be very different for each particular use case. In the absence of a single blockchain standard, a case-by-case assessment therefore remains necessary. It is, however, possible that particular operational factors would allow a signed blockchain transaction to comply with most of the requirements of the advanced electronic signature. Nevertheless, it remains to be seen whether the last requirement – on detecting alterations in the data – can truly be fulfilled by blockchain, as the unalterability of blockchain transactions is a separate process from signing those transactions. Similar conclusions can be drawn with regard to the qualified electronic signature, where most blockchain implementations will not comply with the requirements of the qualified certificate and the qualified electronic signature creation device. However, here it is also possible to set up a particular blockchain implementation in such a way that these requirements could be complied with.

280. Regarding authenticity and integrity, similar conclusions must be drawn with regard to the electronic signature. Given the enormous breadth of different blockchain implementations, it will all come down to the precise operational factors. The basic blockchain technology in itself does not provide for authenticity: it merely uses the PKI technique to sign transactions, without linking the key pairs to any particular person. Moreover, in some blockchain implementations – such as bitcoin – this pseudonymity is even intentional. Nevertheless, it is possible to implement blockchain in such a way, through a permissioned blockchain for instance, that does require a trusted entity to assign key pairs to authorized users, thus supporting authenticity. Given that blockchain transactions can, in principle at least, not be altered after having been recorded on the blockchain, it could be held that such transactions can provide proof of their integrity. However, when the blockchain technology is used in relation to records, the blockchain itself will generally only store a hash, with the actual record remaining outside of the blockchain. While comparing a hash of that record with the hash stored on the blockchain would then attest to the record's integrity, the blockchain in itself would not assure such integrity.

281. In conclusion, it can be held that blockchain technology in itself appears to do little to provide for originality as analyzed in this research. The basic technology does not fulfill the criteria for the advanced and qualified electronic signature, nor does it ensure the authenticity of information or that information's integrity. However, it must be noted that the technology is not standardized, and that many different operational factors may be found in the real-world implementation of blockchain technology. And precisely those operational factors could indeed make blockchain correspond to the second and third tier electronic signature, as well as ensuring authenticity and integrity. While blockchain in itself is therefore not sufficient to ensure originality as analyzed here, additional implementing measures could help the technology to do so.

CHAPTER VII
INTEGRATION & CONCLUSIONS

1. COMMON ELEMENTS OF ORIGINALITY

282. In the previous chapters, we have analyzed how the originality notion is present in the three branches of Belgian law selected for the purposes of this research, namely civil law, administrative law and fiscal law. In those analyses, we first looked at how the originality notion operated in the traditional principles of those branches of law, being the principles that were present before the process of digitalization came into being. Second, we have analyzed how digitalization has affected those branches of law and their respective incarnations of the originality notion.

283. In this section, we will trace the historical roots of the originality requirements analyzed here and assess whether or not a common origin can be found. This will show whether the differentiations that have developed along the way can still be upheld and whether a potential common origin could lead to the formulation of a uniform definition of originality. It therefore requires the integration of the findings of the previous analyses of the different branches of law selected here.

1.1. CIVIL LAW AND ORIGINALITY

284. In chapter III, it was found that Belgian civil law displays a clear preference for evidence in writing. It is in this preference that the originality requirement of this branch of law can be found. The preference for evidence in writing in the Belgian Civil Code was already present in the preparatory works of the 1804 Code Napoleon. It can be found directly in Jean-Étienne-Marie Portalis' *discours préliminaire du premier projet de Code civil.* In that text, Portalis holds that writing is the natural proof of contracts.[740] However, in an attempt to reconcile the different laws applicable in France at that time, he does allow proof to be delivered by witnesses in the case where a beginning of evidence

[740] Portalis, J.E.M. (2007) *Discours préliminaire du premier projet de Code civil*, Saguenay: Chicoutimi, 57.

in writing is present, thus serving as supplementary proof.[741] His rejection of witness statements, as complete evidence on their own, is expressed as fearing that witnesses may be corrupted, or that their memory could fail them.[742]

285. It is in the same writing that Portalis expresses his support for the principle of contractual freedom, holding that the freedom to contract should only be limited by justice, decency and the public good.[743] While this principle can also be understood as giving parties the freedom to decide how they want to conclude their contract – for instance be it oral or in writing – the formalism introduced into civil law by 19th century jurisprudence can be considered as somewhat hollowing out this freedom.[744] Moreover, the courts at that time established the formalism found in the Belgian Civil Code as absolute: when a formality is prescribed, it must be followed.[745] However, current case law does demonstrate a certain leniency when it comes to formalities under the rules on evidence: even when not all formalities are adhered to, a writing could have probative value.[746]

286. Despite this leniency, the late 20th century once again saw the rise of stricter opinions in jurisprudence and doctrine, thus re-establishing formalism in civil law.[747] This time, the goal of this formalism was to protect a particular weaker party, namely the consumer.[748] It is against this background of

741 *Id.*

742 This is expressed in discussing proof of a person's state. Portalis, J.E.M. (2007) *Discours préliminaire du premier projet de Code civil*, Saguenay: Chicoutimi, 50. His reasoning for allowing witness statements in criminal procedures is that in criminal matters written evidence is very rare, thus necessitating the allowance of non-written evidence.

743 Portalis, J.E.M. (2007) *Discours préliminaire du premier projet de Code civil*, Saguenay: Chicoutimi, 57. Note, however, that Portalis was not the first person to subscribe to the notion of consensualism. In fact, this notion can be traced back much further: Montero, E., Demoulin, M. (2004) "La formation du contrat depuis le Code civil de 1804: un régime en mouvement sous une lettre figée", in: Wéry, P. (ed.) *Le droit des obligations contractuelles et le bicentenaire du Code civil*, Bruxelles: La Charte, 6.

744 Demoulin, M. (2014) *Droit du commerce électronique et équivalents fonctionnels*, Brussels: Larcier, 35–36; Montero, E., Demoulin, M. (2004) "La formation du contrat depuis le Code civil de 1804: un régime en mouvement sous une lettre figée", in: Wéry, P. (ed.) *Le droit des obligations contractuelles et le bicentenaire du Code civil*, Bruxelles: La Charte, 3–4.

745 Demoulin, M. (2014) *Droit du commerce électronique et équivalents fonctionnels*, Brussels: Larcier, 36.

746 *Ibid.*, 37–38. Other proof in the leniency regarding evidence can be found in the fact that many of these rules are suppletive, thus allowing parties to deviate from them. Moreover, in cases where certain formalities are not met – such as the requirements of article 1325 Belgian Civil Code – the writing could still be accorded lower probative value, such as that of beginning of evidence in writing.

747 Demoulin, M. (2014) *Droit du commerce électronique et équivalents fonctionnels*, Brussels: Larcier, 41–42.

748 Thus resulting in a number of consumer protection laws that impose a certain formalism in order to balance the inequality between the consumer and the professional. This formalism

renewed formalism – which was of course purely aimed at paper documents and procedures – that technological developments introduced the process of digitalization. The originality requirement should then be viewed in this framework of formalism. More precisely, it constitutes the fixation of the language of the agreement on its first carrier, which must also be signed.[749]

287. The formalities in civil law are, however, not the sole invention of the Code Napoleon or of later jurisprudence. Over a century previously, in 1689, Jean Domat wrote about the need to have the judge ascertain whether the formalities of a proof are adhered to.[750] More specifically, he references the need to assess whether a writing that is to serve as proof consists of an original or a copy.[751] Like Portalis after him, Domat considered writing the best proof for contractual agreements.[752] In this, he references the maxim "*contra scriptum testimonium non scriptum testimonium non fertur*", meaning that witness statements cannot be used against evidence in writing. Moreover, he explicitly mentions the need for a signature in order for a writing to constitute a private instrument.[753] In this, he draws inspiration from the earlier *Ordonnance de Louis XIV* of April 1667.[754] This *Ordonnance*, in turn, finds inspiration in the earlier *Ordonnance de Moulins* of 1566, which deviated from classic Roman law in limiting the cases in which oral proof could be delivered.[755] As such, the *Ordonnance de Moulins* can be considered as the direct precursor to the current article 1341 of the Civil Code.

288. Originality is also considered by Domat to be one of the core formalities in probative law: "*la vérité des actes écrits s'établit par les actes mêmes, c'est-à-dire, par la vûë des originaux*" (the truth of written acts is established by those acts themselves, meaning by viewing the original).[756] Moreover, he states that a person against whom a copy is invoked can always demand the original, a

---

is expressed in requiring written contracts, the inclusion of certain formulations and information, rules on how the document must be drafted, etc.

749 Demoulin, M. (2014) *Droit du commerce électronique et équivalents fonctionnels*, Brussels: Larcier, 71–72.

750 Domat, J. (1695) *Les loi civiles dans leur ordre naturel*, Tome II, Seconde édition, Paris: Jean Baptiste Coignard, 409–410.

751 *Id.*

752 *Ibid.*, 413 & 415. However, Domat does place a higher trust in authentic instruments than in private instruments, precisely due to the involvement of a public notary in the former.

753 *Ibid.*, 417.

754 More in particular: title XX, article II. De Boutaric, F. (1743) *Explication de l'ordonnance de Louis XIV roi de France et de Navarre sur les matieres civiles*, Toulouse: Gaspard Henault et Jean-François Forest, 189–190.

755 More concretely its paragraph 54. Isambert, X., Decrusy, X., Taillandier, X. (eds.) (1829) *Recueil Géneral Des Anciennes Lois Françaises*, Tome XIV, 1e partie, Paris: Belin-Leprieur, 203.

756 Domat, J. (1695) *Les loi civiles dans leur ordre naturel*, Tome II, Seconde édition, Paris: Jean Baptiste Coignard, 419.

principle that can indeed still be found in the Civil Code's article 1334.[757] Domat, however, did not posit a new theory here: he refers back to Justinianus' *Corpus Iuris Civilis*.[758] However, while the distinction between originals and copies can in that sense be drawn back to classic Roman law, the specific formalities of article 1325 of the Civil Code are not so ancient: they were introduced by decisions of the *Parlement de Paris* in the 18th century.[759] Nevertheless, while the rule of the double original – in the cases where there are two parties – was only officialized at that time, practice was already developing to achieve this end. In maritime commerce, for instance, the *charte-partie* came into use in the 16th century, whereby a maritime transport contract would be cut in half, giving each party a piece of the original.[760]

289. Summarizing, it can be held that the notion that an original has more value than a copy was already present in Roman law. The prevalence of written evidence, however, was only later put forward more expressly, and found its way from the *Ordonnance de Moulins* into the Civil Code. The formalities regarding the originality requirement are also a more recent evolution. After developing in maritime practice, the requirements of the current article 1325 of the Civil Code were only first formalized by the *Parlement de Paris* in the 18th century. Further jurisprudence in the 19th and 20th century developed more formalities.

290. The main rationale behind this requirement and its formalities is to provide reliability and protection. Originals are historically preferred to copies, because copies used to be produced by hand, thus potentially exposing them to error or fraud.[761] The formalities developed around the originality requirement can be held to relate mainly to the protection of potentially weaker parties. Here, the requirements of article 1325 of the Civil Code aim to provide all parties with the same probative power.

---

757 *Id.*

758 More precisely, he references the Digest, nr. 22.4.2.

759 Planiol, M. (1901) *Traité élémentaire de droit civil conforme au programme officiel des Facultés de droit*, Tome II, Paris: Pichon, 354. The goal of this formality was to provide all parties with the same probative means. Aubry, C., Rau, C.F., Bartin, E. (1922) *Cours de droit civil français*, Tome XII, Paris: Marchal et Billard, 188–189. Such formalities were unknown in Roman law. Demolombe, C. (1879) *Traité des contrats ou des obligations conventionelles*, Tome VI, Paris: A. Lahure, 325.

760 Boulay-Paty, P.S. (1821) *Cours de droit commercial maritime*, Tome II, Rennes: Cousin-Danelle, 264; Noël, M.F., Carpentier, M.L.J. (1831) *Philologie française ou dictionnaire étymologique, critique, historique, anecdotique littéraire*, Tome I, Paris: Le Normant Père, 194–195; De Miltitz, A. (1837) *Manuel des Consuls*, Tome I, London: A. Asher, 266; Planiol, M. (1901) *Traité élémentaire de droit civil conforme au programme officiel des Facultés de droit*, Tome II, Paris: Pichon, 354.

761 Demoulin, M. (2012) "L'archivage électronique et le droit: entre obligations et precautions", in: Demoulin, M. (ed.) *L'archivage électronique et le droit*, Brussels: Larcier, 32.

1.2. ADMINISTRATIVE LAW AND PRESERVATION

291. As noted in chapter IV, the main element of Belgian administrative law that is important to the purposes of this research is its principles regarding the preservation of information. When looking into the originality notion under Belgian administrative law, we must, therefore, analyze the origins of its notion of preservation.

292. Etymologically speaking, the connection between governmental entities and the preservation of information appears to be fundamental. The word 'archive' itself, though only first recorded around the turn of the 17th century, is said to be derived from the Ancient Greek term '*archeion*', which can refer to a governmental palace or the office of a state administrator, as well as to archival records or a repository for original records.[762] Its stem, '*arch*', refers to power and authority, thus solidifying the connection to the activities of governmental entities.[763] Archives, and the preservation of information therein, are therefore clearly linked to government activities.

293. Indeed, some of the earliest known forms of archives – such as those in which the Ebla and Mari tablets were found – were in fact depositories containing all kinds of commercial, civilian and ownership records, maintained by local authorities.[764] Similar depositories maintained by magistrates existed in the Hellenic city-states, which, as noted, would eventually give us the term 'archive'. In the Roman Republic, a central depository – first the *aerarium* and later the *tabularium* – preserved all important texts, mainly *leges* and *senatus consulta*.[765] In the *Codex Iuris Civilis*, there is a reference to archives as places where public records are preserved.[766] Throughout the ages, the main powers within states continued to preserve their own records, leading to the close connection between archives and the clergy and royal houses.[767] Only the

---

762 Gagnon-Arguin, L. (1994) " Les archives, les archivistes et l'archivistique", in: Rousseau, J.-Y., Couture, C. (Eds.) *Les fondements de la discipline archivistique*, Sainte-Foy: Presses de l'Université du Québec, 10; Van den Eynde, S. (2001) "Digitale archivering: een juridische stand van zaken vanuit Belgisch perspectief. Deel 1", *ICRI research report*, 6.

763 *Id.*

764 DeVries, L. F. (1997) *Cities of the Biblical World*, Eugene, OR: Wipf and Stock Publishers, 27 & 67–71.

765 InterPARES (2001) "Authenticity Task Force Report", *interpares.org*, 21; Cunningham, A. (2005) "Archival institutions", in: McKemmish, S., Piggott, M., Reed, B., Upward, F. (Eds.) *Archives: Recordkeeping in Society*, Wagga Wagga: Centre for Information Studies, 27; Head, R. C. (2013) "Documents, archives, and proof around 1700", *The Historical Journal*, Vol. 56, 914. Though Culham disputes that these were truly archives. Culham, P. (1989) "Archives and Alternatives in Republican Rome", *Classical Philology*, Vol. 84, 100–115.

766 Duranti, L. (1996) "Archives as a Place", *Archives & Manuscripts*, Vol. 24, 242–255. Duranti references *Dig. 48.19.9*, 6.

767 One example being Charles V's Simancas archive. Cunningham, A. (2005) "Archival institutions", in: McKemmish, S., Piggott, M., Reed, B., Upward, F. (Eds.) *Archives:*

French Revolution saw the creation of true state archives, as can now be found in probably every sovereign state.[768]

294. The current Belgian territory was annexed to the French state in 1795, though archival depots had been set up in the Austrian Netherlands already before this.[769] Following the French annexation, the Belgian territory became subject to the Act of 5 brumaire year V (26 October 1796) concerning the departmental archival services.[770] This act imposes a clear obligation on local administrative entities to preserve information and requires that such records are submitted to the central archival authorities. This structure of centralized archival authorities was maintained during the period of the United Kingdom of the Netherlands, and the subsequent independent Belgian state.[771] The French laws regulating the archives remained in place until the adoption of the Belgian Archives Act in 1955.[772] This act reiterates, in its article 1, the general obligation of public law entities to preserve their archival documents.[773] Following the federalization of Belgium, similar texts have been adopted at the regional level.[774] This sub-domain of archival law is part of the broader domain of administrative law, as in this case it is the public sector entities that are subjected to a duty to preserve, in order to account for their actions.[775]

295. When looking at originality, it was found in chapter IV that the originality notion in Belgian administrative law must be interpreted in the sense of the regular use of the word, meaning the first form or source of something, that from which other work is derived or copied.[776]

Recordkeeping in Society, Wagga Wagga: Centre for Information Studies, 28; Daston, L. (2012) "The Sciences of the Archive", *Osiris*, Vol. 27, 171.

768 *Ibid*, 28–30.

769 *Arch.be/index.php?l=en&m=about-the-institution&r=history-of-the-institution.*

770 Loi du 5 brumaire an V qui ordonne la réunion, dans les chefs-lieux de département, de tous les titres et papiers acquis à la République, *Bulletin Officiel du Ministère d l'Intérieur* no. 7 (1841), 24.

771 *Arch.be/index.php?l=en&m=about-the-institution&r=history-of-the-institution.* Currently, there is a central depot and 18 local depots.

772 Act of 24 June 1955 on archives, *Belgian State Gazette* 12 August 1955 (hereinafter: Belgian Archival Act).

773 While under private law there may be a few specific duties to preserve information – such as duty to preserve invoices or merchant books – there is no such general duty in this sphere.

774 Flanders Region: Decree of 9 July 2010 relating to the governmental-administrative archival organization, *Belgian State Gazette* 5 August 2010 (hereinafter: Flemish Archival Decree). Wallonian Region: Decree of 6 December 2001 on public archives, *Belgian State Gazette* 20 December 2001 (hereinafter: Wallonian Archival Decree). Brussels Capital Region: Ordonnance of 19 March 2009 relating to the archives of the Brussels Capital Region, *Belgian State Gazette* 26 March 2009 (hereinafter: Brussels Archival Ordonnance).

775 Van den Eynde, S. (2001) "DAVID: Digitale archivering: een juridische stand van zaken vanuit Belgisch perspectief. Deel 1", *ICRI research report,* 17–18.

776 See the discussion in chapter III.

1.3. FISCAL LAW AND THE ORIGINAL FORMAT

296. Various forms of consumption taxes were introduced in the first half of the 20th century. France and Germany, for instance, introduced this kind of tax during the First World War.[777] These taxes would lead to the idea behind a value added tax or VAT, although it would take until the 1950s and 1960s before some countries started to implement a true VAT system.[778] Today, about 166 countries have implemented a VAT system.[779] This makes VAT law a very recent field of law, much more so than civil law or even administrative law.

297. The EU first proposed rules with regard to VAT in 1967, through a VAT directive.[780] A second directive in this field – issued on the same day as the first one – only mentioned that an invoice must be issued, without reference to originality.[781] The third directive in this field only extended the deadline for transposition of the second directive[782], as did the fourth[783] and fifth[784] directives.

298. In 1977, the framework set by the second directive was replaced by a sixth directive.[785] This directive echoes the provision regarding the need to draft an invoice from the second directive, but adds that every taxable person shall keep a copy of the invoices they issued.[786] This provision can thus be said to have created the original-copy dichotomy in EU VAT law. However, it was not until much later that a direct reference to an original was included, which happened

777 Helgason, A. F. (2017) "Unleashing the 'money machine': the domestic political foundations of VAT adoption", *Socio-Economic Review*, Vol. 15, 798–799.

778 *Ibid.*, 799.

779 OECD (2016) *Consumption Tax Trends 2016: VAT/GST and excise rates, trends and policy issues*, Paris: OECD Publishing, 14.

780 First Council Directive of 11 April 1967 on the harmonisation of legislation of Member States concerning turnover taxes, *OJ* 1301/67 of 14 April 1967, 14–15.

781 Article 12(2) Second Council Directive 67/228/EEC of 11 April 1967 on the harmonisation of legislation of Member States concerning turnover taxes – Structure and procedures for application of the common system of value added tax, *OJ* 71 of 14 April 1967, 1303–1312.

782 Third Council Directive 69/463/EEC of 9 December 1969 on the harmonisation of legislation of Member States concerning turnover taxes – introduction of value added tax in Member States, *OJ* L 320 of 20 December 1969, 34–35.

783 Fourth Council Directive 71/401/EEC of 20 December 1971 on the harmonization of the laws of the Member States relating to turnover taxes – Introduction of value added tax in Italy, *OJ* L 283 of 24 December 1971, 41–42.

784 Fifth Council Directive 72/250/EEC of 4 July 1972 on the harmonization of the laws of the Member States relating to turnover taxes – Introduction of value added tax in Italy, *OJ* L 162 of 18 July 1972, 18–19.

785 Sixth Council Directive 77/388/EEC of 17 May 1977 on the harmonization of the laws of the Member States relating to turnover taxes – Common system of value added tax: uniform basis of assessment, *OJ* L 145 of 13 June 1977, 1–40.

786 Article 22(3)(a) Sixth Council Directive 77/388/EEC.

through the 2001 directive that allowed for electronic invoicing – in holding that Member States may require invoices to be stored in their original format.[787]

299. In Belgium, VAT was introduced in 1969.[788] It required tax subjects to issue invoices.[789] In 1992, a new Royal Decree was adopted.[790] In this Royal Decree, it is confirmed that two copies must be issued of invoices.[791] Similarly as in European law, a direct reference to the original format was only introduced when amending the law to allow for electronic invoices.[792]

1.4. COMMONALITY IN THE ORIGINS?

300. The previous sections have shown how the three branches of Belgian law, analyzed for the purposes of this research, have followed very different paths. While the rules of civil law directly follow from the Code Napoléon, they can be traced much further back in history, with some principles dating at least back to Roman law. Administrative law is in that sense a much more recent field of law – developed in the late 19th and early 20th centuries – even though there were also other principles – such as those relating to the preservation of documents – that could be traced back to Antiquity. Fiscal law, at least the domain of VAT law important for our research, is only a very recent development, dating back to the second half of the 20th century. This makes it clear that these branches of law did not develop out of a single common point of origin.

301. The formulation of the originality requirement in these branches of law also appears – at least at first glance – to be very different.

In *civil law*, the originality notion serves to set apart original documents – meaning documents to which a valid signature has been affixed – from copies. The main reason for this duality is evidence. Civil law displays a clear preference for written documents, according a higher probative value to such means of evidence than to non-written means. Written documents are considered to be more reliable and the pinnacle of reliability has become the signature – thus placing signed documents at the top of the probative hierarchy. While a copy

787 Council Directive 2001/115/EC of 20 December 2001 amending Directive 77/388/EEC with a view to simplifying, modernising and harmonising the conditions laid down for invoicing in respect of value added tax, *OJ* L 15 of 17 January 2002, 24–28.
788 Belgian Act introducing the VAT Code, *Belgian State Gazette* 17 July 1969.
789 Original article 50, §1, 2° Belgian VAT Code.
790 Royal Decree nr. 1 of 29 December 1992 regarding the regulation for the fulfillment of the value added tax, *Belgian State Gazette* 31 December 1992.
791 Article 8 Royal Decree nr. 1 of 29 December 1992.
792 Article 11 Act of 28 January 2004 amending the VAT Code, *Belgian State Gazette* 10 February 2004.

can be a faithful reproduction of a document, it will in principle lack a valid signature. It is this that puts copies at a lower probative level.

In *administrative law*, the originality requirement follows from the principle of preserving information. Here, archives – being governmental entities – have a clear historic duty to preserve original information. To ensure the trustworthiness of those archival records, archival science and diplomatics have historically focused on preserving the original format of the information.

In *VAT law*, the originality notion only came into play further on in the development of this field of law. While it was already clear that an invoice needed to be issued in two copies – one for the recipient and one for the issuer's own accounting – the more direct reference to the original format of the invoice was, somewhat ironically, only raised when introducing the electronic invoice.

302. Nevertheless, despite those ostensible differences in how the originality requirement is raised in these three branches of law, it can be held that there are also clear similarities. In civil law, the preference for written and signed information serves to provide all relevant contract parties with the same and reliable probative means. In administrative law, the focus on the preservation of original information serves to protect against fraud and forgeries, thus also allowing for later probative use of the information. In fiscal law, the principles on the preservation of (original) invoices also serve to ensure later use of those invoices as proof in accounting and for tax audits. While these originality requirements therefore seem different at first glance, and have clearly gone through a different historical development, they do all serve the purpose of preserving information for later probative purposes.

2. INTEGRATION AND CONSTRUCTION OF DEFINITION

303. As shown in the previous section, the originality requirements of the three branches of Belgian law analyzed for the purposes of this research do not stem from a common origin, but developed separately from each other. However, it was found that these originality requirements do, at least to some extent, serve a common goal, namely the preservation of information for later probative purposes. In attempting to formulate a more uniform definition of the originality requirement, the focus will therefore have to be put on this common goal.

304. It is important to understand how a unified originality requirement would need to be operationalized in light of the ongoing processes of digitalization. For this, we can look at how the originality requirements of the three branches of law analyzed here are maintained in the age of digitalization. A recurring theme that can be identified here concerns the preservation of the authenticity and integrity of the information.

In *civil law*, this is exemplified by the different forms of the electronic signature. Particularly the advanced and qualified electronic signature make use of techniques that aim to ensure the authenticity and integrity of the information to which these electronic signatures are affixed. It is the acceptance of electronic signatures that allow electronic 'originals' to be procured. Moreover, recent developments with regard to qualified archival services aim to allow for a limited form of substitution.

In *administrative law*, preserving the authenticity and integrity of the information have always been key concerns in the fields of archival science and diplomatics. Here, the originality requirement can also, therefore, be said to be operationalized through ensuring the authenticity and integrity of archival information.

In *VAT law*, the introduction of electronic invoices was initially paired with the introduction of the use of the advanced – or qualified – electronic signature and EDI as techniques to ensure the authenticity and integrity of the electronic invoices that are to be preserved. More recent rules no longer impose the use of any particular technique, thus leaving the choice on how to ensure the authenticity and integrity up to the tax subject. Moreover, VAT law is marked by clear rules on the substitution of paper invoices by electronic reproductions, again subject to the requirement of preserving the information's authenticity and integrity.

305. As a result of these findings, we can propose to define a more unified originality requirement not in terms of the traditional original-copy dichotomy, but rather in terms of being a state in which the authenticity and integrity of the information to be preserved is guaranteed. This would correspond to what all three branches of law analyzed here aim to accomplish, namely the preservation of information for later probative use. Moreover, focusing on the need to preserve the authenticity and integrity of the information can easier be effectuated through digitalization processes than the classic original-copy dichotomy.

306. Given the normative nature of this question, an assessment can be made according to the normative criteria formulated in chapter I: legal certainty, inclusivity and proportionality.

In terms of *legal certainty*, a unified originality requirement should allow citizens to determine with reasonable certainty whether or not their information passes the test of authenticity and integrity, and can thus be considered as original under the redefined requirement. In this regard, it can be argued that leaving the choice for the technique with which to ensure authenticity and integrity completely up to the citizen could reduce this certainty, as the final word will be left entirely up to the judge of the matter – *e.g.* a court in civil proceedings or tax administrations in fiscal matters. On the other hand, imposing one particular technique as the sole means of ensuring authenticity and integrity risks becoming outdated in the face of rapidly evolving digitalization processes. As a middle ground, inspiration can be sought in the more recent amendments in VAT law, which still list the techniques of the advanced electronic signature and EDI as a means to ensure authenticity and integrity, but also leave open the possibility for the tax subject to determine its own set of business controls to do so. This approach allows for new techniques to be used, while at the same time providing a fall-back option of techniques that are certainly acceptable. In that sense, such an approach can provide legal certainty regarding the compliance of the information with the authenticity and integrity aspects of the redefined originality requirement, even in the face of new digitalization processes.

In terms of *inclusivity*, a redefined notion of originality should be applicable to all branches of law analyzed in this research. Here, we have already determined that the focus on preserving the authenticity and integrity of the information could serve the purposes of the different originality requirements identified in those branches of law. The reorientation of originality towards authenticity and integrity – rather than the traditional original-copy dichotomy – can therefore be considered as being inclusive for all three branches of Belgian law analyzed here.

In terms of *proportionality*, it can be held that a redefined originality requirement should not establish obligations that are too burdensome for the citizen. Moreover, a redefined originality requirement should facilitate digitalization processes in the branches of law analyzed here and should not be counterproductive to that evolution. Here, it can be held that the reorientation of originality toward authenticity and integrity can certainly support ongoing and future processes of digitalization, more so than the traditional focus on the original-copy dichotomy. As noted in discussing the criterion of legal certainty, it is not the aim of a redefined originality requirement to impose the use of any particular technique to ensure the authenticity and integrity of the information, although examples of acceptable techniques can be provided, as is the case in VAT law. Allowing citizens to determine their own means of establishing the authenticity and integrity of their information, therefore, does not impose requirements that can be considered to be overly burdensome.

3. CONCLUSION

307. The goal of this research has been to analyze the originality requirement as present in three distinct branches of Belgian law, namely civil law, administrative law and fiscal law. First, it was analyzed how these originality requirements operate under the traditional principles of those branches of law.

Second, it was analyzed how those originality requirements are influenced by ongoing processes of digitalization. The aim of that analysis was to establish if those originality requirements stemmed from a common origin, and whether we can formulate a more uniform definition of originality to be used across different branches of law.

308. For civil law, it was found that this branch of law displays a clear preference for evidence in writing, a principle that can be traced all the way back to Roman law. This is mainly because written evidence is assumed to possess a greater trustworthiness, and in order to provide all parties with the same probative means. The originality requirement is manifested in the original-copy dichotomy, whereby an original – being a document bearing a valid signature – is accorded a higher probative value than copies – lacking a valid signature. As a result, it is the signature that makes an original under Belgian civil law. In terms of digitalization, the main focus has therefore been put on the introduction of the electronic signature, in order to allow for electronic originals to be produced. However, the way in which electronic information is created and exchanged makes the distinction between originals and copies meaningless. More recently, the Belgian legislator has taken steps to allow for the substitution of paper information by electronic reproductions, albeit under strict conditions.

309. For administrative law, it was found that in this branch of law the focus of the originality requirement is put on the preservation of information. Ideally, information is preserved in its original format, as this is assumed to provide the highest degree of trustworthiness. While administrative law in itself is a much more recent branch of law than civil law, archives have been linked to the preservation of information by public authorities since Antiquity. In terms of digitalization, it is clear that the preference for preserving the original format clashes with evolutions such as substitution or emulation or even preservation strategies such as migration.

310. For fiscal law – or more precisely: for VAT law – it was found that the originality requirement relates to the figure of the invoice. Traditionally, such invoice must be issued as an original for the recipient and a copy for the issuer. Unlike original documents in civil law, however, invoices are normally not signed. Both the issuer and the recipient must preserve their copy of the invoice for later probative use. In terms of digitalization, VAT law has long since embraced electronic invoices. Originally, such electronic invoices had to be created and preserved using either an advanced electronic signature or EDI, but more recent EU-wide legislation allows for other techniques to be used as well. Moreover, VAT law fairly liberally allows for the substitution of paper invoices by electronic reproductions, as long as the authenticity and integrity of the invoice is maintained.

311. It is clear that the originality requirements of these three branches of Belgian law have very different origins. Civil law can of course be traced throughout history back to Roman law. Administrative law is a much more recent branch of law – dating to the late 19th century – but here there are also elements – particularly regarding archives – that find their origins in Antiquity. VAT law, on the other hand, is a product of the second half of the 20th century, without clear links to what came before. It is, therefore, not possible to identify a single root from which these three originality requirements developed.

312. Nevertheless, despite their different origins and their (at first glance) different formulations, it can be argued that the originality requirement serves as a means to ensure the trustworthiness of information for later probative use in all three branches of law analyzed here. In that sense, it can be proposed to redefine originality as pertaining to a state in which the authenticity and integrity of information is guaranteed, rather than in terms of the classic original-copy dichotomy.

313. Moreover, such reorientation of originality in terms of authenticity and integrity also works in various contexts of digitalization. In civil law, for instance, the advanced and qualified electronic signature makes use of the digital signature technique which precisely aims to preserve the authenticity and integrity of information. Similarly, preserving the authenticity and integrity of information has always been the core aim within archival science and diplomatics. As in civil law, VAT law has introduced techniques to ensure that the authenticity and integrity of information is preserved, except that that recent VAT law is more lenient in allowing for more diverse techniques.

314. From a normative point of view, it can be argued that the recommendation of certain techniques – yet, as is the case in current VAT law, without prescribing any particular technique – to ensure the authenticity and integrity of information can result in more legal certainty for those who need to preserve information. A redefined originality notion in terms of authenticity and integrity would also be more inclusive, as it can be argued that such notion could apply across different branches of law. Last, a redefinition of originality in terms of authenticity and integrity, would be operable in light of different current and future processes of digitalization. It can therefore support such processes without imposing requirements that would create disproportionate burdens.

315. One of such possible future processes of digitalization could potentially use the blockchain technology, as analyzed in chapter VI. While it was found that the basic tenets of this technology in itself do not ensure the authenticity and integrity of information, additional operational measures could be implemented toward that end. In so doing, future blockchain processes could then possibly ensure authenticity and integrity, and therefore originality.

316. Putting these findings together, it can be held that a redefined and unified originality requirement should be interpreted as being the state in which the authenticity and integrity of information is ensured. This corresponds to the underlying goals of the existing originality requirements in Belgian civil law, administrative law and VAT law, namely to ensure the reliability and trustworthiness of information for later probative use. By providing examples of techniques that can ensure such authenticity and integrity, yet without imposing the use of any particular technique – as is the case in current VAT law – it can be ensured that legal certainty is provided to the citizen, while at the same time leaving the door open for the introduction of new techniques as part of ongoing and future processes of digitalization – such as the use of blockchain technology perhaps. This approach would furthermore be proportionate to the goals it aims to achieve, without being overly burdensome. Moreover, this integrated reformulation is inclusive, as it can apply to all three branches of law analyzed here.

BIBLIOGRAPHY

1. LEGISLATION

1.1. EUROPEAN UNION

1.1.1. Regulations

Regulation (EC) No 1137/2008 of the European Parliament and of the Council of 22 October 2008 adapting a number of instruments subject to the procedure laid down in Article 251 of the Treaty to Council Decision 1999/468/EC, with regard to the regulatory procedure with scrutiny – Adaptation to the regulatory procedure with scrutiny – Part One, *OJ* L 311 of 21 November 2008, 1–54.

Regulation (EU) No 910/2014 of the European Parliament and of the Council of 23 July 2014 on electronic identification and trust services for electronic transactions in the internal market and repealing Directive 1999/93/EC, *OJ* L 257 of 28 August 2014, 73–114.

1.1.2. Directives

First Council Directive of 11 April 1967 on the harmonisation of legislation of Member States concerning turnover taxes, *OJ* 1301/67 of 14 April 1967, 14–15.

Second Council Directive 67/228/EEC of 11 April 1967 on the harmonisation of legislation of Member States concerning turnover taxes – Structure and procedures for application of the common system of value added tax, *OJ* 71 of 14 April 1967, 1303–1312.

Third Council Directive 69/463/EEC of 9 December 1969 on the harmonisation of legislation of Member States concerning turnover taxes – introduction of value added tax in Member States, *OJ* L 320 of 20 December 1969, 34–35.

Fourth Council Directive 71/401/EEC of 20 December 1971 on the harmonization of the laws of the Member States relating to turnover taxes – Introduction of value added tax in Italy, *OJ* L 283 of 24 December 1971, 41–42.

Fifth Council Directive 72/250/EEC of 4 July 1972 on the harmonization of the laws of the Member States relating to turnover taxes – Introduction of value added tax in Italy, *OJ* L 162 of 18 July 1972, 18–19.

Sixth Council Directive 77/388/EEC of 17 May 1977 on the harmonization of the laws of the Member States relating to turnover taxes – Common system of value added tax: uniform basis of assessment, *OJ* L 145 of 13 June 1977, 1–40.

Council Directive 87/54/EEC of 16 December 1986 on the legal protection of topographies of semiconductor products, *OJ* L 24 of 27 January 1987, 36–40.

Council Directive 91/250/EEC of 14 May 1991 on the legal protection of computer programs, *OJ* L 122 of 17 May 1991, 42–46.
Directive 96/9/EC of the European Parliament and of the Council of 11 March 1996 on the legal protection of databases, *OJ* L 77 of 27 March 1996, 20–28.
Directive 98/34/EC of the European Parliament and of the Council of 22 June 1998 laying down a procedure for the provision of information in the field of technical standards and regulations and of rules on Information Society services; *Official Journal* L 204 of 21 July 1998, 37.
Directive 1999/93/EC of the European Parliament and of the Council of 13 December 1999 on a Community framework for electronic signatures, *OJ* L 13 of 19 January 2000, 12–20.
Directive 2000/31/EC of the European Parliament and of the Council of 8 June 2000 on certain legal aspects of information society services, in particular electronic commerce, in the Internal Market ('Directive on electronic commerce'), *OJ* L 178 of 17 July 2000, 1–16.
Council Directive 2001/115/EC of 20 December 2001 amending Directive 77/388/EEC with a view to simplifying, modernising and harmonising the conditions laid down for invoicing in respect of value added tax, *OJ* L 15 of 17 January 2002, 24–28.
Council Directive 2006/112/EC of 28 November 2006 on the common system of value added tax, *OJ* L 347 of 11 December 2006, 1–118.
Council Directive 2010/45/EU of 13 July 2010 amending Directive 2006/112/EC on the common system of value added tax as regards the rules on invoicing, *OJ* L 189 of 22 July 2010, 1–8.

1.1.3. Preparatory documents

Report from the Commission to the European Parliament and the Council of 15 March 2006 on the operation of Directive 1999/93/EC on a Community framework for electronic signatures", *COM(2006) 120 final.*
Communication from the Commission to the European Parliament, the Council, the European Economic and Social Committee and the Committee of the Regions of 26 August 2010, A Digital Agenda for Europe, *COM(2010) 245 final/2.*
Commission proposal for a regulation of the European Parliament and of the Council of 4 June 2012 on electronic identification and trust services for electronic transactions in the internal market, *COM(2012) 238 final.*
Commission staff working document of 7 June 2012 impact assessment accompanying the document proposal for a regulation of the European Parliament and of the Council on electronic identification and trust services for electronic transactions in the internal market, *SWD(2012) 135 final.*

1.2. BELGIUM

1.2.1. Codes

Articles 22 and 32 Belgian Constitution.
Articles 1315 – 1356 Belgian Civil Code.

Book XII Belgian Code of Economic Law.
Articles 20 and 25 Belgian Commercial Code.
Articles 259*bis* and 314*bis* Belgian Criminal Code
Articles 883 – 894 Belgian Judicial Code.

1.2.2. Acts

Act on the Profession of Notary, 16 March 1803 (25 ventôse XI).
Archival Act of 24 June 1955, *Belgian State Gazette* 12 August 1955.
Act of 2 May 1956 concerning the postal cheque, *Belgian State Gazette* 13 June 1956.
Act introducing the VAT Code, *Belgian State Gazette* 17 July 1969.
Act of 4 December 1990 concerning financial transactions and financial markets, *Belgian State Gazette* 22 December 1990.
Code of Income Tax 1992, *Belgian State Gazette* 30 July 1992.
Act of 8 December 1992 protecting the personal sphere against the processing of personal data, *Belgian State Gazette* 18 March 1993.
Act of 11 April 1994 concerning the publicity of governance, *Belgian State Gazette* 30 June 1994.
Act of 20 October 2000 introducing the use of means of telecommunication and of the electronic signature in judicial and extrajudicial proceedings, *Belgian State Gazette* 22 December 2000.
Act of 9 July 2001 concerning the determination of certain rules regarding the legal framework for electronic signatures, electronic certified mail and certification services, *Belgian State Gazette* 29 September 2001.
Act of 11 March 2003 concerning certain legal aspects of services of the information society, *Belgian State Gazette* 17 March 2003.
Act of 28 January 2004 amending the VAT Code, *Belgian State Gazette* 10 February 2004.
Act of 13 June 2005 concerning electronic communication, *Belgian State Gazette* 20 June 2005.
Act of 27 December 2005 holding diverse provisions, *Belgian State Gazette* 30 December 2005.
Act of 15 May 2007 holding the establishment of a legal framework for certain providers of trust services, *Belgian State Gazette* 17 July 2007.
Act of 21 August 2008 concerning the foundation and organization of the eHealth platform and other provisions, *Belgian State Gazette* 13 October 2008.
Act of 6 May 2009 holding diverse provisions, *Belgian State Gazette* 19 May 2009.
Act of 15 February 2012 amending the Act of 9 July 2001 concerning the determination of certain rules regarding the legal framework for electronic signatures, electronic certified mail and certification services, *Belgian State Gazette* 7 March 2012.
Act of 17 December 2012 amending the VAT Code, *Belgian State Gazette* 21 December 2012
Act of 4 May 2016 holding internment and diverse provisions in the field of justice, *Belgian State Gazette* 13 May 2016.
Act of 21 July 2016 executing and supplementing Regulation 910/2014 of the European Parliament and of the Council of 23 July 2014 concerning electronic identification and trust services for electronic transactions in the internal market and repealing

Directive 1999/93/EC, inserting title 2 in book XII "Law of the electronic economy" in the Code of Economic Law and inserting the definitions for title 2 of book XII and of the enforcement rules of title 2 of book XII in the books I, XV and XVII in the Code of Economic Law, *Belgian State Gazette* 28 September 2016.

Act of 6 July 2017 holding simplification, harmonization, informatization and modernization of provisions of civil law and of civil procedural law, as well as of the notary and holding diverse provisions concerning justice, *Belgian State Gazette* 24 July 2017.

1.2.3. Royal Decrees

Royal Decree nr. 1 of 29 December 1992 regarding the regulation for the fulfillment of the value added tax, *Belgian State Gazette* 31 December 1992.

Royal Decree of 16 February 2004 amending Royal Decree nr. 1 of 29 December 1992 regarding the regulation for the fulfillment of the value added tax, *Belgian State Gazette* 27 February 2004.

Royal Decree of 15 December 2009 amending Royal Decree nr. 1 of 29 December 1992 regarding the regulation for the fulfillment of the value added tax, *Belgian State Gazette* 21 December 2009.

Royal Decree of 18 August 2010 executing articles 1, 5 and 6*bis* of the Archival Act of 24 June 1955, *Belgian State Gazette* 23 September 2010.

Royal Decree of 19 December 2012 amending Royal Decree nr. 1 of 29 December 1992 regarding the regulation for the fulfillment of the value added tax, *Belgian State Gazette* 21 December 2012.

1.2.4. Preparatory documents

Parl. St. Senaat B.Z. 1991–92, nr. 100–49/20, 8–10.

Gedr. St. Kamer 1992–93, nr.839/1, explanatory note, 5.

Proposal introducing new means of telecommunication in the judicial and extrajudicial procedures, *Parl. St. Kamer* 1997–1998, 1501/1.

Proposal to introduce new means of telecommunication in the judicial and extrajudicial procedures, *Parl. St. Kamer* 1999–2000, 0038/6.

Proposal for an act regarding informatics crime, *Parl. St.* Kamer 1999–2000, 0213/1, 12.

Proposal concerning the working of certification services regarding the use of electronic signatures, *Parl. St. Kamer* 1999–2000, 0322/1, 5.

Parliamentary question of 24 February 2001, *www.senate*.be, 5–1485.

Proposal to introduce an Act concerning certain legal aspects of the services of the information society, *Parl. St. Kamer* 2002–2003, 2100/1, 14–15.

Proposal for an Act amending the Act of 9 July 2001 concerning the determination of certain rules regarding the legal framework for electronic signatures, electronic certified mail and certification services, *Parl. St. Kamer* 2010–2011, 1450/1, 3–4.

Proposal to amend the legislation introducing the law of electronic commerce, *Parl. St. Kamer* 2012–2013, 2745/1.

Proposal to amend the legislation introducing the law of electronic commerce – Committee report, *Parl. St. Kamer* 2012–2013, 2745/7.

1.2.5. *Regional decrees*

Brussels Ordonnance of 30 March 1995 concerning the publicity of governance, *Belgian State Gazette* 23 June 1995.
Wallonian Decree of 6 December 2001 on public archives, *Belgian State Gazette* 20 December 2001.
Flemish Decree of 26 March 2004 concerning the publicity of governance, *Belgian State Gazette* 1 July 2004.
Flemish Decree of 9 July 2010 relating to the governmental-administrative archival organization, *Belgian State Gazette* 5 August 2010.
Brussels Ordonnance of 19 March 2009 relating to the archives of the Brussels Capital Region, *Belgian State Gazette* 26 March 2009.
Brussels Ordonnance of 13 February 2014 concerning communication using electronic means in the framework of interactions with the governments of the Brussels Capital Region, *Belgian State Gazette* 5 March 2014.
Brussels Capital Region Parliament 2012–2013, *A-444/1.*

1.3. FRANCE

Loi du 5 brumaire an V qui ordonne la réunion, dans les chefs-lieux de département, de tous les titres et papiers acquis à la République, *Bulletin Officiel du Ministère d l'Intérieur* no. 7 (1841), 24.
Décret n°80–533 of 15 July 1980 pris pour l'application de l'article 1341 du code civil, modifié par article 56 Décret n°2004–836 of 20 August 2004, *JORF* 22 August 2004.

1.4. GERMANY

Gesetz vom 13. Juni 1997 zur Regelung der Rahmenbedingungen für Informations- und Kommunikationsdienste (Informations- und Kommunikationsdienste-Gesetz – IuKDG), *BGBl. I* 28 July 1997, 1872–6.

1.5. ITALY

Legge n. 59 15 marzo 1997 Delega al Governo per il conferimento di funzioni e compiti alle regioni ed enti locali, per la riforma della Pubblica Amministrazione e per la semplificazione amministrativa, *Gazzetta Ufficiale* n. 63 of 17 March 1997.

1.6. LUXEMBOURG

Règlement grand-ducal of 1 August 2008 concernement le basculement en euro le 1er janvier 2002, *Mémorial A n° 117* of 18 September 2001.

1.7. THE NETHERLANDS

Act of 4 June 1992 on general administrative law, *Stb.* 1992, 315.
Archival Act of 28 April 1995, *Stb.* 1995, 276.
Archival Regulation of 15 December 2009, *Stcrt.* 2010, 70.

1.8. UNITED KINGDOM

An Act for the Encouragement of Learning, by Vesting the Copies of Printed Books in the Authors or Purchasers of such Copies, during the Times therein mentioned of 5 April 1710, *c.19.*

1.9. UNITED STATES OF AMERICA

Article I, Section 8, Clause 8 of the United States Constitution.
Fed. R. Evid. 1001(d) – 1004.
Utah Digital Signature Act, Utah Code §46–3–101 – 504.

1.10. INTERNATIONAL

Convention for the Protection of Literary and Artistic Works, signed at Berne on 9 September 1886.

2. CASE LAW

2.1. COURT OF JUSTICE OF THE EUROPEAN UNION

CJEU, John Reisdorf *v.* Finanzamt Köln-West, C-85/95.
CJEU, Société générale des grandes sources d'eaux minérales françaises *v.* Bundesamt für Finanzen, C-361/96.
CJEU, Infopaq International A/S *v.* Danske Dagblades Forening, C-5/08.
CJEU, Eva-Maria Painer *v.* Standard VerlagsGmbH and Others, C-145/10.

2.2. BELGIUM

2.2.1. Court of Cassation

Cass. 14 November 1901, *Pas.* 1902, I, 37–38.
Cass. 4 November 1926, *Pas.* 1927, 84.

Cass. 29 September 1955, *Arr. Cass.* 1955, 53–55.
Cass. 24 November 1961, *Pas.* 1962, I, 367.
Cass. 2 October 1964, *jure.juridat.just.fgov.be.*
Cass. 1 March 1973, *jure.juridat.just.fgov.be.*
Cass. 25 October 1979, *jure.juridat.just.fgov.be.*
Cass. 17 June 1981, *jure.juridat.just.fgov.be.*
Cass. 30 April 1982, *jure.juridat.just.fgov.be.*
Cass. 28 June 1982, *jure.juridat.just.fgov.be.*
Cass. 19 May 1983, *jure.juridat.just.fgov.be.*
Cass. 13 June 1986, *jure.juridat.just.fgov.be.*
Cass. 18 January 1990, *jure.juridat.just.fgov.be.*
Cass. 25 mei 1992, *jure.juridat.just.fgov.be.*
Cass. 26 February 1993, *jure.juridat.just.fgov.be.*
Cass. 21 December 1999, *jure.juridat.just.fgov.be.*
Cass. 7 March 2002, *jure.juridat.just.fgov.be.*
Cass. 16 December 2004, *jure.juridat.just.fgov.be.*
Cass. 20 December 2007, *jure.juridat.just.fgov.be.*
Cass. 10 March 2008, *jure.juridat.just.fgov.be.*
Cass. 18 April 2008, *jure.juridat.just.fgov.be.*

2.2.2. Council of State

Council of State 10 december 1968, nr. 13.270, Rijksdienst voor de Sociale Verzekering der Zelfstandigen – Tops, *Arresten en Adviezen van de Raad van State 1968,* 962–965.
Council of State 8 May 2009, nr. 193.106.
Council of State 22 December 2010, nr. 210.056, *RW* 2011–2012, case note Dirk de Bruyn, 615.

2.2.3. Court of Appeals

Ghent, 21 November 2002, *NJW 2003*, nr. 33, 634, note by Brewaeys, E.
Mons 27 February 2007, note by Mougenot, D. (2007) "Le statut probatoire de la photocopie: nuageux avec éclaircies", *TBBR*, 468–475.

2.2.4. Local courts

Rb. Turnhout 21 May 1987, *TBBR,* 1989, 171.
Rb. Antwerpen, 5 June 2015, nr. 14/1851/A.

2.3. GERMANY

Bundesgerichtshof, Urt. *v.* 09.05.1985, *Az.* I ZR 52/83.

2.4. UNITED STATES OF AMERICA

United States *v.* Steffens, United States *v.* Witteman, and United States *v.* Johnson, 100 US 82 (1879).
Bleistein *v.* Donaldson Lithographing Co., 188 US 239 (1903).
Feist Publications *v.* Rural Telephone Service, 499 US 340 (1991).

3. LITERATURE

"best-evidence rule" (2009) *Black's Law Dictionary* (9th ed.), Thomson Reuters.

"original" (2015) *Cambridge Advanced Learners Dictionary & Thesaurus,* Cambridge University Press.

"original" (2015) *Collins English Dictionary,* HarperCollins Publishers.

"original" (2015) *Merriam-Webster.com,* Merriam-Webster.

"original, adj. and n." (2015) *OED Online,* Oxford University Press.

"originality" (2009) *Black's Law Dictionary* (9th ed.), Thomson Reuters.

"originality" (2015) *Cambridge Advanced Learners Dictionary & Thesaurus,* Cambridge University Press.

"originality" (2015) *Collins English Dictionary,* HarperCollins Publishers.

"originality" (2015) *Merriam-Webster.com,* Merriam-Webster.

"originality, n." (2015) *OED Online,* Oxford University Press.

Abrams, H.B. (1992) "Originality and creativity in copyright law", *Law and Contemporary Problems,* vol. 55, 3–44.

Allemeersch, B., Schollen, P. (2002) "Behoorlijk bewijs in burgerlijke zaken. Over de geoorloofdheidvereiste in het burgerlijk bewijsrecht", *RW,* 41–60.

Amand, C. (2008) "De gemiste besparingen van de elektronische facturatie in Europa", *Tijdschrift voor Fiscaal Recht,* nr. 343, 573–578.

Aps, F. (2000) "Het "recht op nieuwsgierigheid tussen echtgenoten" en de toelaatbaarheid van geluidsmateriaal in het kader van een echtscheidingsprocedure op grond van bepaalde feiten", *Echtscheidingsjournaal,* 31–34.

Archief 2020 (2014) "Handreiking vervanging archiefbescheiden", *archief2020.nl.*

Aubry, C., Rau, C.F., Bartin, E. (1922) *Cours de droit civil français,* Tome XII, Paris: Marchal et Billard.

Ballon, G. (2008) "Inleiding", in: Ballon, G., Samoy, I., Byl, T., Deschoolmeester, F., Dumortier, J., Goethals, T., Govers, M., Swaenepoel, E. (Eds) *De factuur en verwante documenten,* Brugge: Vanden Broele.

Ballon, G.L. (2009) "De bewijswaarde van een e-mailbericht", note to Ghent Appeals Court 10 March 2008, *T.G.R.,* 29.

Bayern, S. (2014) "Of Bitcoins, independently wealthy software, and the zero-member LLC", *Northwestern University law Review Online,* Vol. 108, 1485–1500.

Bedos-Rezak, B. M. (2011) *When Ego Was Imago: Signs of Identity in the Middle Ages,* Leiden: Brill.

Bollen, R. (2013) "The Legal Status of Online Currencies: Are Bitcoins the Future?", *Journal of Banking and Finance Law and Practice,* vol. 24, nr. 4, 272–293.

Boudrez, F. (2005) "Digitale handtekeningen en archiefdocumenten", *edavid.be.*

Boudrez, F., Dekeyser, H. (2004) *Handboek Digitaal archiefbeheer in de praktijk*, Antwerpen: Stadsarchief.

Boudrez, F., Dekeyser, H., Dumortier, J. (2005) *Digital Archiving: The New Challenge?*, Mont Saint Guilbert: IRIS.

Boudrez, F., Drossens, P. (2010) "Substitutie: Magda?", *edavid.be*.

Boulay-Paty, P.S. (1821) *Cours de droit commercial maritime*, Tome II, Rennes: Cousin-Danelle.

Brito, J., Castillo, A. (2013) *Bitcoin: A Primer for Policymakers*, Arlington: George Mason University Mercatus Center.

Bushey, J. E. (2005) *Born digital images as reliable and authentic records*, Unpublished thesis University of British Columbia, Vancouver.

Caboor, P. (2001) "De wet van 20 oktober 2000 tot invoering van het gebruik van telecommunicatiemiddelen en van de elektronische handtekening in de gerechtelijke en de buitengerechtelijke procedure: een eerste verkenning", *A.J.T.*, 637–642.

Certipost (2009) "Certification Practice Statement Citizen CA – Verklaring met betrekking tot de certificatiepraktijk", *repository.eid.belgium.be*.

Chaum, D. (1983) "Blind signatures for untraceable payments", *Advances in Cryptology Proceedings of Crypto*, Vol. 82, 199–203.

Circular AAFisc Nr. 14/2014 (*nr. E.T. 120.000*) of 4 April 2014.

Circular AFZ nr. 02/2013 (*AFZ/2011-0272*) of 23 January 2013.

Circular letter nr. AOIF 16/2008 (E.T.112.081) of 13 May 2008.

Circular letter of 13 May 2008, nr. AOIF 16/2008 (E.T.112.081).

Cloquet, A. (1954) *Factuur*, Brussels: Larcier.

Cook, T. (1997) "What is past is prologue", *Archivaria*, Vol. 43, 17–63.

Cornelis, L. (2000) *Algemene theorie van de verbintenis*, Antwerpen: Intersentia.

Cornelis, L., Goethals, P. (2000) "Contractuele aspecten van e-commerce", in: X, *De elektronische handel*, Antwerpen: Kluwer.

Culham, P. (1989) "Archives and Alternatives in Republican Rome", *Classical Philology*, Vol. 84, 100–115.

Cunningham, A. (2005) "Archival institutions", in: McKemmish, S., Piggott, M., Reed, B., Upward, F. (Eds.) *Archives: Recordkeeping in Society*, Wagga Wagga: Centre for Information Studies.

Dai, W. (1998) "B-money", *weidai.com/bmoney.txt*.

Daston, L. (2012) "The Sciences of the Archive", *Osiris*, Vol. 27, 156–187.

De Boeck, A. (2006) "De bewijskracht van de onderhandse akte: voorzichtige versoepeling van de vormvereisten; op weg naar meer? Enkele bedenkingen bij Cass. 26 april 2001", *Rev. Gén. Droit Civ. Belge*, 346–349.

De Boutaric, F. (1743) *Explication de l'ordonnance de Louis XIV roi de France et de Navarre sur les matieres civiles*, Toulouse: Gaspard Henault et Jean-François Forest.

De Bruyn, J., Van Eecke, P. (2011) "Afdeling 3 – Elektronische facturatie", in: Van Eecke, P. (Ed.) *Recht en elektronische handel*, Gent: Larcier.

De Cock, D., Wolf, C., Preneel, B. (2006) "The Belgian Electronic Identity Card (Overview)", in: Dittmann, J. (ed.), *Sicherheit 2005, Sicherheit – Schutz und Zuverlässigkeit, Beiträge der 3rd Jahrestagung des Fachbereichs Sicherheit der Gesellschaft für Informatik e.v. (GI), Lecture Notes in Informatics (LNI) LNI P-77*, Bonner Köllen Verlag.

De Corte, R. (2001) "Elektronische handtekening en identificatie in de virtuele wereld", *P&B*, 207–234.

De Filippi, P. (2014) "Bitcoin: a regulatory nightmare to a libertarian dream", *Internet Policy Review*, vol. 3, nr. 2, 1–2.

De Groote, B. (2001) "Het bewijs in de elektronische handel – Enkele bedenkingen", *A.J.T.*, 880–889.

De Miltitz, A. (1837) *Manuel des Consuls*, Tome I, London: A. Asher.DeVries, L. F. (1997) *Cities of the Biblical World*, Eugene, OR: Wipf and Stock Publishers.

De Page, H. (1967) *Traité élémentaire de droit civil Belge, Tome Troisième (Les Obligations)*, Brussel: Bruylant.

Dekeyser, H., Dumortier, J. (2004) "Juridische obstakels voor de elektronische handel op het vlak van archivering en datering", *FPS Economy, SME, Self-employed and Energy*.

Del Castillo, M. (2017) "Fight for Your Right: Universal Music Veteran Launches Ethereum IP Platform", *CoinDesk*, 5 October.

Demolombe, C. (1879) *Traité des contrats ou des obligations conventionelles*, Tome VI, Paris: A. Lahure.

Demoulin, M. (2012) "L'archivage électronique et le droit", in: Demoulin, M. (Ed.) *L'archivage électronique et le droit*, Brussels: Larcier.

Demoulin, M. (2014) *Droit du commerce électronique et équivalents fonctionnels*, Brussels: Larcier.

Demoulin, M., Soyez, S. (2012) "L'archivage électronique dans le secteur public", in: Demoulin, M. (Ed.) *L'archivage électronique et le droit*, Brussels: Larcier.

Demoulin, M., Soyez, S. (2012) "L'authenticité, de l'original papier à la copie numérique – Les enjeux juridiques et archivistiques de la numérisation", in: Duranti, L., Schaeffer, E. (eds) *The Memory of the World in the Digital Age: Digitization and Preservation*, Conference proceedings of UNESCO: Vancouver, 26–28 September 2013.

Den Teuling, A.J.M. (2003) *Archiefterminologie voor Nederland en Vlaanderen*, 's-Gravenhage: Stichting Archiefpublicaties, nr. 8.

Depoortere, R. (2010) "Substitutie in België, magda?", presented at VVBAD studiedag Substitutie: Magda?, Brussels, 1 April.

Deschoolmeester, F. (2008) "De factuur in het bewijsrecht", in: Ballon, G., Samoy, I., Byl, T., Deschoolmeester, F., Dumortier, J., Goethals, T., Govers, M., Swaenepoel, E. (Eds) *De factuur en verwante documenten*, Brugge: Vanden Broele.

Devolder, K., Verachten, L. (2013) *Overbrenging van digitale archieven*, Brussels: Belgian State Archives.

Dion, D. (2013) "I'll gladly trade you two bits on Tuesday for a byte today: Bitcoin, regulating fraud in the e-conomy of hacker-cash", *Journal of Law, Technology & Policy*, 165–201.

Domat, J. (1695) *Les loi civiles dans leur ordre naturel*, Tome II, Seconde édition, Paris: Jean Baptiste Coignard.

Dujardin, J., Van Damme, M., Vande Lanotte, J., Mast, A. (2009) *Overzicht van het Belgisch Administratief Recht*, Mechelen: Kluwer.

Dumortier, J. (2004) "Legal status of qualified electronic signatures in Europe", in: Paulus, S., Pohlmann, N. and H. Reimer (eds), *ISSE 2004-Securing Electronic Business Processes*, Wiesbaden: Springer Vieweg, 281–289.

Dumortier, J. (2008) "Elektronische facturen", in: Ballon, G., Samoy, I., Byl, T., Deschoolmeester, F., Dumortier, J., Goethals, T., Govers, M., Swaenepoel, E. (Eds) *De factuur en verwante documenten*, Brugge: Vanden Broele.

Dumortier, J. (2010) *ICT-Recht*, Leuven: Acco.

Dumortier, J. (2015) "Goede praktijken digitaal-vriendelijke regelgeving voor de Vlaamse overheid", presented at workshop digital-friendly regulation, Brussels, 26 January.

Dumortier, J. (2015) "Naar een Vlaams beleid inzake substitutie?", *vlaanderen.be*.

Dumortier, J., Dekeyser, H. (2003) "Hoofdstuk V. Ruimen van juridische obstakels bij contracten langs elektronische weg", in: Van Eecke, P., Dumortier, J. (ed.) *Elektronische Handel - Commentaar bij de wetten van 11 maart 2003*, Brugge: die Keure.

Dumortier, J., Graux, H., Debusseré, F. (2013) *ICT-Recht*, Leuven: Acco.

Dumortier, J., Somers, G. (2006) "Het bedrijfsgebruik van elektronische post juridisch doorgelicht", *C.J.*, 2.

Dumortier, J., Somers, G. (2007) "De wet van 15 mei 2007 tot vaststelling van een juridisch kader voor sommige verleners van vertrouwensdiensten: een eerste verkenning", *T.B.H.*, 649–659.

Dumortier, J., Van Den Eynde, S. (2001) "De juridische erkenning van de elektronische handtekening", *Computerrecht*, 185–194.

Dumortier, J., Vandezande, N. (2012) "Trust in the proposed EU regulation on trust services?", *Computer Law & Security Review*, 568–576.

Dumortier, J., Vandezande, N. (2014) "Legal evidence in a digital context: will signatures disappear?", in: Savin, A., Trzaskowski, J. (eds.), *Research Handbook on EU Internet Law*, Cheltenham: Edward Elgar, 432–457.

Duranti, L. (1996) "Archives as a Place", *Archives & Manuscripts*, Vol. 24, 242–255.

Duranti, L. (1998) *Diplomatics: New Uses for an Old Science*, Lanham: Scarecrow Press.

Duranti, L. (2001) "The impact of digital technology on archival science", *Archival Science*, Vol. 1, 39.

Duranti, L. (2009) "From Digital Diplomatics to Digital Records Forensics", *Archivaria*, Vol. 68, 39–55.

Duranti, L. (ed.) (2002) "The Long-term Preservation of Authentic Electronic Records: Findings of the InterPARES Project - Authenticity Task Force Report", *interpares.org*.

Febelfin (2015) "Samen streven naar digitalisering van de economie", *febelfin.be*.

Federal Public Service Finance (2007) "I. Verplichting tot bewaring", *FisconetPlus*, nr. 557/2–558.

Finck, M. (2017) "Blockchain Regulation", *Max Planck Institute for Innovation and Competition Research Paper No. 17-13.*

Gagnon-Arguin, L. (1994) " Les archives, les archivistes et l'archivistique", in: Rousseau, J.-Y., Couture, C. (Eds.) *Les fondements de la discipline archivistique*, Sainte-Foy: Presses de l'Université du Québec.

Gencer, A. E., Basu, S., Eyal, I., van Renesse, R., Gün Sirer, E. (2018) "Decentralization in Bitcoin and Ethereum Networks", *arxiv.org/pdf/1801.03998.pdf.*

Gobert, D. (2001) "Vers une discrimination de traitement entre la facture papier et la facture électronique?", *Cahier du Juriste*, nr. 4–5/2001, 45–54.

Gobert, D. (2003) "La Directive du 20 Décembre 2001: Vers une discrimination de traitement entre la facture papier et la facture électronique?", in: Montero, E., Demoulin, M., Gobert, D. (Eds.) *Commerce électronique: de la théorie à la pratique, Cahiers du CRID, n° 23*, Brussels: Bruylant.

Gobert, D., Montero, E. (2000) "La signature dans les contrats et les paiements électroniques: l'approche fonctionelle", in: Montero, E. (ed.) *Commerce électronique: le temps des certitudes*, Brussels: Bruylant.

Gobert, D., Montero, E. (2001) "L'ouverture de la preuve littérale aux écrits sous forme électronique", *J.T.*, 114–127.

Govers, M. (2008) "De factuur en verwante documenten in het fiscaal recht", in: Ballon, G., Samoy, I., Byl, T., Deschoolmeester, F., Dumortier, J., Goethals, T., Govers, M., Swaenepoel, E. (Eds) *De factuur en verwante documenten*, Brugge: Vanden Broele.

Graux, H. (2011) "Rethinking the e-signatures directive: on laws, trust services and the digital single market", *Digital Evidence & Electronic Signature Law Review*, Vol. 8, 9–24.

Haig, S. (2017) "MIT to Issue Diplomas Using Bitcoin Blockchain", *Bitcoin.com*, 22 October.

Hariani, K., Hariani, A. (2011) "Analyzing "Originality" in Copyright Law: Transcending Jurisdictional Disparity", *IDEA The Intellectual Property Law Review*, vol. 51, 491–501.

Head, R. C. (2013) "Documents, archives, and proof around 1700", *The Historical Journal*, Vol. 56, 909–930.

Helgason, A. F. (2017) "Unleashing the 'money machine': the domestic political foundations of VAT adoption", *Socio-Economic Review*, Vol. 15, 798–799.

Hern, A. (2015) "Nasdaq bets on bitcoin's blockchain as the future of finance", *The Guardian*, 13 May 2015.

Higgins, S. (2017) "Air France Tests Blockchain for Supply Chain Tracking", *CoinDesk*, 5 October.

Iansiti, M., Lakhani, K. R. (2017) "The Truth About Blockchain", *Harvard Business Review*, January-February, 118–127.

Intercontinental Exchange (2015) "NYSE to Launch NYSE Bitcoin Index, NYXBT", *Business Wire*, 19 May 2015.

InterPARES (2001) "Authenticity Task Force Report", *interpares.org*.

InterPARES 2 (2008) "The InterPARES 2 Project Glossary", *interpares.org*.

Isambert, X., Decrusy, X., Taillandier, X. (eds.) (1829) *Recueil Géneral Des Anciennes Lois Françaises*, Tome XIV, 1e partie, Paris: Belin-Leprieur.

ITU-T (2008) "Recommendation X.500", *itu.int*.

Jaszi, P. (1991) "Toward a Theory of Copyright: The Metamorphoses of "Authorship", *Duke Law Journal*, 455–502.

Jaszi, P. (1994) "On the Author Effect: Contemporary Copyright and Collective Creativity", in: Woodmansee, M., Jaszi, P., *The construction of authorship: textual appropriation in law and literature*, Durham: Duke University Press.

Judge, E.F., Gervais, D. (2009) "Of silos and constellations: comparing notions of originality in copyright law", *Cardozo Arts and Entertainment*, vol. 27, 375–408.

Kaplanov, N. (2012) "Nerdy Money: Bitcoin, the Private Digital Currency, and the Case Against its Regulation", *Loyola Consumer Law Review*, Vol. 25, 111–174.

Kien-Meng Ly, M. (2014) "Coining Bitcoin's 'legal-bits': examining the regulatory framework for Bitcoin and virtual currencies", *Harvard Journal of Law & Technology*, vol. 27, nr. 2, 587–609.

Kohavi, R. (2001) "Mining e-commerce data: the good, the bad, and the ugly", in: X., *KDD '01 Proceedings of the seventh ACM SIGKDD international conference on Knowledge discovery and data mining*, New York: ACM.

Lamensch, M. (2006) "La règle de la primauté de la preuve écrite: une application delicate", *TBBR*, 46–55.

Lemieux, V. (2016) "Trusting records: is Blockchain technology the answer?", *Records Management Journal*, Vol. 26, 110–139.

Lemieux, V. (2017) "Blockchain Technology for Recordkeeping", *SSHRC Knowledge Synthesis Grant Competition on "How can emerging technologies be leveraged to benefit Canadians?"*, Volume 1 - Report.

Liivak, O. (2005) "The Forgotten Originality Requirement: A Constitutional Hurdle for Gene Patents", *Journal of the Patent and Trademark Office Society*, vol. 87, 261–297.

Macneil, H. (1994) "Archival Theory and Practice: Between Two Paradigms", *Archivaria*, Vol. 37, 6–20.

Massin, I. (2014) "'Bedrijfscontrole': zelfcontrole en (externe) audit 'aanbevolen'", *Fiscoloog*, nr. 1383.

Massin, I., Vanderstichelen, B. (2002) "Nieuwe algemene vergunning inzake elektronische facturatie", *Fiscoloog*, nr. 848.

May, T.C. (1994) "Cyphernomicon", *spinnaker.com/crypt/cyphernomicon/CP-FAQ*.

McMillan, R. Metz, C. (2013) "The rise and fall of the world's largest bitcoin exchange", *Wired*, 6 November 2013.

Meehan, J. (2003) *Towards an archival concept of evidence*, unpublished University of British Columbia thesis.

Metz, C. (2015) "Bitcoin May Never Make It to Wall Street, But Its Tech Will", *Wired*, 12 May 2015.

Minjauw, H., Vandendriessche, J. (2008) "Titel VI. Het bewijsrecht in burgerlijke zaken", in: Roodhooft, R. (ed.), *Bestendig Handboek Verbintenissenrecht*, Mechelen: Kluwer.

Montero, E. (2009), "À propos de la valeur probante des e-mails", note to Ghent Appeals Court 10 March 2008, *D.A.-O.R.*, 314–319.

Montero, E., Demoulin, M. (2004) "La formation du contrat depuis le Code civil de 1804: un régime en mouvement sous une lettre figée", in: Wéry, P. (ed.) *Le droit des obligations contractuelles et le bicentenaire du Code civil*, Bruxelles: La Charte.

Mougenot, D. (2002) *Droit des obligations: la preuve*, Brussel: Larcier.

Mougenot, D. (2007), "Paiement et commencement de preuve par écrit", *P&B*, 288–290.

Mourlon Beernaert, F. (2006) "Partie VI. Le droit de la preuve - Introduction", in: X, *Obligations. Traité théorique et pratique*, Brussel: Kluwer.

Nakamoto, S. (2008) "Bitcoin: A Peer-to-Peer Electronic Cash System", *bitcoin.org/bitcoin.pdf*.

NIST (2012) "Secure Hash Standard (SHS)", *FIPS PUB 180-4*.

Noël, M.F., Carpentier, M.L.J. (1831) *Philologie française ou dictionnaire étymologique, critique, historique, anecdotique littéraire*, Tome I, Paris: Le Normant Père.

Nordén, A. (2006) "Electronic Invoicing in the Light of European Community Directive 2001/115/EC", in: Schulz, A. (Ed.) *Legal Aspects of an E-Commerce Transaction*, Munich: Sellier.

O'Leary, R. R. (2017) "Shipping Giant Maersk to Deploy Blockchain Maritime Insurance Solution", *CoinDesk*, 6 September.

OECD (2016) *Consumption Tax Trends 2016: VAT/GST and excise rates, trends and policy issues*, Paris: OECD Publishing.

Pandectes Belges, v° Signature, nr. 1.

Pearce-Moses, R. (2005) *A Glossary of Archival and Records Terminology*, Chicago: The Society of American Archivists.

Peck, M. (2012) "The cryptoanarchists' answer to cash", *IEEE Spectrum*, June 2012, 51–56.

Pflaum, I., Hateley, E. (2014) "A bit of a problem: National and extraterritorial regulation of virtual currency in the age of financial disintermediation", *Georgetown Journal of International Law*, Vol. 45, 1169–1215.

Planiol, M. (1901) *Traité élémentaire de droit civil conforme au programme officiel des Facultés de droit*, Tome II, Paris: Pichon.

Portalis, J.E.M. (2007) *Discours préliminaire du premier projet de Code civil*, Saguenay: Chicoutimi.

PriceWaterhouseCoopers (1999) "Study on the requirements imposed by the Member States, for the purpose of charging taxes, for invoices produced by electronic or other means – final report 23 August 1999", *ec.europa.eu*.

PricewaterhouseCoopers (2005) "e-Invoicing and e-Archiving taking the next step", *pwc.com*.

Raadgevend Comité voor de Telecommunicatie (2015) "Memorandum aan de Minister bevoegd voor Telecommunicatie en de Digitale Agenda: Een digitale agenda voor België", *rct-cct.be*.

Rose, M. (1988) "The Author as Proprietor: Donaldson v. Becket and the Genealogy of Modern Authorship", *Representations*.

Rosenthal Kwall, R. (2007) "Originality in context", *Houston Law Review*, 871–899.

Ross, S. (2007) "Digital Preservation, Archival Science and Methodological Foundations for Digital Libraries", Keynote Address at the 11th European Conference on Digital Libraries (ECDL), Budapest (17 September 2007).

Rothenberg, J. (1995) "Ensuring the longevity of digital documents", *Scientific American*, Vol. 272, 42–47.

Rothenberg, J. (1999) *Avoiding Technological Quicksand: Finding a Viable Technical Foundation for Digital Preservation*, Washington D.C.: Council on Library and Information Resources.

Rothenberg, J. (2000) *An experiment in Using Emulation to Preserve Digital Publications*, Amsterdam: Koninklijke Bibliotheek.

Saelemans, S. (2017) "An analysis of the legal effect of an electronic signature used to sign an agreement in a blockchain application, under Dutch law", *Master thesis Vrije Universiteit Amsterdam*.

Samyn, B. (2013) "Sms is maar begin van bewijs", *De Juristenkrant*, nr. 276, 2.

Santos, M. (2018) "CEO of Overstock.com buys world's first Bitcoin bond for $500,000", *99bitcoins.com*, 2 January.

Siegel, D. (2016) "Understanding The DAO Attack", *CoinDesk*, 27 June.
Siracusa, J. (2003) "About the Finder...", *Ars Technica*, 2 April 2003.
Steennot, R. (1999) "Juridische problemen in het kader van de elektronische handel", *T.B.H.*, 664–676.
Stevens, O. (2010), note to Brussels 14 March 2008, *T.B.H.*, 109–116.
Stijns, S. (2009) *Leerboek Verbintenissenrecht Boek 2*, Brugge: die Keure.
Stokes, R. (2012) "Virtual money laundering: the case of Bitcoin and the Linden dollar", *Information & Communications Technology Law*, vol. 21, nr. 3, 221–236.
Storme, M.E. (2001) "De invoering van de elektronische handtekening in ons bewijsrecht", *RW*, 1505–1525.
Suneetha, K.R., Krishnamoorthi, R. (2009) "Identifying User Behavior by Analyzing Web Server Access Log File", *International Journal of Computer Science and Network Security*, 327–332.
Taylor, H. A. (1987) "Transformation in the Archives: Technological Adjustment or paradigm Shift?", *Archivaria*, Vol. 25, 12–28.
Thomassen, T. (2011) "A first introduction to archival science", *Archival Science*, Vol. 1, 373–385.
Turpin, J. (2014) "Bitcoin: the economic case for a global virtual currency operating in an unexplored legal framework", *Indiana Journal of Global Legal Studies*, Vol. 21, 335–368.
Twomey, P. (2013) "Halting a shift in the paradigm: the need for Bitcoin regulation", *Trinity College Law Review*, Vol. 16, 67–90.
Van Baeveghem, B. (2006) "De paraaf: "Slip of the pen" of geldige handtekening?", *Tijdschrift voor Belgisch Burgerlijk Recht (TBBR)*, 593–601.
Van den Eynde, S. (2002) "DAVID: Authenticiteit, integriteit en originaliteit van elektronische archiefstukken", *ICRI research report*.
Van Eecke, P. (2003) "Hoofdstuk I. Artikelsgewijze bespreking van de wetten elektronische handel", in: Van Eecke, P., Dumortier, J. (eds.), *Elektronische Handel – Commentaar bij de wetten van 11 maart 2003*, Brugge: die Keure.
Van Eecke, P. (2004) *Naar een juridische status voor de elektronische handtekening: Een rol voor de handtekening in de informatiemaatschappij?*, PhD thesis KU Leuven – Faculty of Law.
Van Eecke, P. (2009) "De elektronische handtekening in het recht", *T.B.H.*, 322–354.
Van Gerven, W., Covemaker, S. (2006) *Verbintenissenrecht*, Leuven: Acco.
Van Kildonck, K. (2010) "Privacy Werknemers. Onrechtmatig verkregen bewijs op het werk", *NJW*, 180–183.
Vandenabeele, V. (2002) "De elektronische handtekening: rechten en plichten van de certificatiedienstverlener, de certificaathouder en de vertrouwende derde", *TBBR*, 609–615.
Vandezande, N. (2018) *Virtual Currencies: A Legal Framework*, Cambridge: Intersentia.
Wagner, K. (2008) "Recente ontwikkelingen met betrekking tot het bewijs in burgerlijke zaken", in: Serrus, D. (ed.), *Actualia Gerechtelijk Recht*, Gent: Larcier.
Wagner, K. (2009) "Actualia burgerlijk bewijsrecht", *P&B*, 153–172.
Wallace, B. (2011) "The rise and fall of bitcoin", *Wired*, 23 November 2011.
Wéry, P., Gobert, D., Kerzmann, L. (2003) "La preuve", in: Coipel, M., Wéry, P., Durant, I., Cruquenaire, A., *Guide juridique de l'entreprise*, Brussel: Kluwer.

Wüst, K., Gervais, A. (2017) "Do you need a Blockchain?", *IACR Cryptology ePrint Archive 2017*, 375.

X (1804) *Code civil des français. Édition originale et seule officielle.* Paris: Imp. de la République.

KU Leuven Centre for IT & IP Law

The KU Leuven Centre for IT & IP Law Series brings together the results of research activities of the Centre for IT & IP Law. The central research themes of the series concern the legal and ethical aspects of information technology, innovation and intellectual property.

Each book in the series focuses on the essential developments in the current legal framework, necessitated by the rapid evolution of technology in various fields, such as government, media, health care, informatics, digital economy, banking, transport and culture. The research is characterised by an interdisciplinary approach, constantly cross-fertilising legal, technical, economic, ethical and socio-cultural perspectives.

Books are published in English, Dutch and/or French.

Recently published in this series:

1. Rán Trygvadóttir, *European Libraries and the Internet: Copyright and Extended Collective Licences*, 2018.
2. Niels Vandezande, *Virtual Currencies*, 2018.
3. Aleksandra Kuczerawy, *Intermediary Liability and Freedom of Expression in the EU: From Concepts to Safeguards*, 2018.

www.ingramcontent.com/pod-product-compliance
Ingram Content Group UK Ltd.
Pitfield, Milton Keynes, MK11 3LW, UK
UKHW051847100926
8556IPUK00005B/500

9 781780 687605